Principles of Devotion

Principles of Devotion

Charles G. Finney

Compiled & Edited by
Louis Gifford Parkhurst, Jr.

Gospel Truth
P.O. Box 6322
Orange, CA 92863

BETHANY HOUSE PUBLISHERS
MINNEAPOLIS, MINNESOTA 55438
A Division of Bethany Fellowship, Inc.

Published by Bethany House Publishers
A Division of Bethany Fellowship, Inc.
6820 Auto Club Road, Minneapolis, Minnesota 55438

Printed in the United States of America

Library of Congress Cataloging-in-Publication Data

Finney, Charles Grandison, 1792-1875.
   Principles of devotion.

   1. Prayer. I. Parkhurst, Louis Gifford, 1946-
II. Title.
BV215.F56   1987   248.3'2   86-28315
ISBN 0-87123-872-1

THE
CHARLES G. FINNEY
TRILOGY ON PRAYER

ANSWERS TO PRAYER

Remarkable answers to prayer in the life and ministry of one of America's greatest evangelists.

PRINCIPLES OF PRAYER

An introductory devotional guide on prayer for the Christian's daily encouragement in prayer, based on the 1835 lectures on prayer for revival found in *Lectures on Revival of Religion*.

PRINCIPLES OF DEVOTION

The most comprehensive study on how and why God answers prayer today. Finney's sermons preached in America and England, first published in *The Oberlin Evangelist* and *The Penny Pulpit*, from the years 1845 to 1855.

CHARLES G. FINNEY was one of America's foremost evangelists. Over half a million people were converted under his ministry in an age that offered neither amplifiers nor mass communications as tools. Harvard Professor Perry Miller affirmed that "Finney led America out of the eighteenth century." As a theologian, he is best known for his *Revival Lectures* and his *Systematic Theology.*

LOUIS GIFFORD PARKHURST, JR., is pastor of First Christian Church of Rochester, Minnesota, and teaches Ethics/Philosophy at Minnesota Bible College. He garnered a B.A. and an M.A. from the University of Oklahoma and an M.Div. degree from Princeton Theological Seminary. He is married and the father of two children.

CONTENTS

INTRODUCTION

Charles G. Finney walked with God. God heard his prayers, and he heard God. "At one time a young lady attending Oberlin College happened to fall into very great need of money. Not knowing what to do, she made the matter a subject of prayer, and then, without mentioning the trouble to any other person, determined to speak to President Finney about it at the next inquiry and conference meeting. The evening came and the President was going from one to another, counseling and encouraging, when, coming to this young lady, he thrust a five dollar bill into her hand and passed on without a word."[1]

Finney was a powerful preacher, because he knew when and how to pray. "In the year 1840, a young man named Weed became so impressed by Mr. Finney's powerful preaching one Sabbath that he cried out aloud in his anguish over his sins. The preacher stopped and called upon him to come to the altar; the convicted one did so, and then Mr. Finney prayed that as the Lord had lifted the veil a little so He would fully disclose to the penitent one the riches of His grace. The young man was converted."[2]

Charles Finney was also a man of prayer in action. He prayed for individuals to find salvation and have all their needs met, and he was willing to be used by God for these purposes. He prayed for his nation's leaders and their decisions.

"Before President Abraham Lincoln was fully converted to the anti-slavery movement, President Finney wrote three letters to him. 'On bended knee,' said he, 'I wrote one, and then I prayed God

---

[1] A. L. Shumway and C. D. Brower, *Oberliniana* (Cleveland: Home Publishing Co., 1883), p. 74.
[2] *Ibid.*, p. 75.

so earnestly all the while that it might move him. But no answer came. I could not be at peace. I wrote again and waited. This time there came a little note, giving no thanks nor promises, only asking a question. I answered it, and knew that God had prevailed.' It was not long after that the Emancipation Proclamation was made."[3]

If you want to serve God with all your heart, mind, soul, and strength, because you love Him, this collection of Finney's sermons on prayer will teach you how to walk with God. If you want to love and serve your neighbor, as Christ has loved and served you, God will hear your prayers, just as He heard Finney's.

You will notice from the contents that I have organized the sermons after the order of the Scripture texts in the Bible from the Psalms to 1 John. I have also included the dates the sermons were published should you choose to study them in chronological order. You will find these dates on the first page of each sermon in the footnote. I also believe it is interesting to discover which sermons Finney preached in America and which in England.

The sermons in this book were kindly provided from collections of Finney's sermons by the Oberlin College Library and the Burke Library of the Union Theological Seminary. I also owe much thanks to Mr. Homero Ferreyra and his family, who provided my wife and me extended Christian hospitality as I was seeking to find and acquire the sermons from the Burke Library in New York City. I wish to thank Mr. Thomas Lukashow for the book *Oberliniana*, from which the quotations in this Introduction are taken. I wish to thank Mr. Jack Key for use of the research facilities of Mayo Clinic Library, and Mrs. Fred Kirkham for typing portions of the first draft of the manuscript. Finally, I owe tremendous gratitude to the entire staff of Bethany House Publishers for seeing the value of reprinting Finney's works for today's readers,

For the sake of His Kingdom,
L. G. Parkhurst, Jr.
April 30, 1985

---

[3]*Ibid.*, p. 76.

1

DELIGHT IN THE LORD*

"Delight thyself also in the Lord; and he shall give thee the desires of thine heart" (Psalm 37:4).

In speaking from these words, I shall show:

▶ *What is implied in delighting ourselves in the Lord.*
▶ *What is implied in the promise "He shall give thee the desires of thine heart."*
▶ *Why this promise is thus conditioned.*

What is implied in delighting ourselves in the Lord.

The promise implies supreme sympathy with God. No one can properly be said to delight himself in the Lord any further than he sympathizes with God respecting the great end on which His heart is set and in the means by which He is attempting to accomplish that end. He must adopt God's principles and enter into His views and feelings. He must be able to respond with a hearty amen to all the announcements of God's Word, to all the dispensations of His providence, to His character, works, and ways. One who has this supreme sympathy with God, and who deeply interests himself in God's character, government, policy, ends, and means, will of course delight himself in the Lord—and no one else will.

Delighting ourselves in the Lord implies a supreme complacency or deep satisfaction in Him. Complacency in God is benevolence or goodwill toward Him, modified by a consideration

*The Oberlin Evangelist, July 2, 1845.

of His character and relations. Complacency is often spoken of as wholly a *delight* existing in the sensibility or feelings and emotions of the soul. In reality, this is not so. When considered as a virtue, complacency belongs to the will or heart, and always implies a corresponding state of the sensibility or emotions: a delight or pleasure in view of the character, government, relations, works and ways of God. Without this complacency of heart in God, we cannot be said to truly delight ourselves in Him.

Delight in the Lord implies that He is chosen as the supreme good of the soul. We must set our supreme affections on Him. We must choose Him as our all-satisfying portion, making Him the great center in which our affections and sympathy delight to rest.

Delight in God implies universal confidence in Him. We could never be said to delight ourselves truly in God unless we have supreme and universal confidence in His character, providence and Word. Nothing could be chosen by us as an all-satisfying portion unless the mind regarded it as infinite and perfect. The mind is so constituted that it cannot be satisfied with anything else. The mind is naturally and necessarily dissatisfied in varying degrees with whatever is seen to be imperfect. Delight in God implies that the mind regards Him as possessing infinite fullness, perfection, truthfulness, and every attribute that can fill and satisfy the soul. Commonly, men seek what they suppose will make them happy, and endeavor to find happiness in the creature. However, nothing but the infinite perfect Creator can satisfy our needs and demands. To delight ourselves in the Lord, in the sense of the text, implies that we are satisfied in God, that His fullness and perfection meet all the demands of our being. In Him we have enough, and the mind regards Him as an exceeding great reward, as a portion infinitely abundant, satisfying, full, overflowing, glorious and eternal.

Delight in God implies universal submission of our will to His. Therefore, the soul that is not entirely submissive to God cannot be delighted in Him. He is like a child whose will is not subdued to the will of his parent. He is restless under the divine government, often made unhappy by the dispensations of divine providence and by the requirements of God's Word. To have true delight in God implies that we have no will of our own, only that the will of God should be done. Delight in God implies that the soul has come practically to regard God as infinitely wise and good, to feel the fullest satisfaction with His appointments and His dispensations whatever they may be.

Delight in God implies a spirit of universal obedience to Him; a state of mind that asks God what He would have us do with a determination to do all His will without hesitation, devoting ourselves entirely to pleasing Him. In short, our whole being must be given up to God's will so that our only purpose or design is to live wholly for Him in all things, at all times, in all places and forever.

Delight in God implies delight in obeying Him, or delight in His service. It is one thing to obey, and another thing to delight in obedience. Our nature is such that true obedience always produces delight. But obedience and delight are not the same thing. Where the true spirit of obedience exists, we will find our delight and happiness very naturally in the service of God. We are always delighted with the course on which our heart is supremely set. When, therefore, our hearts are given to pleasing God and we live to this end, when we are heartily and universally consecrated to God's glory and interests, nothing will give us as great a pleasure. We shall be delighted in nothing else but serving God, doing His bidding, and in everything engaging in His service. The service of God will be our meat and drink. We shall know what Christ meant when He said, "I have meat to eat that ye know not of." "It is my meat to do the will of him that sent me." "I delight to do thy will, O my God."

Delight in God implies a deep interest in His honor and glory. Everything we do and say will have reference to God. He will be the supreme end of all we say and do. In this we shall sympathize with God himself. God has a supreme regard to His own interest and glory, the chief end of all His works. However, this does not mean God is selfish. He has a supreme regard for His own glory only because this concern achieves the greatest good. God's well-being is infinitely more valuable than the aggregate of the well-being of all creatures that ever were or could be made. God's well-being is infinite; whereas the well-being of all creatures will always be finite. Nothing can be infinite that is not eternally and necessarily so. Nothing finite can ever grow and increase until it becomes infinite. Therefore, the aggregate well-being of all finite creatures must always be finite and infinitely less than the well-being of God.

Now, if God regards things according to their relative value, He must of necessity lay infinitely more stress upon His own happiness and glory than upon the happiness and glory of all other beings together. There is no comparison between the finite and the infinite; therefore, the aggregate value of the endless happiness of all creatures is absolutely nothing when compared with the well-being of God. God so regards this; and it is reasonable and right and infinitely important that He should. Consequently, His own glory and well-being are the supreme end of all His works.

When I saw this fact announced in President Jonathan Edwards' writings many years ago, I did not at once perceive its truthfulness. And I have often since heard people speak as if they were stumbled by such an announcement, as if it implied selfishness in God. Now, selfishness is preferring our own interests to our neighbors, simply because it is our own. We are not selfish to prefer our happiness to the happiness of a goose, because ours is really more valuable. But it is selfish for us to prefer our happiness to our neighbor's, when his is equally valuable to our own. I repeat it again; it is not because the happiness or glory is God's that His heart is set supremely on it, but because of its intrinsic value, because it is so infinitely the greater good. Now, delight in God implies that we regard His interests as the supreme and infinite good, and delight ourselves in promoting His glory and honor in the universe. We find our supreme happiness and satisfaction of soul in promoting God's glory.

Delight in God implies that we supremely seek and desire eternal union and communion with Him. So far as our own happiness is concerned this is all we ask: to have eternal union and communion with the ever-blessed God. If He gives us this, we would lack nothing essential to our happiness; but deprive us of this, and nothing in the universe could satisfy us.

What is implied in the promise "He shall give thee the desires of thine heart."

The promise implies that we shall have those things on which we set our affections, or in other words, that our really cherished desires shall be gratified. If we delight ourselves in the Lord, we shall have all things on which we set our hearts. "He shall give thee the desires of thine heart," means there is no limit; it is plainly implied that what we set our hearts on and pray for shall be granted. It seems to me that the text means that not every transient desire or awaking of appetite shall be gratified, but that the supreme desire of the soul, that on which we can properly be said to fix our affections and our hearts, shall infallibly be granted to us.

Why this promise is thus conditioned.

Without this condition, the promise would be unsafe to the universe. For God to promise unqualifiedly to give us the desires of our hearts, unless He knew that we were in complete sympathy with Him, would be unreasonable, unsafe, and what He could not do without blame or guilt. What would happen if He were to make such a promise without this condition? Why, our selfish desires would be granted. When we make God the great end and center of our desires, then it is both consistent with the will of God and with the highest good of being for Him to grant us our desires. When God gives himself to the soul, He gratifies its desires.

God could not safely make such a promise except on this condition, because it would be impossible to fulfill it. Suppose He should unqualifiedly promise every individual the desires of his heart. With the endless lustings of people after objects around them, different people would often desire the same things, when only one could possess them.

It is perfectly safe for God to make such a promise on the condition of our delighting ourselves in the Lord, because whosoever delights himself in the Lord can never desire anything inconsistent with the will of God. The Spirit of God dwells in him. All his affections and desires are under the influence of the Spirit of God. And while he delights himself in God, he is sure not to set his heart on anything unless he is drawn to it by the Spirit of God. In this case certainly he cannot at the same time be lusting after a forbidden object and delighting himself in the Lord.

This promise is conditional, because God delights to bestow that on which the heart is set when that heart delights in Him. He loves to bestow himself, to communicate His own fullness to those who set their hearts on Him. He loves those who love Him. There is also a sense in which God loves His enemies, but His love for them is not a delight in their moral character. He greatly enjoys the communication of himself to those who delight themselves in Him. He loves to draw them into a participation of His joy so they may drink of the river of His pleasure. He delights in making them partakers of His own divine nature, of His own holiness and of His own happiness.

It is of the highest importance to the universe that God should grant the desires of the heart which delights itself in Him. It is for the highest good of being that He should do so. It is for His glory. It contributes to the stability of His government. It is not only highly honorable to God, but highly useful to His creatures to know that He will grant the desires of those who set their hearts on Him.

REMARKS

Those who delight themselves in God will of course manifest their cheerfulness of mind, because this delight in God is of itself a cheerful state of mind, and because they have the desires of their hearts.

An unsatisfied craving of mind that produces unhappiness, gloom, despondence and despair is not the condition of a mind that delights itself in God. The soul that delights itself in God is pleased with whatever comes to pass. It has no way or will of its own, and therefore cannot be disappointed. It has no craving or lusting of a selfish nature, and therefore is not made unhappy by being crossed and denied things on which its affections are set, because its affections are set on nothing but God. While it delights itself in God, it is of course cheerful and happy under all circumstances, can rejoice always and pray without ceasing, and in everything give thanks.

From what has been said, we may see why so few prayers prevail with God. The fact is, there is so much dissatisfaction with God and so much lusting after other things that God cannot fulfill the desires of such people. It would be infinitely unwise and unsafe to do so. As a condition of prevailing prayer, we must delight ourselves in the Lord. When we do this, our prayer will be dictated by God's Spirit; and of course will be answered.

In these days, how few seem to have their supreme delight in God. How few are seeking communication and fellowship with God. How few make union with God the supreme end of their lives. It is not strange that their prayers are not answered. The conditions of prevailing prayer are not fulfilled. Many pray because they are pressed up to it by conviction, not because their soul pants after communion with God and delights itself in God. Instead of loving to dwell in the Bible, in the house of God, in the closet in prayer; in short, instead of delighting themselves in God, they constantly rove about here and there to see if they cannot find some good. "Who will show us any good?" seems to be their constant inquiry. Now, those who are in this state of mind cannot have their desires granted.

Another reason why many desires are ungratified is that they are not the right kind of desires. The truth is, where an individual delights himself in the Lord, he will have the desires of his heart. Instead of being wretched all the time, and setting his heart on something he cannot get, when he comes to delight himself in the Lord, all this scrambling and lusting after what is beyond his reach will be gone. He will be like a weaned child, all peace. When the mind has God, it has enough.

Much prayer, or that which is called prayer, is after all nothing but lusting in the Bible sense of the term. It is a craving of the mind after some selfish good. Much prayer is nothing but the pouring out of the cravings of a selfish heart. The Apostle James speaks of this state of mind: "Ye lust, and have not: ye kill and desire to have, and cannot obtain: ye fight and war, yet ye have not, because ye ask not. Ye ask, and receive not, because ye ask amiss, that ye may consume it upon your lusts."

When there is delight in God, the supreme desire of course will be for union and communication with God: this will be the all-absorbing desire of the mind. For example, we often see one state of mind or desire swallow up all the others. The mind becomes so engrossed with one object of desire that it cares for little else. We see this state of mind often in this world. One desire seems to eat up and swallow up all the rest. We see this, too, sometimes in the case of individuals that are very wicked. The drunkard's appetite for strong drink sometimes will kill and completely destroy every other appetite; even natural affection seems to be annihilated by it. Sometimes a husband's affection for his wife is so strong that he cares for almost nothing else. If the object of his affection is lost, he says, "What do I have left? I have nothing to care for now." His interest in everything else is destroyed. Let me illustrate. When a person becomes acquainted with God and his sensitivity is rightly developed toward Him, as it always must be before he can be at rest, and when all his desires center in God, He comes to be the supreme end of the soul in such a sense that you can take anything that you will from him except his God, and you cannot affect his happiness. This one desire so swallows up all the rest. With such a soul, nothing else weighs a straw in comparison to the love of God.

Christ was so swallowed up at one time with this one great idea that when He was told, "Behold, thy mother and thy brethren stand without desiring to speak with thee," He replied, "Who is my mother? And who are my brethren?" And He stretched forth His hand toward His disciples and said, "Behold my mother and my brethren! For whosoever shall do the will of my Father which is in heaven, the same is my brother, and sister and mother." He meant to rebuke the idea that our blood relatives are to be considered so much dearer than our spiritual relatives. He would say to those who sustain this relation to God of supremely desiring union and communion with Him, "Ye are my mother and my brethren."

Whoever has his sensitivity well developed toward God comes to feel that everything must sustain some relation to this end, or it is of no value. Nothing else pleases. It must bear a relation to God, to His government and to His glory, to make it of any regard to such a mind. The thing nearest and dearest to people naturally, if it does not sustain this relation, will be cast off as of no value.

A person said some time ago, "I am praying that the Lord will destroy your influence." "Well," remarked the other, "I hope the Lord will answer your prayers if my influence is not good. For it is of no use to my mind unless it can glorify God. And if it does no good, I hope it will be destroyed." Now I suppose that individual answered just as he felt. He felt that his influence was worth nothing unless it would do some good to the universe. He cared nothing about it in itself or apart from its value in glorifying God. Now when an individual comes into this state of mind, he regards everything in this light. It must be valuable to God or he cares nothing about it.

We often see people so attached to others in this world that it seems they really enjoy nothing unless it sustains some relation to the object of their affection. Husbands and wives sometimes sustain this relationship so that everything is valued according to the relation it sustains to the one or the other. Now, I suppose the mind becomes so completely swallowed up in God, so "sick of love," and so ravished with the love of God, and comes to take such delight in Him as to say with the Psalmist, "Whom have I in heaven but thee, O God?" The Psalmist knew what he said, "Whom have I in heaven but thee?" His father, mother, and many whom he had greatly loved had gone to heaven, but still he exclaims, *"Whom have I in heaven but thee?"* His children, and those to whom he was greatly attached, were all around him; and yet when he comes to think of God, his whole soul cries out, "There is none upon earth that I desire besides thee." This is the case with a mind that is ravished and carried away with the love of God. There is such a dying of the mind to all other things—to self, to the world, to friends, to every-thing—that the individual comes to care for nothing, not even to eat, unless for the glory of God. He is dead to all but God. How safe is it, then, for God to make such a promise as this to an individual who thus delights himself in God!

An individual who delights himself in the Lord will also postpone everything that competes with communion with God. You will not find him making excuses for not attending prayer meetings, for not spending time in his closet and holding much communion with God. You see people who seem to be really honest say they would like to commune with God: they would like to attend the prayer meeting, but they have worked very hard today, or they have so much to do, or there is some good excuse and they cannot attend. Now, I have learned that when people really come to delight themselves in the Lord, such ex-cuses don't appear to be very important. Show me a man whose soul is panting after God, who can say with the Psalmist, "As the hart panteth after the water brooks, so panteth my soul after thee, O God." Such a man will love to go where he can have communion with God. He will as naturally postpone everything else that interferes with his communion with God as he draws his breath. The truth is, when people make such excuses about reading their Bibles and attending meetings, the secret is they have lost their keen relish for communion with God and are beginning to lose their delight in Him.

If we delight ourselves in God, He will delight himself in us. He will delight himself in us in proportion to our delight in Him. As we seek communion with Him, so will He seek com-munion with us. God loves society—the society of the holy. If we embrace Him, He will embrace us. If we pant after Him, He will pant after us. If we are drawn to Him, He will be drawn to us. This is the law of the mind. It is impossible that He should not delight in the person who delights in Him; impossible that He should not seek after the person who seeks after Him. It would be the same thing as denying himself, not to delight in those who delight in Him. Whenever a mind seeks union with God, God sets His heart on that person. He is as dear to Him as the apple of His eye. He loves him as He loves His own soul. Why should He not? He is like Him; he is a part of himself. He is, so to speak, flesh of His flesh and bone of His bone. He has come to be assimilated to His own nature. He comes to love him as He loves the man Christ Jesus, and for the same reason. And He will no more turn from him and not hear him than He would turn from His own beloved Son, Jesus Christ.

Now we ought to understand this, that whenever we find ourselves strongly drawn to God, God is infinitely drawn toward us. When our heart is panting after God, He is panting after us. In fact, it is God panting after us that draws us toward Him! We should fix this truth in our minds, that when our mind is tending toward God, He is tending toward us. "Draw nigh to me," God says, "and I will draw nigh to you. Turn unto me, and I will turn unto you. Love me and I will love you."

The person who delights in God will greatly moan if for any reason communion is withheld. Those will be days of mourning when, for any reason, God withholds the light of His countenance. It is impossible for him, then, to be cheerful and happy. He may have confidence and say as David, "Why art thou cast down, O my soul? and why art thou disquieted within me? hope thou in God: for I shall yet praise him, who is the health of my countenance, and my God." In this case, though the Psalmist had confidence in God, he mourned. He tried to cheer up his soul, but he could only mourn. In such a case the soul is ready to cry out, "My God, my God, why hast thou forsaken me?"

I have often thought that there is not so much mystery in what Christ said from the cross as many would make us believe. The Christian who knows what it is to commune and walk with God, and to have God withdraw His countenance from him, will naturally use this same language. And he will cry out with the Psalmist, "Will the Lord cast off for ever? and will he be favorable no more? Is his mercy clean gone for ever? Doth his promise fail for evermore? Hath God forgotten to be gracious? hath He in anger shut up his tender mercies?" It is not strange that Christ should cry out as He did. God's countenance was withdrawn from Him, and He could not help crying out to God to know why this was so.

Where a person has come to delight himself in God and falls into this state of mind in which he grieves, his mourning will be very submissive and peculiar. It will be nothing like the mourning of the world—a rebellious, complaining state of mind. It will be the mourning of a "weaned child," very submissive—a peculiar kind of mourning and submission. It is not rebellious nor complaining, and yet it is not joyful. It is not distrustful. "Hope thou in God," is its language, "for I shall yet praise him." It expects good from God. "I shall rejoice. Yes, for my Father will not always hide His face from me."

When these seasons last long, they lead the soul into such a state, and so show the individual to himself, that he is filled with deep grief and led to utter unearthly, heart-rending groans. At the same time, he has an expression of holy submission, a childlike dependence on God and a confidence and hope in Him. Oh, if the sinner could listen to such an individual when he supposed none but God near, he would go away and say, "Now I know, as I exist, I know there is such a thing as communion with God. Oh, such expressions! Such language! I know God was there!"

When I was an unrepentant sinner, I had been out to attend to some law business. Returning and passing by a schoolhouse, I heard a man praying. That prayer did more to impress my mind with the subject of religion than all I had ever heard before. I have not the least doubt that such a prayer would affect almost any man of reflection, could he hear it. The man did not know that anyone could hear him. He had left his work in the field, and had retired to the schoolhouse for secret communion with God. And as I rode along, I heard him and stopped and listened to what he said. Oh, how it set my mind on fire! I had never witnessed such praying before. It seemed as if I was brought right into the presence of God! The very tone of his voice, before I could understand what he said, seemed to come down upon me, like the voice of God from heaven. Every word he spoke seemed to come right from the bottom of his heart. His voice was frequently choked with groans and sighs. It was the voice of a man pleading with God!

When an individual is in this state of mind, when he has fallen into darkness for any reason whatever, although he mourns, he will not turn to any other source but God for happiness. He has travelled too far with God to go anywhere else for happiness. When a person has only a little grace, he will sometimes go to other objects, run with friends, going here and there, trying this thing and that to get happiness. But when one has come to delight himself in God, and the supreme desire of his soul has centered in Him, if he should fall into such circumstances as I have mentioned, he will not take a detour to other places and scenes to make himself happy! No, he will say, "O God, I cannot, I will not go anywhere else for happiness. O God, thou hast taught me to love thee; thou hast weaned my soul from everything else, so that I cannot love anything but thee, and now, wilt thou take thyself, thou who art my all, from me? O my God, I will find my joy in thee, or joy I will never have." Such will be the language of a soul in this state.

Do you know what this is? You will know if you will give your whole being up to God so as to be completely absorbed in Him. If this is not true with you, you need to be crucified with Christ and die to your self.

The happiness which the soul that delights itself in God finds in Him is so different from all other delight, so peculiar, it is like no other happiness in the world. All other joy is as nothing by comparison. It has such a peculiarity, such purity— there is nothing else that can compare with it. The intellect, the heart, the emotions, the whole being is utterly satisfied in God. Oh! I wish I had some words to describe this union with God! But we need some unearthly language to express what every Christian experiences when he comes into such a complete communion with God. He is so elevated in God. He is drinking of the very river of which God drinks. There is such a peculiarity, such sweetness in this, that the soul abhors all other joy. It cannot go and sip and sip in the polluted fountains of this world. What are they by comparison! Shall a person who has bathed in the very atmosphere of heaven sip of the filthy cups of this world? Never! Never! Only as he delights in God can he find any delight whatever. He cares for nothing else but what comes from God.

Be sure when you pray that you fulfill these conditions, that you delight yourself in God. For he who will be content with God will really be satisfied with Him and have as much of God as he wills. And just in proportion as we give ourselves up to find our delight in God shall we have delight in God. Search the universe over and you will find that just in proportion as the soul gives itself up to God, just in that proportion, will it find its fullness in God. If you divide your enjoyment, how can God fill your cup? Just empty your whole heart of self and of everything else, then hold it up to God, and He will fill it with His own purity, with His own love and blessedness. Yes, you will have it filled with the ocean of God.

2

PRAYER FOR A PURE HEART*

Create in me a clean heart, O God, and renew a right spirit within me" (Psalm 51:10).

The term rendered "right" in this passage is in the margin, "constant," and this seems to be its precise meaning. A constant, steadfast spirit as opposed to the fickle and unstable state in which he had so sadly fallen before temptation, was the thing David now desired and sought in earnest prayer.

In discussing the subject brought before us in this passage, I shall show:

► *What this petition really means.*
► *What is implied in offering it acceptably.*

What this petition really means.

The terms *heart* and *spirit* are used in the Bible in various senses. The term *heart* often denotes the *will*, or the voluntary attitude or state of the will. Sometimes *heart* is opposed to flesh, and then is synonymous with *mind* as distinct from body. In our text, both heart and spirit seem to be used in their widest and most general sense, including the whole mind—not its voluntary powers and states only, but also those which are involuntary. We must suppose that these terms as used here include other powers than the will, for it is manifest that his will was substantially in a right state already. He did not regard his will as opposed to God, for his will goes out in this earnest and

---

*The Oberlin Evangelist, March 14, 1849.

apparently most sincere prayer that his whole being might be made pure and be put in such a state that he should never sin again. It lies on the very face of this psalm that David's will was right before God. Hence he prays for something which he calls a clean heart and a right spirit, which is more than merely a right state of the will. It may be wisely sought in prayer after one's will is subdued, humbled, yielded to God and submissive.

Of course a clean heart and a right spirit, as used in this Psalm, imply a thorough cleansing or sanctification of the whole mind. Having a right spirit would include the regulation or cleansing of the imagination, the thoughts, desires, feelings—all those modifications of the capacity to perceive, and all those habits of thought and feeling which so often annoy the Christian and become most distressing and dangerous snares to his soul. These are often spoken of in the Bible as fleshly, "fleshly lusts which war against the soul." David obviously prays that God would do for him all that His omniscient eye saw needful to make and keep him pure from all sin, forever. He prays to be *made right* throughout all the powers and states of his being.

What is implied in offering it acceptably.

The petition must be offered *intelligently*. The petitioner must understand what he needs and have a practical and just apprehension of it. There can be no real *prayer* without this.

The person praying this prayer must have a *deep conviction of past sin*. One who is not convicted by the Holy Spirit has no conception of what this language means. Indeed, without the illumination and convicting agency of the Spirit, the sinner has no conceptions of anything of a spiritual nature. Hence, he needs to be convicted so as to understand thoroughly the nature of sin; then he will see his need and *feel* it deeply. This deep feeling, based on a just apprehension of his sin and guilt, is essential to acceptable prayer for a clean heart.

A sincere offering of this prayer implies *sincere repentance,* a real turning of the will from all sin; for without this there cannot be sincere prayer for a clean heart.

The prayer also implies *confession of sin to God.* By this I mean more than simply uttering our acknowledgment of sins before God; I mean confessing them as *sins committed against God.* We must deeply realize the power and self application of David's words: "Against thee, thee only, have I sinned, and done this evil in thy sight." Now, it is easy, and cheap too, for some men to confess their sins. But truly to understand the nature of sin in its relations to God, and to see how odious and how abominably guilty one's own sin is in view of these relations, is much more than mere oral confession. And yet the petitioner must enter deeply into those views of sin and realize that for his great sins against God he deserves the divine wrath forever, or he cannot throw his whole soul into this prayer for a clean heart and a right spirit.

There must also be a deep apprehension of one's danger of falling under temptation. It is plain that David in praying for a clean heart and right spirit made use of popular language. By it he really referred to those things in his constitution and habits which had been to him *occasions* of great sin. Who does not know that after the will is set right, and has done all it can do toward consecrating the whole being to God, the *occasions* of sin still exist and may still act with great energy. For example, the imagination—long trained in the course of sin, long corrupted, polluted, filled with foul images, and terribly under control of impure associations—remains to be regulated, renovated, and *cleansed* before it can be something other than a snare and a most unfit associate of a right will.

It should, however, be understood that sin, strictly speaking, belongs to *acts of the will* only. And when sin or moral defilement is applied to other faculties or states of the mind, the language is used in a popular and not a metaphysical sense. While this is true and important to be understood, it still remains true also that our mental associations, our states and habits of both mind and body, have been during our life of sin such that they continue after conversion to be active and fruitful occasions, but not causes, of sin.

This is illustrated in the case of David. His imagination had not become so regulated nor had his passions been so crucified and sanctified as to cease to act as occasions and temptations to sin. His lusts and appetites had long been so indulged and so developed by indulgence that though his will was converted to God, it might still be overpowered by their temptations. Every Christian knows more or less of the presence and power of these temptations. He is also conscious that these appetites, feelings, passions, imaginations and habits create within the mind a certain uneasiness and sense of loathing as if they were really unclean.

The Bible speaks of "the motions of sins" while we are in

the flesh, as working "in our members to bring forth fruit unto death." It seems to speak of our members in popular language as being sinful. In the case of David, whoever has had any experience in the government of corrupted feelings and of indulged passion cannot read this psalm without seeing what was working in his mind. Deeply convicted of his great sin, his mind turns within upon those propensities or inclinations of such fearful power—those appetites, habits and vile imaginations which had so woefully ensnared his soul and dishonored his God—and he cries aloud, "Oh, my God, give me a pure heart. Create in me a clean heart, O God, and renew a right spirit within me. Wash me thoroughly from mine iniquity, and cleanse me from my sin."

Hence this prayer implies a clear apprehension of those things which become occasions of sin, and involves especially a request for their entire subjugation and cleansing.

Those of you who have read Madame Guyon noticed that in speaking of the great work wrought in her she alludes to the fact that her imagination had been greatly polluted, but was at length, through sanctifying grace, so brought under the power of a holy will as to be no longer a source of conflict as before. So in the case of all Christians, the correction of all these states of mind and wayward imaginings and physical inclinations constitutes an important part of the work of moral cleansing.

This prayer offered acceptably implies a loathing of these occasions of sin and a deep dread of them. Take, for example, the man who has a polluted imagination. If he is a Christian, will he not find this an occasion of great self loathing? Deeply ashamed of himself, he often feels as if it would be a relief to him if he could spue out of his very self all those vile pollutions of thought and imagination, and be a new and pure creature. For although the action of the imagination is not itself sin, not being directly a voluntary state of mind, yet it often becomes a most disgusting and loathsome *occasion* of sin, and consequently in the renewed mind an occasion of great conflict. Hence the strong desire to be made pure in these respects.

God Is Willing To Help Us.

Prevailing prayer also involves an apprehension of our dependence on God to subdue habits of sin. Everyone who has tried to manage them himself has learned his own weakness; but ordinarily we learn our weakness and dependence no faster than we gain this experience by efforts to master inclinations to sin. How often does the Christian find himself thrown into deep agonizings, struggling in vain to overcome all within which creates temptations and occasions to sin! When this painful and dear-bought experience has thoroughly taught a man his dependence on God, he can then sincerely ask God to do the great work of moral cleansing for him. Without the teachings of experience, you can scarcely expect anyone to be sincere and heartily earnest in prevailing prayer. Every Christian should know, beyond all doubt or hesitation, that he needs God's aid, and can do nothing without it.

Prevailing prayer also implies a confidence in the ability of God to do this work of cleansing. I speak now only of the masses of professed Christians, for some individuals hold different views and pray as David did for entire moral cleansing to take place in this life. There is no evidence in this psalm that David prayed or expected death to do this work of cleansing. On the other hand, he most obviously prayed for this work to be done here and now. He expected to live after it was done, and tells God what he shall do after his heart is made clean in answer to his prayers. "Then," he says, "will I teach transgressors thy ways, and sinners shall be converted unto thee."

But most Christians in these latter ages expect death to do this work of cleansing, and of course they anticipate nothing better than to carry these loathsome things with them till they die. If indeed this *were* an allotment of God, it would be a severe condition for a Christian to impose upon himself by failing to embrace the proposal of almighty aid in the speedy accomplishment of a universal renewal unto holiness.

Certain others have thought that subduing the propensities, these inclinations, is equivalent to their annihilation. This, however, is a great mistake; for David who prayed that his whole being might be cleansed evidently did not expect to lose his imagination altogether, nor indeed did he think of having any other faculty of mind or body annihilated, as if God had created some faculties which are intrinsically evil and must therefore be removed from the system before it can be morally pure! David did not think or pray with this notion; on the contrary, he prayed that God would regenerate his whole being— overhaul it, make it over, mold it into purity and order—till it should subserve and not derange the right action of a sanctified will.

This prayer of David's implies confidence that God is *able* and *willing* to answer it; moreover, that to do so is in accordance with the plans and purposes of His moral government. If he had believed only that God is able, but that He has no purpose, plan or will to do such a thing under any circumstances of our earthly life, would it not have been blasphemous for him to have offered this prayer? Look at it! Suppose David had believed, as some now are understood to hold, that God, though able, had no intention or will to give the Christian a clean heart during this life. Would not this prayer of his have been impious? It would be as much as to say, "Lord, I know thou hast no desire or intention to give thy children a pure heart in this world; but, Lord, we want this blessing, and we want it *now*, and we cannot be denied. Let thy purposes stand ever so much opposed to granting the blessing; we want it." Nor could the Psalmist have offered such a prayer without tempting God. Hence, we may infer that he doubtless believed it to be in accordance with God's government and plans to bestow this blessing when earnestly sought by prayer.

I have often known men who had great uncertainties as to whether God intended in all cases to lead Christians through life pure, their hearts cleansed in the sense of our text. Consequently, if they ever ask for these blessings, they are afraid to believe, and hence they cannot possibly cast themselves upon the Lord in such confidence as is essential to prevailing prayer. They know that God is able, but they do not believe He is willing; hence, they are greatly troubled, and there can be no strong confidence, no childlike trust in their prayers.

Not so with David. He held God to be willing as well as able. You must certainly admit that David assumed God's willingness to do the very thing he asked, whatever you may suppose that thing to be. The real thing requested in his prayer he must have supposed God most willing to perform.

We must be willing to submit to God.

The sincere prayer that God would create in us a clean heart implies that on our part *we are willing to have the thing done.* People often have strong desires that something should be done, yet they are not willing that it really be done. A tooth aches painfully; they know it ought to come out. Oh, how they wish it were out now! But are they *willing* to have it done? That's the trying point. Their desires in the matter are very strong but they don't amount to a willingness. So, often, this is the case with regard to wishing and praying for a clean heart. People think they want a pure heart; but when they come to see all that is implied in it, they shrink back, and say, "No. We cannot meet all those consequences."

A striking case of this sort once fell under my observation. A young lady claimed she was willing to become a Christian, and I suppose honestly thought so. I often pressed her with the fact that she was not really willing to become a Christian, but she as often resisted my position and my arguments. Ultimately she heard a sermon which greatly affected her, and brought her to determine that she would not live in her sins any longer. She turned her thoughts in deep earnest toward God and began to ask Him to take away all her sins. But suddenly when she saw so clearly how much would be involved in this, she shrank back and withdrew her petition. She rose from her knees and went her way. She had found that she did not want to be *such a Christian.*

So often this is the way with people who profess to be Christians. When they see all that is implied in a clean heart, they turn away. They may have offered this prayer often without apprehending how much it implies. When they come to see the whole matter, they are conscious of shrinking from meeting such results.

Hence, an acceptable offering of this prayer implies that we are willing to have this whole work done. We are willing to have every constitutional appetite, passion, tendency and function of either flesh or spirit so modified as to come perfectly under the control of right reason and of God's revealed will. We must be willing to have our bodies become fit temples for God's indwelling Spirit—every function or faculty of our entire nature being in harmony with a holy heart, being such as would not soil an angel's purity, if his spirit were to inhabit our body, and act through our physical organs.

This prayer offered acceptably implies that we are willing for God to do His own work *in His own way.*

Often people will dictate to God the *manner* in which they want things done. They ask only with certain reservations and qualifications, as if they would say, "May God be pleased to do this thing provided it shall not touch my idol. May God sanctify all my appetites, so as to bring them under the law of enlightened reason, except this favorite one—spare me this, for I am very partial to it and it has been such a comfort to me so long!" Or perhaps they are afraid to pray right out (without qualification or exception) that God would actually give them a heart universally clean and a spirit altogether right, lest, if their prayer should be answered, it might smite some of the precious things they love. As a woman once said to me, "I dare not ask for sanctification, lest if I should, *God should take away my husband!*" "But why such fears?" "Because I am conscious that my heart is greatly bound up in him, and I am terribly afraid that God could not sanctify me without tearing him away from my heart."

Of course this woman could not pray, "Create in me a clean heart, O God, and renew a right spirit within me." This prayer implies that we are willing to have any sacrifice made which God sees to be necessary; that we yield ourselves to all the outward training, and also to all the inward training, which in the eye of God may appear to be necessary. We submit ourselves to His discretion as to the things to be done as to time, the manner, and all the circumstances of doing it. We do most fully and freely consent that God should use His own infinite wisdom. Let Him smite whatever He sees best. Let my soul commit itself into His hands to suffer any pain and endure any sacrifice which His wisdom may choose and His love can inflict. Let me never fear any unreasonable severity *from such a Father!*

But how often Christians have their own way marked out for God to walk in. They would have Him be careful to deal with themselves very gently, and especially beware not to use His providential rod too roughly. It would suit them well if the Lord would come down upon them as with an electric shock and shake their very souls into purity and holiness. Some sudden and purely spiritual agency is often the thing they are dreaming of, and they prefer that the clean heart shall come in this way rather than by any form of sore trial. They seem not to realize that there are some attachments of such a character that God cannot rectify them without seizing upon the loved object, butting it down, tearing up its very roots, and rending asunder all those tender ligaments which bind our hearts in selfish, idolatrous love to our idol. Every Christian ought to consider that asking God sincerely to create in us a clean heart involves the submission of our entire case to His management with full permission from us to use the *knife* or anything else He may find necessary for a thorough cure.

This prayer, to be acceptable, must involve not only a willingness to have the thing done, but to take with it the consequences which will naturally follow. If the gift of a clean heart involves new relations and new duties, we must meet them cheerfully. And what is more, in anticipation of them we must not shrink; for if we do, we cannot have the gift. Thus, for example, it is obviously the duty of those whom God thus blesses to glorify His name. Let them, like the leper, go into the temple to bear their public testimony to saving grace. Or like David, let them be able to say, "I have not *hid* thy righteousness within my heart; I have not concealed thy lovingkindness and thy truth from the great congregation." Even beforehand, let them say as he did, "Deliver me . . . and my tongue shall sing aloud of thy righteousness. . . . open thou my lips: and my mouth shall show forth thy praise."

Now many would be very willing to be religious if they might accomplish it all without any consequent reproach. They might even be happy to be sanctified if they might have the blessing of no attendant dishonor, no sacrifice of reputation. If nobody would talk about them. If none would observe their conduct and their spirit more closely than before. But all such compromises for reputation's sake are vain and ruinous. You must be willing to lay your very self upon God's altar. Your self I say, your all: reputation, name, leisure, your estate if need be, your personal liberty if God's providence calls for it, and even your life. Go up with firm unfaltering step and lay your all upon that altar; then let God do with that offering what He will: blast it, burn it, blow it to every quarter of the heavens. Yet lay it down and say, whether in the fear or the face of all losses, "These things are thine, O my God; do with them all as thou please. Spare me nothing which thou pleases to take. I trust thy wisdom and thine infallible love."

Now, every Christian should know that the gift of a clean heart and a right spirit comes not from God till he is willing to take with it its legitimate consequences, till he is willing to trust the results to the wisdom of his great Father. You must be willing to be made a spectacle to angels and to men, for God will never light a candle to put it under a bushel. You may lift up your cry the hundredth time for the blessing; still the question will return, "Will you glorify God? Will you let your light shine? Will you do all you can to make the gift, if bestowed on you, available to the glory of the Blessed Giver?" God asks, "Are you willing I should put you in the furnace and heat up the fire to sevenfold fury, and let the world look on to see what grace can do?" You are wrong if you suppose God does such works of sanctifying mercy for your sake alone. "Not for *your* sake, be it known unto you, O house of Israel, saith the Holy One, but for my holy name's sake."

Let it be well understood that you must be willing to meet and bear the trials which God sends. You must expect trials, such trials as will probably call the attention of others to your case. Perhaps God would eagerly profit others by the blessings He gives you. If so, should you rebel? Perhaps He would glorify himself. If so, shall you shrink? Never! It places you rather under obligation to glory in tribulation, outward or inward: for it is sweet even by suffering to be made the passive instruments of glorifying our Father in heaven. Let the burning trial come, if the grace of God thereby shines the more brightly. It is the manner of our God to make the holiness of His people and the riches of His own grace shine most gloriously in the furnace of affliction.

REMARKS

I remark first what I have already said in substance but repeat here, that David intended to be sanctified in the present life. His will at the time he offered the prayer in the text was already right, but he had other things about him which were not right, and his soul was fixed to have them corrected. His vile imagination must be regulated. His lusts subdued and slain. He wanted the whole man set in such tone that he would not be continually falling into sin from temptations. All these were blessings which he needed in the present life if ever, needed *then*, which moreover he prayed he might obtain *then*, and which he manifestly expected then.

Many are in the habit of using this language of prayer frequently without really apprehending what it means. Consequently their prayers obtain no particular answer. No one need expect a specific answer to prayer unless he prays specifically and knows what it is. It is impossible that there should be intelligent desire for objects unless those objects are apprehended by the mind with considerable distinctness.

Many do not fulfill the conditions so as to offer the prayer acceptably. They lack the requisite confidence in God. Not asking in faith, they cannot receive, for their unbelief places it beyond the power of God to bless them without sacrificing His own honor.

We do not understand the recorded prayers of Scripture, nor the promises, until we are brought into a state of mind similar to that of the writer. As to David, I do not mean that none can understand this prayer in our text until they have committed

David's sins, but I do mean that we must see ourselves to have committed some sins, and that we must be greatly humbled and deeply penitent as he was, and be filled with utter self-loathing as was the case with him. Such a state of mind brings out the full and precious meaning of the promise. It unfolds it like a charm in luster and glory such as none but the humbled soul can possibly appreciate.

It is moreover quite essential that we should *understand* our liabilities to fail before temptation actually comes. Probably David, before his sin, was not aware of his great danger. He did not know how powerful those occasions to sin actually were. He might have been entirely unaware that any circumstances could ever have involved him in such dreadful sin. First seduction and adultery, then betrayal and murder in their meanest form. Who can believe that David previous to his sin understood all his own fearful liabilities to such sins as these? What, therefore, must have been his amazement when these terrible tendencies and occasions of sin came to be developed! How did he then cry out in deep anguish of his soul, "O my God, save me from myself! O my God, create in me a clean heart, and renew a right spirit within me." So must every Christian see himself in these dark, fearful aspects of his character before his prayer will be like David's, a prayer of deep agony of soul.

It is not uncommon for Christians to have a right will and of course be in this respect acceptable to God while yet their previous habits have been so bad as to subject them to continual struggles and warfare. The imagination takes its filthy course, rioting in its pollutions unless constantly held in check by the pressure of some great considerations. Now the thing needed by such people is to see their dangers and liabilities, and then to throw themselves upon the saving strength of the Most High God.

The unsanctified involuntary states of mind are great enemies to the soul. These appetites are the "fleshly lusts" that war against the soul's peace and purity. If these were removed, there would still remain the devil to war against. With them we have both Satan from without and our unsubdued propensities and ungoverned imagination within.

Formerly it was supposed that these conflicts with appetite were a real warfare with inborn and inbred sin. I hold no such doctrine. These appetites are not themselves sin, but they are the occasions of sin: the means of temptation to sin; and hence, are objects of dread and loathing to the Christian.

In proportion as these lusts are subdued, there will arise in the mind a sense of purity. I have said that the soul loathes these appetites and passions which become occasions of sin, and loathes itself on account of them and their vile associations. For the same reason, when purified from these loathed abominations, there will ensue a sweet consciousness of being pure, such as can by no means exist prior to their subjugation and cleansing.

This rectification of the appetites, sensibilities and imagination has been commonly called sanctification, because people have really supposed that these things were themselves sinful. If they really were so, then their rectification would be genuine sanctification. In popular language there seems to be no strong objection to their being called this now. Indeed the Bible, ever using popular language, speaks of sanctification as affecting "spirit, soul and body." "The very God of peace sanctify you wholly. And I pray God your whole spirit and soul and body be preserved *blameless*"; as if blame might attach to either. The writer doubtless intends simply the sanctification of the whole man, in which state the body would no longer be the occasion of sin to the mind.

This blessing is exceedingly valuable and desirable. It is hardly possible to estimate adequately its great value. Let one experience what David did. Have reason to loathe himself as he had. Have occasion to know the dreadful power of those inward foes—those terrible snares to his soul. Let him see how his tyrant lusts have overpowered him and laid him prostrate and bleeding in the dust. Then may he see how greatly desirable it is to have even the hottest fires of providential discipline seize upon him and burn up all his tin and dross till nothing remains but gold well purified. Oh, how he will rejoice in spite of such a process to come forth redeemed and cleansed, so that he may stand henceforth perfect and complete in all the will of God!

This blessing is indispensable to inward tranquillity and peace of mind. No further than this entire work is advanced can one enjoy repose in God. The will may be right; but the mind will almost continually experience those terrible agitations which result from conflict with unsubdued, ungoverned sensuality. There can be no abiding grace till the whole man is brought into harmony with God's service with a holy will and a holy life.

Especially is this blessing greatly desirable as a condition of passing tranquilly through difficult outward trials. When men have received this blessing, it seems to be the order of God's providence to test them and cause them to exhibit great calmness to the praise of victorious grace. Then observers will wonder how they can pass so calmly and so sweetly through such fiery trials. The three children in Daniel walked within the burning furnace, amid its hottest flames, and came forth with no smell of fire on them, for the Son of God had been there. Likewise, when Christians have their lusts subdued and slain beforehand, so that Jesus can walk with them through the furnace, no fires can burn upon them from without or within. All is calm and is safe. A man once said of a Christian sister who was under the most distressing trials, "I wonder how she can live." But she was calm and quiet as a lamb. God can purify us so that we can pass through the most terrible trials unruffled as the air of a summer evening.

The blessing of sanctification is very important to our highest usefulness. People have been useful without this, but if they would be useful in the highest degree, they must go to God, imploring Him to do all He sees they need. This is the very spirit in which we should apply to God for this blessing. "O my God, do all thy will in me; then put me in any position in the universe which will most fully illustrate and extol thy grace. No matter what it is, only let it greatly glorify thy name."

Until this work is done, Christians will more or less frequently be a great stumbling block to the world, and indeed to all others. So was David. His heart was not thoroughly made pure; hence, a constant liability to such dreadful sins as those into which he fell. President Edwards made and put on record this most excellent resolution: "When I fall into any sins, I will not rest until I have searched out and found the occasion and have removed it." This great man had learned enough from his own experience to show him that he must look for the *occasions of sin*. When a patient is sick, you would not attack the symptoms, but would look for the occasions or causes and would seek to remove them. So in the occurrence of sin, you must look for the occasions and give yourself no rest till they are thoroughly removed. Hence the fitness of this prayer made by the Psalmist, and hence the reason why you should go to God and cry, "O my God, create in me a clean heart. Take away all these distressing occasions of sin, or I shall continue to dishonor thee and bring reproach on thy name."

3

THE JOY OF GOD'S SALVATION*

"Restore unto me the joy of Thy salvation" (Psalm 51:12).

In speaking from these words, I shall show:
- ► *What the Psalmist prayed for.*
- ► *Why he prayed for it.*
- ► *The conditions upon which this prayer can be answered.*
- ► *What is implied in offering such a prayer acceptably.*

What the Psalmist prayed for.

Our first inquiry respects the elements which enter into the Christian's joy, or in other words, the joy of God's salvation.

It is pertinent to observe here that there are elements in this joy which do not belong to the holy joy of beings who have never sinned. The saved sinner has some forms of joy that the unfallen angel has not and cannot have. From this I do not infer that the sinful, when saved, are more happy than the sinless who have never needed salvation. I only say that the joy of each has elements in it which are unlike those of the other, and this everyone must see who enters at all into the peculiar circumstances and state of mind of each class.

The words of our text are found in what is called David's penitential psalm. This psalm, as the caption states and as the scope sufficiently shows, was written with reference to David's great sin in the matter of Bathsheba and Uriah. It may have been written at the very time of his being rebuked by Nathan,

*The Oberlin Evangelist, April 13, 1849.

and of his becoming penitent, as the caption of the psalm would seem to indicate. Or if written sometime, more or less, afterward, it was evidently *in recollection of those scenes*; so that we must regard these circumstances as being the *occasion* of the prayer in our text.

Our question now is: What are the principal ingredients or elements of this state of mind?

A sense of pardon. Some might repent and yet not have in full measure the joys of God's salvation; for one element of this joy is a *sense of pardon.* The sinner needs a revelation from God that God has forgiven him.

A sense of divine reconciliation. We can conceive of a person who may be truly penitent and yet have no manifestations made to his soul of God's forgiving grace. He might not see that God is reconciled to him, might not think of or believe any such thing. But it is plain that some degree of divine manifestation on this point is essential to constitute the joy of God's salvation in the case of a sinner convicted of sin. It might not be essential to a sinless being, but must be to one who like David has sinned, and feels himself to have fallen under the divine displeasure.

The love of complacency. The Scriptures speak of "the love of God shed abroad in the heart by the Holy Spirit." The experience of Christians shows that this shedding abroad of divine love in the heart by the Holy Spirit usually follows deep exercises of penitence and of faith in Christ's redeeming blood.

This love is a state of the sensibility as opposed to any action of the will. It consists substantially in emotions of pleasure and delight in God and in His ways and works, and differs essentially from the love of benevolence. It is one of the elements of a forgiven sinner's joy.

A sense of inward purity. I do not suppose an individual could have the joy of God's salvation unless he had a sense of inward purity. He could not have real and rich joy unless he felt as Brainerd expressed himself, "I am clean from both past and present sin." Without this element one may have excitement, but he cannot have the real joy of God's salvation. For he still lacks the real *salvation* itself, that in which the real blessedness of a saved soul chiefly consists; namely, inward purity, positive deliverance from present sin. When God applies the energy of His Spirit to renew the soul, and in place of selfish lusts to shed abroad his own love in the heart, there is begotten a sweet sense of present purity, and the soul has the witness in itself that sin is put away and divine love has taken its place.

A sense of inward harmony. By this I refer to a state of mind which is in harmony with God and with all other holy beings in the universe, as well as with itself. Its own powers are brought into such fitting correlation with each other, and all together are in such relations to God, that the very working of their perfect machinery produces harmony. Perhaps there is no word which so well expresses this delightful result as *harmony.* It is indeed like the harmony of sweet music. Each separate vibration fits every other, and together they produce the result of most exquisite harmony. None will understand this unless they have a keen apprehension of what the word *harmony* means. I have often been struck to see how differently men will understand the meaning of words or language. It is so with the word *harmony.* Some minds have no just conception of what harmony is. But one who has a keen relish for harmony in sounds, who has a cultivated taste, and an ear well attuned, can understand what is intended by harmony of soul when all its powers are in tune. He can understand it too by the law of contrast. Let him listen to the grating discord of a piano, or worse still of an organ when utterly out of tune. Oh, how it rakes his sensibilities! So is the mind in its unconverted state; and so too as it passes along slowly in its progress toward becoming attuned to the sweet harmony of love. But when God himself puts it in tune, putting every pipe and every string in order, so that He can run His divine fingers over it and make it breathe forth the very harmony of heaven, then, oh, what music! No words can describe it! But if you will commit your own soul into God's hands that He may put it in spiritual tune, you may learn by experience what it is. You will find it a most blessed experience. When every power, every affection, every element of your soul's activities is in such tune that not a note, not even a sentence can be found in it which is not perfectly in tune, then what rich harmony it will produce! Peace will be an all-pervading element in the atmosphere of your soul—every opinion, every emotion, every affection is in harmony with God.

Of course there will be implied in this a delight in the whole revealed will of God—in all His character, in all He does, and in all He omits to do. It involves acquiescence in all His providential arrangements, including all He accomplishes and all He neglects to accomplish. When this state of mind exists in its purity, there is a universal satisfaction of mind in God. Every want and demand both of our nature and of our circumstances is seen to be perfectly met in God. A deep apprehension of this forms a prominent part of the joy of God's salvation.

Why he prayed for it.

David prayed for this blessing because it was desirable in itself. It is in itself good, and therefore lawful to pray for.

Possessing this joy is honorable to God. Such happiness ought to characterize the children of so great and bountiful a Father. Its absence greatly dishonors God. Is it not dishonorable to a king that his "children should go mourning all their days"? How strange that those who profess to be children of God should have no joy! Would it not dishonor God to have His people lean and ill-favored, going about the streets like walking skeletons? It is as though He could endure this himself, and not only so, but even liked Christians better for their rags and filthiness! Who can believe this? What prince on earth ever kept his court and above all, his children, looking in such style?

Christians who live without spiritual joy and peace not only dishonor God, but highly disgrace Him. What is implied when a Christian complains of the absence of spiritual joy? He must imply either that God is very careful about giving His children occasions of joy, or that they are loathe to embrace and enjoy those occasions.

The joyful Christian is exceedingly helpful to others. Who can estimate the value of a living fountain of waters in a barren desert? A Christian who always has something to say of the joy of God's salvation is like Siloam's well in a land of drought, or like an oasis in a wilderness. His words and his spirit are all the more reviving because so many are always complaining. How often are we grieved and distressed with these complaints!

A single joyous-hearted Christian is a priceless blessing in a family. To have one such Christian in each household who should be so full of the joys of God's salvation that he could not help speaking it out on all fit occasions; this would be like planting a well-spring of water in every acre of earth's desert sands. How soon the wilderness would rejoice and blossom as the rose! How often has one such Christian set a whole community on fire with desire to get rid of their darkness and come forth into God's glorious light!

The spiritual joy of Christians is exceedingly helpful to sinners. Sinners know that Christians ought to rejoice in God, and of course are not surprised that they should. The sinner is impressed to see the Christian at rest in God! Oh, he knows nothing of that peace himself, and the view of it as enjoyed by the Christian reveals his own desolation. What sinner was ever in the habit of mingling in the society of Christians whose heart and lips are full of joy, without himself feeling unutterable yearnings of heart for such joys as these! I can well recollect that some of my earliest impressions of a serious nature were occasioned by hearing a young man speak of his joy in God. I went home from that meeting weeping. I said to myself—that joy is rational; it is a joy worthy of a human soul. I walked along with many tears, and when alone, I sought a retired and dry place to kneel down and pray that God would give me what that young man had. All I had ever heard of sermons and lectures had not made half so much impression as that young man's religious joy.

Sinners know that they really lack joy; hence, when they see the Christian's joy, they cannot help contrasting it with their own, and the result can scarcely fail to reveal to them their own wretched state.

These struggles of the sinner for joy are indeed altogether selfish. My prayers at the time alluded to were so; but yet they were helpful, for they served to enforce conviction of the value of Christian faith and of the worthlessness of everything short of it. The Psalmist understood the value of Godly joy. "Restore unto me," said he, "the joy of thy salvation; *then* will I teach transgressors thy ways, and sinners shall be converted unto thee." He knew this would make a powerful impression on their minds for good.

The absence of this spiritual joy is a great stumbling block to all classes of people. What a stumbling block to a church to have a minister who is perpetually in spiritual darkness and trouble! How can he serve the Lord's Supper if his own heart is cowering with spiritual fears, or if he is suffering under spiritual agonies for himself? The more important the position of a man, the more desirable it becomes that he should be full of the joy and peace which the Holy Spirit inspires. Deacons in a church, parents in a family, professors in a college, how can people who hold such stations of responsibility ever think of fulfilling their responsibilities without possessing grace enough to give them the joy of God's salvation?

In saying this I would not be understood to imply that Christians never have trials and sorrows; they will have them doubtless, but even in these very trials and sorrows, how precious will be the joys of God's salvation to their souls.

The joy of God's salvation is especially indispensable to one who preaches the Gospel. A person might preach *something* without it, but not the Gospel. He might deliver moral essays, or might contend valiantly for his polemic creed; but as for preaching the vital matters of salvation, how can he if he knows nothing about them by experience? He needs such faith as brings peace, such communion of soul with God as brings joy of heart. This is something more than being penitent or merely pious. The Psalmist knew that he was penitent, yet he knew also he needed something more. God had not yet revealed the light of His own face to him. Hence, when he had confessed and humbled himself before God, it still remained that he should pray, "Restore unto me the joy of thy salvation."

David had known well what it was to be full of joy before God. He had danced for joy with all his might before the ark of the Lord, and often we find him preparing songs of joy and praise; but now, alas, his harp is silent and all unstrung! He has sinned grievously against God. A thick cloud has come over his soul. And though he has confessed, yet still he has occasion to pray, "Restore unto me the joy of thy salvation." Why does he want this joy? Because without it he cannot teach transgressors to any good purpose.

What Christian does not know how to sympathize with David in this state of mind? Who has not known by experience the state of those who have sinned and confessed, but still have the greatest occasion to ask God to restore to them the lost joy of His salvation? The soul cries out, "Lord, how can I live, shut out in the darkness from thee? Oh, if thou canst, wilt thou not reveal thy reconciled face and restore again the joys of thy salvation?"

The conditions upon which this prayer can be answered.

We must have a sense of our own sins and their deep and damning guilt. I said that some of the elements in the Christian's joy do not exist in the joy of angels or beings without sin. In the Christian's case, it is indispensable that his joy should be preceded by a sense of sin and guilt. Otherwise, he cannot appreciate the grace of pardon, cannot really appreciate anything about the Gospel. He needs such a sense of sin as to understand how great a thing it is to be delivered from sin, rescued from its further commission, and pardoned of its horrible guilt.

To experience the joy of gospel salvation a person must confess his sin and really repent of it. God would be poorly employed if He restored the joys of salvation to one who has not repented.

Making restitution must also be a condition of receiving the joy of salvation. This is essential to real repentance.

One must have an apprehension of the atonement and way of acceptance. I have said that one might repent and yet not have this sense of restored joy. I know this to be true; and I believe every Christian reading this knows it. In order to have this joy, we need a sense of pardon, but this is not all. We need *such* a sense of it and such a view of its *manner* in being granted as shall justify God—such a view as will show that God is just in pardoning the sinner. The sinner in the state of mind supposed is not selfish; hence, he desires God to be justified, and could not be happy to receive pardon in any way which he did not see would fully acquit and greatly glorify God. Hence, he needs to see that the gospel manner of pardon is such as most fully justifies and honors God. He needs to see that the atonement through Jesus Christ most perfectly answers all these great and most desirable ends. I do not believe it possible for a man to enter into the joy of God's salvation without some just notions of the atonement as the way in which God can be glorious in forgiving sin.

Another essential condition is the acceptance of Christ in the fullness of His relations. Unless we see what relations Christ sustains to us and what He consequently can do for us, it is impossible to experience this joy. Unless we apprehend Christ's fullness, we cannot receive fully the joy of His salvation.

The condition of universal confidence in God is indispensable. If there is anything in which we have no confidence in God, there will be chafing and trouble. The soul is not right toward God.

An entire renunciation of self is a condition. Whoever does not renounce himself cannot have this joy. You must renounce all idols. What would you think of God if He were to give this joy to those who are sipping at every fountain of earthly pleasure, trying to find some little joy besides that from God?

There must also be a sympathy of will with God. Our will must be so thoroughly with His that we can go with Him in all He does without the least reluctance of misgiving.

Furthermore, subdued appetites and passions are essential; for while these are clamoring for indulgence, it is utterly impossible for the soul to experience the joys of God's salvation.

Another condition is the indwelling Spirit of God; for who will have his appetites subdued, or indeed, who will fulfill any of these conditions without the Holy Spirit?

It is essential that there should be a clear medium of communication between our souls and God. A man who does not have communion with God cannot have the joys of gospel salvation. When for any reason the soul is shut out from God and the communion is not free, God hides His face and the soul cannot rejoice in the joy of His great salvation.

What is implied in offering such a prayer acceptably.

We need a sense of our necessities; for until we feel our needs, we never will pray with any fervency. As long as we are sipping at every accessible fountain of earthly pleasure and accumulating for ourselves poor broken cisterns as well, we are never likely to come to the gospel fountain. The soul needs to have a sense of its great necessities, a consciousness of being altogether empty, and hence a conviction of its need of access to the divine fountain, or there is no hope it will ever come to this fountain for the waters of life.

Another requirement is a sense of dependence on God for this state of mind. People may feel their need of the blessing and yet not realize their dependence on God. But this feeling of dependence must exist in the mind before one can deeply and earnestly rest upon God for the blessing. People need to know and to realize that although they have power to repent, they cannot get access to this fountain of divine pleasures without God's help. His angel must come down and trouble the waters of this "house of mercy"; and lend us a kind hand to help us down therein; then our soul is made whole of "whatsoever disease it had."

Acceptable prayer implies fulfilling the conditions. If not, we only tempt God. He who knows the revealed conditions and yet prays God to bestow the blessing without fulfilling the conditions insults God to His face. It amounts to demanding that God should ignore or abolish His expressed conditions; a thing which of course He can never do, and which no man can even impliedly ask Him to do without abusing God exceedingly.

It is especially important that this prayer is not selfish. The person must be consecrated to God, fully purposed to use the blessing if obtained. And if not obtained, yet to use everything it has for the glory of God and the highest good of man. David felt this way: "Then will I teach transgressors thy ways, and sinners shall be converted unto thee." There is a great danger in asking for spiritual joy: our hearts may be selfish instead of disinterestedly seeking to glorify God in all things, even with the religious joy and peace which He may graciously impart to us.

A sense of the great value of this joy is another requirement. This should be coupled with the realization that you do not deserve it. If you combine these two sentiments in their great strength, you are in small danger of seeking in vain the joy of salvation.

In connection with these, there must be great confidence in God's willingness to bestow the blessings sought. David seems to have had this. There must be a willingness to have God use all the necessary means to open the way for this result. There may be a great many springs of earthly joy to be dried up, many idols to be removed, many a cup of earthly pleasure to be dashed, before we are prepared to receive the joy of God's salvation. Consequently, there must be on our part a willingness to have God do anything He pleases with us to prepare the way. Unless we are thus willing that God should take His own course, we are making conditions for God which show that we are real hypocrites. We are trying to get the joy of holiness without the holiness itself.

There must also be a willingness to leave the time, the way, and the conditions of conferring the blessing wholly in the disposal of Infinite Wisdom. All must be left in His hands with the most unqualified submission, ourselves ready to do or suffer anything that is necessary so we may glorify God.

There must also be a fixed purpose to make a wise and holy use of the blessings which we receive. It must be in our heart to use this blessing wholly for God. Unless we pray with the sincere intention of asking it *for* God, we have no reason to expect it. A person would be poorly employed to pray for this blessing just to put it under a bushel. The great Giver eagerly seeks to make His goodness known. Why shouldn't you lend your aid in so noble an enterprise, for an end so glorious?

If God fills your cup, you must be willing to pass it around and let others be refreshed from the same fountain. Show them where the fountain is and how good its waters are. They do not know much about these things, and they need the hints you can easily give them if your own heart is full of that divine joy.

REMARKS

Many who profess to be Christian know nothing of the joys of God's salvation. I was impressed with this long before my conversion. At that time I was in the habit of conversing with Christians about their own experiences. Having much curiosity on this subject, I felt free to inquire about it and took frequent opportunities to do so. It was with me a matter of speculation, being then, as now, much struck with the apparent fact that so few Christians had much real joy in God. The impression was often made on my mind that most Christians were wretched, unhappy, muttering, grumbling, and full of trouble. Hence, the conviction ripened more and more in my mind that they had little or no real joy in God. They might have repented of sin and lost their burden at the cross, but they did not seem to know much, if anything, about the joys of God's salvation. On this subject they were generally silent, having little or nothing to say of the salvation of God and the light of His countenance.

A great many who profess to be Christian seem not to care for this blessing. They scramble after dress or money, are anxious after worldly goods as if there were no other good for them to seek, and live for this world as if God had told them to seek first the kingdom of this world and its good things. So they press on, running to this concert, to that show or party of pleasure, always lusting after something sensual and worldly. Such are their pursuits, and such of course is their character. They would rather go to a circus than into their closet or to a prayer meeting. They cannot imagine how any one can wish to go like Francis Xavier into his closet, who spent seven hours at once in such deep and holy communion with God that his countenance glowed like an angel's. They can form no just conception of the attractiveness of such a scene and of such employments.

When a Christian has really tasted this joy in God, and then subsequently been deprived of it, he will go with his head bowed down like a bullrush. He looks as if he had lost all the friends he ever had. Having once drunk from the sweet waters of life, oh, how insipid are the draughts of earthly joy! I do not mean to imply by this that Christians cannot enjoy earthly things. They can. None can enjoy earthly good with half so solid a relish as those who have God in all their earthly good, and take all as His gift from His hand. But let a man who has experienced these joys once get away from God and into sin, as David did, and his peace and joy are spoiled. He looks ashamed before God and before men. He cannot hold up his head. If you meet him in a Christian spirit, he cannot look you in the face—especially if you show him that your heart is full of the joys of God's salvation. How often I have seen this, and so probably have many of you. Look around you. There is a professed Christian fallen into sin. Let someone arise before him, full of the joys of God's salvation, and oh, how self-condemned he is. How full of agony and trouble! Poor man; he is far from God and can find no rest there.

Some people care just enough for these joys to pray for them selfishly, but in no other way. I remember a man with whom I was boarding during a revival. Being greatly troubled about his own spiritual state, he asked me, "What would you think of a man who prays for the Spirit of God week after week but never receives?" My reply was, "I should think the man prayed selfishly. I presume that is all the trouble. The devil might pray for spiritual joy in the very same way, his only end being his own spiritual enjoyment. The Psalmist did not pray so. He prayed that God would restore to him the lost joys of his salvation; but his motives were not selfish. No, for he adds, "Then will I teach transgressors thy ways, and sinners shall be converted unto thee." This seemed to the man a hard saying, and he went away, as he afterward told me, in great anger, and prayed that God would kill him. However, a little more thought, together with the melting power of the Spirit, subdued him, and he became as docile and humble as a lamb.

So it often happens that people want God to meet their selfishness; and when they find He does not, they often have a long struggle before they really humble themselves so as to meet God on His own grounds.

Many think that caring for the joy of God's salvation is necessarily selfish. They do not realize the value of this joy to the church, to God, and to the world; hence, they cannot realize that any motives other than selfish ones can induce Christians to pray for it. Consequently, with these views of the selfish character, they pray for it very little, if at all.

Few realize the importance of having this joy of the Lord in their souls. They seem not to appreciate its important bearings upon the interests of vital godliness.

Many Christians have special seasons and states of mind in which they are very desirous to have this blessing; but on the whole they are unwilling to yield up the sources of their carnal joys. They would gladly have both if they could; but since they cannot, they cleave to the carnal and forego the spiritual. A most unwise, most wretched, and most guilty choice!

Spiritual joy often abounds when all other sources of joy are dried up. By this I do not mean that joy in God precludes all enjoyment of the world and its pleasures; this is far from true. When worldly sources of pleasure are cut off from us or are dried up, then God comes in to fill the void with richer spiritual joys. Poverty and losses may have withdrawn from you many of the comforts of life. God can make His grace abound so much more that your soul will rejoice exceedingly in the exchange. Sickness may have robbed you of the joy which health affords; but God can make your soul prosper and be in health to such a degree that your physical loss shall be more than counterbalanced by your spiritual gain. God knows how to fill up the chasms of earthly happiness which His providence makes. Often He apparently makes them for the very purpose of filling them with the more precious material of His own spiritual blessings. He sometimes finds himself under the necessity of cutting off every source of earthly joy in order that He may shut us utterly to himself. When He finds us unwilling to let go of our idols voluntarily, in mercy He dashes them to pieces before our eyes that He may make us feel our need of something better. Or sometimes, if men will not let go of earthly idols, God leaves them to their own choice, saying, "They have loved idols and after them they will go. They are joined to their idols; let them alone." But if we are willing to serve God, then we may find sources of spiritual joy springing up in the most barren of earth's deserts. Nothing earthly is so desolate that God cannot gladden it with the intermingled joys of His salvation.

On the other hand, if you will selfishly cleave to earth, and thrust away the offered joys of God's love, then if He would save you, there remains no alternative but to scatter desolation widely over all your earthly joys. God will blight them if He can. And surely He who has the resources of the universe at His command can never lack the means of filling your cup with dregs of wormwood and gall. It would be the worst form of folly if you should compel your loving Father to do this as a last resort in order to save and bless your soul.

Very few realize how much the absence of spiritual joy and its manifestations will dishonor God. Few realize how great a stumbling block it is to people to see professed Christians go about with a sorrowful heart, bowed down and hatefully selfish; no trust—or almost none—in God; no joy in the light of His countenance, and no preparation of heart for doing anything efficiently in God's service. It is a living reproach to the name of Jesus that His people should appear thus before either their brethren or the world.

Legalists greatly stumble at those who possess the joy of God's salvation. Legalists are never happy in themselves. Always in a strait-jacket, every muscle drawn up with a tightness never to be relaxed, they don't know about such a joyous state of mind. They see a great many things that look suspicious. When they see souls rejoicing greatly in the Lord, they are perplexed. If a Christian's soul triumphs in his God, "Alas," they say to themselves, "what can that mean? There is nothing like that in *my* religion!" Often there is too much cheerfulness in other people's religion to suit their taste or to tally with their own experience. Never having had any experience in such joys as these, they are greatly scandalized.

So it seems to have been with one of David's wives when she saw him running and dancing before the ark of the Lord in the overflowings of his joy. *Indeed,* she thought, *this looks very unbecoming for a king, for the king of Israel.* Christians of a somber, heavy countenance, who have never known anything of the glad joy of holy love, who cannot explain to themselves even the peaceful look of the saint who is communing with God, and above all who know not the first element of his state of mind whose soul pours forth the gushing tides of its affection before God as if it could never express the half it feels—those who look on amazed at such manifestations because they know nothing of them in their own experience will doubtless be greatly stumbled. But notwithstanding all their stumbling, if this spiritual joy is sustained by a holy, consistent life, it cannot fail to exert its power upon their hearts. They may be at first offended; but soon they must see that there is both reason and reality in the peaceful joy of those who walk humbly with God. "O Lord," they will be compelled to say, "I don't know that experience. *There* is something to which I am a stranger. I must know what that is. I doubt whether my religion is worth straw. It gives me no joy in the Lord like what I see in these other Christians."

Few things are a greater curse than legalism. It is often as bad as open wickedness, if not worse. Often it is such a misrepresentation of Christianity that little children become more afraid of a religious man than of a fiend. Does he recommend Christianity? He could not possibly disparage and misrepresent it more than he does. Better far if he were never thought to be a Christian at all; for then his somber, morose and harsh spirit would be ascribed to its true cause—the unsubdued selfishness of his heart, and the utter absence of the gentle spirit of gospel love.

Many fall short of this joy because they do not ask for it. Will you lose it through lack of prayer and of faith? It is too choice a blessing to be missed for such a reason.

4

THE REWARD OF FERVENT PRAYER*

"Open thy mouth wide, and I will fill it" (Psalm 81:10).

These words were addressed by God to the Church. There is nothing in the context in which they are found that particularly demands explanation. I would, therefore, proceed at once to say that this promise and injunction being addressed to the Church was also, of course, addressed to individual Christians. Whenever a promise or an injunction is applicable to the Church, it is also applicable to each individual composing the Church. This reveals to us the principle on which God deals with His people. The spirit of what is written here is even more true. In briefly considering this subject, I propose to show:

▶ *What this language means.*
▶ *What it implies.*
▶ *What its relationship is to our responsibilities.*

What this language means.

Of course it is figurative: "Open thy mouth wide, and I will fill it." Does it mean *literally* to open the mouth wide and He will fill it with something without our understanding what?

"I am the Lord thy God, which brought thee out of the land of Egypt." This was addressed to the Church of old, and the

---

*From *The Penny Pulpit*, delivered May 15, 1850, at the Tabernacle, Moorfields, No. 1,522. From the collection: "Miscellaneous Sermons, 6 713 F6," and published by courtesy of the Burke Library, Union Theological Seminary, New York, New York.

spirit of it is addressed to the Church in all ages. It is said in the eighth verse, "Hear, O my people, and I will testify unto thee: O Israel, if thou wilt hearken unto me; there shall no strange god be in thee; neither shalt thou worship any strange god. I am the Lord thy God, which brought thee out of the land of Egypt: open thy mouth wide, and I will fill it." The language, then, is figurative, and is to be understood in the following ways.

God enjoins us to *ask of Him great things*. The injunction is not only, "Open thy mouth," but open it *wide*; open it fully to its utmost capacity; by which it is to be understood that we are to ask of God great things, as great as we can conceive. We are merely creatures, and therefore our conceptions are low, and the spirit of the injunction tells us that we should ask great things of our heavenly Father. With our finite powers, we can conceive of Him "who is able to do for us abundantly above all that we can ask or think." Let the request be ever so great, He can grant it. In your petitions to Him, therefore, "open thy mouth wide," ask for things as great as you can conceive.

Another thing we are to understand by this language is, we are *to expect those great things* for which we ask. We are required to ask believingly in expectation that He will give the things which we ask.

The spirit of this injunction also means that we are to attempt *to accomplish great things* for God. We are to ask earnestly, to ask largely, to ask perseveringly in order that we may honor and glorify Him. Here, I might add, we are to understand that all our petitions must be addressed in the name of Christ from right motives.

What it implies.

The injunction "open thy mouth wide" is followed by the promise "and I will fill it."

This language implies that God is interested in us. What would motivate Him to say this to us if He were not interested in us? Why should He exhort us to open our mouths wide and ask of Him great things if He had no interest in us? This language must surely imply that for some reason or other He has great interest in His Church, and, of course, in each individual composing that Church.

It implies that He is interested in those things He requires us to do. He is interested in giving us the great things which

He has promised, and in our possessing them to enable us to do what He requires of us.

God's Full Provision

God has made provision for us in every situation. He does not require great things of His people without promising the grace to help them perform that which He requires of them. But He does require many and great things of His people. He requires them to go forth to the conquest of the world, and many other things He requires of them in the various relations that they sustain to the world and to society.

Now, you must not complain that you cannot accomplish what is required of you, that you cannot do this or that because of your littleness or insufficiency. For God says, open your mouth wide for ability to do His will and He will fill it. He will enable you to do what is required of you. I say, then, that this language implies His interest in us *personally*, and that He is greatly interested in giving us the things for which we ask. He is quite able out of His fullness to supply all our need, to give us everything we want to enable us to accomplish everything He requires of us.

This language is addressed to different classes of individuals who maintain particular relationships in life regarding special and particular circumstances. For example, it is addressed to local authorities, ministers, parents, and private Christians. Whatever the circumstances, this language relates to your particular needs: "open thy mouth wide, and I will fill it."

It is of great importance for everyone to understand that God is interested in each individual. He takes all things into account. He placed us in our various relationships; therefore, He must be interested in us. He is able to make His grace sufficient to enable us to do all that is required of us so we may honor and glorify His name. People can never be too well assured of this: "I am Jehovah, thy God." What is implied in that? *"Thy* God." "Open thy mouth wide," therefore, "and I will fill it." These words apply to every individual in all the relationships of life.

Now, think of what your relationships are. Think of your circumstances, of your peculiar trials, difficulties and responsibilities, and the duties you are called upon to perform—no matter what they are. Only understand God as addressing you by name—old and young, rich and poor, influential or otherwise—no matter, only understand God as saying to you, "I am

Jehovah, thy God: open thy mouth wide, and I will fill it." He is interested in your maintaining these responsibilities in a manner worthy of Him, as being His children.

I have often thought of the magnitude of unbelief. The unbelief of many is so great that they entirely overlook the secret depths of meaning that the promises of God contain, and they stumble at some of the plainest things in the Bible.

Suppose the King of England should send his son to travel on the Continent or in America, and should say to him, "Now, son, you are going among strangers, so remember your great responsibilities: you are my son, and you are my representative. When the people see you they will form an opinion of me, and they will estimate my character very much by yours, as a natural consequence. Now, remember, wherever you are, that the eyes of the people are upon you and my honor is concerned in your behavior. I have great interest in you; first, because you are my son; and second, because you are to be my representative among those who do not know me personally. I am, therefore, greatly concerned that you should not misrepresent me. For particular and weighty reasons, therefore, I want you to conduct yourself like a prince, and that you may do so, you shall always have the means. Remember never to exercise any kind of economy that will disgrace your father and the nation you represent. Draw upon me liberally. Of course, you will not squander needlessly upon your lusts, for such conduct would disgrace yourself and dishonor me: but what you want for the purpose of representing fully the Sovereign of England you can have. Draw largely; always remember this."

Now observe, God has placed His people here in a world of strangers to Him. He has placed them in various relationships. He has admonished them to remember that they are His children and they are also His representatives in this world. God says to them, "I have placed you in these relationships that you may honor me. I love you as my own children. I have given my Son to redeem you, and thus I have proved my personal regard for you. I always desire that you should walk worthy of the high vocation wherewith you are called. Remember, you are my representatives in the midst of a rebellious world; therefore, 'let your light so shine before men, that others, seeing your good works, may glorify your Father which is in heaven.' "

God's own interest in us leads Him to tell us to ask largely of Him. His intrinsic regard for us as our Father, as His redeemed children, is very great. Indeed, in every point of view,

He has the deepest interest in us. That we may not dishonor Him, He tells us He will give us grace to meet all our responsibilities and discharge our duties. "Open your mouths wide," He says, "and I will fill them." "I will 'supply all your needs.' I am glad to do it. I shall delight to do it. I am interested in doing it."

Now, don't you ever forget this. Ask largely enough, ask confidently enough, and ask perseveringly enough to meet all your needs. I suppose that no one is disposed to call in question the truth of any of these principles.

These words, "open thy mouth wide, and I will fill it," imply that provision is made to supply our needs, and that God's capability is so great that He does not fear that we shall need anything, or be able to conceive of anything, beyond His power to grant. Hence, He tells us that His grace is sufficient for us. Observe, He does not caution us about asking too much, but He tells us here, as in many other parts of the Bible, to make our requests unlimited: "Ask what you will, and it shall be done unto you." Of course it means "what you will" for a right reason, not for a selfish and improper reason.

We are not restricted at all in Him. It is not intended that we should hesitate to accomplish anything which He requires of us. We are not restricted in Him, for He says, "open thy mouth *wide*, and I will fill it." In any of the circumstances or relationships in which we may ever be placed, or whatever we may be called upon to accomplish, we are never to regard ourselves as restricted in Him.

If He requires His people to go forth to the conquest of the world, they are abundantly able to take possession of the land. We are to have confidence in Him, and to take possession of it in His name and in His strength. If He tells us to compass the city and blow with the ram's horns, the walls of Jericho shall surely tumble down—there is no mistake about it.

In this injunction and promise is implied that if we fail in anything to perfectly represent or obey Him in every respect, and in all things to be and do what He requires of us, the fault is not His but ours. It is not to be resolved into "the mysterious sovereignty of God," for the fault is ours. If we fail, it is not because God by any arbitrary sovereignty withheld the power, but because as a matter of fact, in the possession of our liberty we failed to believe and appropriate the promises.

God Is Honored By Big Requests

This injunction and promise implies that God considers himself honored by the largeness of our requests. If we ask but a trifling thing, it shows that we find ourselves either unable or unwilling to expect or believe any great thing of Him. What does it imply when people ask small favors of God? I know very well what people say—they are so unworthy that they cannot expect to get any great things in answer to their poor requests. But is this real humility, or is it a voluntary humility? Is it a commendable state of mind? "Our prayers are so poor, are so unworthy, that we cannot expect to receive much in answer to them; therefore, we have not confidence enough to ask great things, and so we only ask for small things that we may without presumption expect to receive." Is this a right disposition of mind? This is that voluntary humility which God denounces: it is self-righteousness. What state of mind must that individual be in, who, instead of measuring his requests by the greatness of God's mercies, the greatness of His promises and the largeness of His heart, shall measure them by his own worthiness or unworthiness? Why, the fact is, if an individual will measure his requests by such a standard, he will ask nothing better than hell, and he may expect nothing better. This is applicable to all men in all ages, if they make themselves the standard of their requests. But if we are to rely upon God's promises, God's faithfulness, God's abounding grace in Christ Jesus and God's eternal love, then there are infinite blessings in store for His people, which the goodness of His heart is trying to force upon them. Then, pray, what has our great unworthiness to do, only to commend us to God's grace and mercy? Whenever, therefore, we ask great things of God, and expect great things from Him, we honor Him, inasmuch as we say, "Lord, although we are infinitely unholy and unworthy of thy blessings, yet we judge not of what thou art willing to give us, measured by our unworthiness, but by thine own wonderful love to the world as shown in the gift of thine own and well-beloved Son, the Lord Jesus Christ. Therefore we will not ask small things of so great a God. We will ask great things because it is in thine heart to give them, and thou findest it more blessed to give than we do to receive." Now, it is by this sort of confidence that we honor God.

Some ask scantily, sparingly, for fear of overtaxing or overburdening God. What a mean, low, and contemptible view this is of God! Suppose the prince, whom we referred to, had been very sparing in drawing upon his father's accounts. Suppose that he drew only five or ten dollars at a time. The strangers among whom he was living would have noticed it. They would have said, "What can it mean? Why does he not draw more? How is he so poor? Is his father so miserly or so poor?" Thus dishonor would be brought upon his father and his country because the prince drew so sparingly when he might have had plenty.

Now, God has sent His children to this land, and He has told them that they are the "light of the world," the "salt of the earth," a "city that is set upon a hill." And He says, "Let your light shine"; show yourselves worthy of your heavenly Father. Now, suppose that from a lack of confidence, or for some other reason, they draw very sparingly. Everybody will see that they get but little from God in answer to prayer. A miserable, lean, famishing supply is all they get from their heavenly Father. There is but a slight spiritual distinction between them and the world in which they live; they have so little grace, so little faith, so little of anything that one might suppose God would surely provide for His children. Is this honorable to God? What, profess to be children of God and never realize your high distinction! Living in a world of rebels, having no more grace than you have, you never thought of the dishonor you bring upon God. What do you think of your Father? Do you think that God your Father is satisfied? To see you, people would think you had no Father, that you were poor orphans. And yet God says, " 'open thy mouth wide, and I will fill it'; ask of Me such things as you need. Why, then, do you go about in such a miserable condition? Why live at such a dying rate, always in doubt, darkness and trouble? Do you not know that I am the Lord your God, and that if you open your mouth wide, I will fill it?"

Now, brethren, is not this true? Is this some new-fangled doctrine not taught in the Bible? Or is it true that professing Christians generally have infinitely misconceived this matter, not understanding what God requires of them, or that they have dishonored Him in the highest degree by such conduct. They the light of the world! Why, their lamps are gone out! They cannot get any oil; and if they could, they have no money to buy it. Why is your lamp gone out? Has God your Father failed to send you a remittance? At all events, the lamp's gone out and left you in obscure darkness—a worldly spirit has come over you. What is the matter? You have been going by little and little till you have lost almost all confidence in God, and scarcely expect to receive anything from Him in answer to your prayers.

I don't know how it is with you, but I know that the great

mass of professing Christians are in this miserably low state. They seem neither to know that they dishonor God by their conduct, nor that God is ready and willing to give them abundance of grace if they will believingly seek for it.

Of course, if God considers himself honored by the largeness of our requests, it must be upon the condition that we really have confidence in Him, expecting to receive those things for which we ask. If we should ask great things in words but not mean what we ask, or if we do not expect to receive answers to our petitions, we dishonor God by mocking Him. Always observe and remember this: a man who really expects great things from God and asks of God in faith with right motives will receive them. Those who honor God, God will honor.

God regards himself as honored by everything we accomplish in His name: by our asking great things of Him, and by our attempting great things in His name.

God Is Dishonored By Feeble Requests

Suppose a man goes forth in the name of the Lord Jesus to carry the Gospel to those who are in darkness, believing what Jesus has said, "Lo, I am with you always, even unto the end of the world." Suppose that in this confidence he attempts great things, and aims at the conquest of cities and nations. The greater his aims in God's name and strength, so much the greater is the honor that God receives. He goes forth relying on God, as God's servant, as God's child, to accomplish great things in His name and strength. God considers himself honored by this. God considers himself honored by the high attainments of His children and *dishonored* by their low attainments. He is honored in the fact that their graces so shine forth that it shall be seen by all around that they have partaken largely of His Spirit.

Exalted piety is honorable to God. Manifestations of great grace and spirituality of mind honor God. He is greatly honored by the fruits of righteousness His people bring forth. Christ himself says, "Herein is my Father glorified that ye bring forth much fruit." Ministers should be greatly fruitful. They should bring forth the fruits of the Spirit in their tempers, in their lives, in the strength of their faith and labors of love. Can you doubt that God has great interest in these things? Indeed His great desire, that you should bring forth fruit to His glory, is shown in the fact that He says, "open thy mouth wide, and I will fill it."

And it must imply, also, that He is greatly dishonored by the opposite of this. Professing Christians who have but little faith make but feeble efforts, and have but very little to distinguish them from the world around them. Nothing can be more offensive to God than for His professed servants to have so little confidence in Him that they ask sparingly to receive sparingly. It must be admitted, I suppose, that the conceptions of the general population of Christians are very low—they expect but small things from God. But this is dishonorable to God, as I have said, and He is endeavoring by every possible means to encourage our faith. At one time He will go into the nursery, where the mother is with her children, and say, "Mother, if thy son should ask for bread, would you give him a stone? or if he should ask a fish, would you give him a serpent? or if he should ask an egg, would you give him a scorpion to sting him to death?" The mother is surprised, and can scarcely contain herself. "Well," He says, "I did not suppose you would do so; but if these things would be far from you—if you would by no means do them, and feel indignant at the bare suggestion of the possibility of such a thing, 'how much more will your heavenly Father give good things to them that ask him?' " "How much?" Why, as much as He is better than you are.

A parent has no higher happiness than to give his little ones what they ask for if it is for their good. A father or a mother purchases some dainty thing; they can hardly bear to taste it themselves—the children must have it. "If ye, then, being evil"—compared with God, infinitely evil—"know how to give good gifts unto your children, how much more shall your heavenly Father give?" Oranges, sweets, candy? No; "the Holy Spirit to them that ask him." That is the great blessing which you need. Oh, if we could only have more of the Spirit!

Christians live as if God had but little of the Holy Spirit to give. But is this the representation of the Scriptures? No, indeed; but infinitely the reverse of this. Some professing Christians live like spiritual skeletons, and, if they are reproved for it, they say, "Oh, we are dependent on the Holy Spirit." Indeed, and is that the reason you are so much like the world? Why you do not prevail with God to convert your children, and the clerks and people around you? Grieve not the Holy Spirit with such excuses; seek, and ye shall find. God is infinitely more ready to give you His Holy Spirit than you are to give good gifts to your own children.

When God exhorts His people to open their mouths wide,

and promises to fill them, we are to understand that He seeks in them a clear medium through which to communicate His blessings to those around them. This is a natural law of the divine economy. If you are parents and have unconverted children, or have those around you unconverted, God seeks to make you an agent by which He can communicate the blessings of salvation to them.

When God thus urges people to open their mouths wide in order that He may fill them, we are to understand that His heart is very much set upon their having the things which He is seeking to give them. He takes the highest interest in their having these things—a greater interest than they do themselves. He restrains not His gift at all; the infinite fountain of His love and blessing flows everlastingly, so that every empty vessel may be filled; and, when they are all full, this living stream still flows on forever.

We must not be afraid of asking too much. When we seek a favor from a finite being, we might ask so much as to be thought unreasonable; but, when we come to an infinite being, we cannot ask too largely. Oh, brethren, always remember that.

What its relationship is to our responsibilities.

We are entirely without excuse to God for not being and doing what would in the highest degree satisfy His divine mind. We are not restricted in Him, but in ourselves.

We are not only without excuse to God, but we are cruel to ourselves. How cruel a man would be to himself if he starved himself to death in the midst of plenty, of which he might freely partake. Now, what excuse can a Christian have for all his doubts, fears, darknesses and perplexities, and how cruel he is to himself when such marvelous provision is made to set the Christian free from all such unhappy experiences. Do we live under such circumstances, and yet have a life of complaining? Indeed! And is it a law of God's house that His children almost starve? Is it a rule of God's house that His children should not have grace enough to lift them above perplexities and unbelief? Does God starve His children to death? "They do all they can; can't they get grace enough," says the devil, "to prevent their living so much like my own servants? So much alike are they, indeed, that nobody can distinguish them from my children!" Dear children, is there not an infinite mistake here? Are we not dishonoring God if we do not avail ourselves of the great things which God has provided us?

It is cruelty to the world also. God has said, "Go forth and conquer the world: disciple all nations." Has He said this to His people, and do they slumber, do they hesitate? What is the matter, brethren? Are not the words, "Come over and help us," borne on the four winds of heaven? "Come over into Macedonia and help us"; send us missionaries, send us Bibles, send us tracts, send us the Gospel? And is the Church unable to do it? What is the matter? Do let me ask, is there not something entirely wrong here? Does God require His people to make brick without straw? Has the world any right to expect the gospel of salvation to be sent to them by the Church? Brethren, consider!

What cruelty it is to those around us and those who sustain relations to us. We have such a promise in the Bible, yet our children remain unconverted! Think of it!

If Christians would but avail themselves of all the blessings which God has provided and really become filled with the Spirit, what do you suppose would be the result? Let me ask this question, "Suppose every Christian in your city should really comply with the appeal and be filled with the Holy Spirit, what do you suppose would be the natural effect upon the populace? Suppose every Christian were to open His mouth wide, and should receive the Holy Spirit, do you not believe that in one year a very great change would occur in the city, so that you would scarcely know it?" I have not the least doubt that more good would be done than has been done before in your city. If one church could be thoroughly awakened, another and another would follow, till the whole city would be aroused and every chapel would be filled with devout inquirers after salvation. This has been the case frequently in American cities; and the like may occur in any city if Christians are but thoroughly alive to their duties and responsibilities. If every Christian in your city would make up his mind to take hold of the promise of God, and thus come into deep sympathy and fellowship with Him, the effect would be astonishing. Like the lamps of the city, Christians are scattered over it so they may give light to the multitudes around them; but if they are not lighted up, the purpose for which they were intended is not accomplished. Let every Christian in your city be filled with the Holy Spirit, and what would be the result? Your city would move! Your state would move! America would move! Europe would move! Asia would move! The world would move!

Now, brethren, does this appear extravagant? If so, it is because you do not consider the power of the promises of God and what the churches are able to effect in His name. The guilt and the weakness of the Church is her unbelief. This is so great that she does not expect to do much. We must now conclude with a few remarks.

REMARKS

Many people so confound faith with sight that they are ready to say, "If God should make windows in heaven, then might this thing be." A great many people have no faith except in connection with sight: give them the naked promise and they cannot believe it; they must have something they can see. Few individuals can walk by faith. When they see a thing accomplished, they think they have strong faith; but only let this appearance be put out of sight and their faith is gone again. Now, what a Christian ought to be able to do is this: take God's promises and anchor right down upon them without waiting to see anything; because, somebody must believe simply on the strength of God's testimony, somebody must begin by naked faith, or there will be no visible testimony.

God always honors real faith. He is concerned to do so. God often greatly honors the faith of His people. He frequently gives them more than they expect. People will pray for one individual, and God will often honor their faith by not only converting that individual but many others also.

I once knew a man who was sick, and a neighbor of his, an unconverted man, frequently sent from his store things for his comfort. This poor man said to himself, "I cannot recompense Mr. Chandler for his kindness, but I will give myself up to pray for him." To the surprise of all the neighborhood, Mr. Chandler became converted; this he testified before the whole congregation, which had such an effect that a great revival ensued and many souls were brought to God. This poor man gave himself up to pray for one individual, and God honored his faith by converting many, thus fulfilling the declaration of His Word, that He will "do exceeding abundantly above all we can ask or think."

Instead of finding that God gives grudgingly and sparingly, He gives abundantly. God always acts worthy of himself. You ask a blessing of God in faith and He says, "Be content, and take a great deal more so that your cup shall run over." The fact is, where but little is attempted, little expected, little will be received; but where little is really obtained, the fault is not with God, but entirely with us.

5

HEART SEARCHING*

"Search me, O God, and know my heart: try me, and know my thoughts, and see if there be any wicked way in me, and lead me in the way everlasting" (Psalm 139:23, 24).

In speaking from this text, I shall of course be obliged to assume many things as true without attempting to prove them. This indeed is almost always the case in preaching. It is taken for granted that certain things are agreed upon both by the speaker and the hearer, and unless this was assumed we could scarcely preach at all. Therefore I shall take it for granted that you believe in the existence and attributes of God, and that you also admit that He exercises a providential government over all the affairs of the universe. Directly or indirectly He is concerned in everything that takes place—either positively bringing it about, or when it is about to occur He knows it and permits it in order that He may make some use of it. I shall take it for granted that you believe that no event occurs without God either positively causing it, or else permitting it to occur with a design to overrule or make some use of it for His own glory and the good of man. I cannot of course enter into a discussion upon the divine perfections, but must assume that my readers admit that God's providence is in some sense universal, and that it extends to every individual. In speaking from these words I design to show:

The Penny Pulpit, delivered November 27, 1849, at the Borough Road Chapel, Southwark, No. 1,479.

▶ *What is implied in the sincere and acceptable offering of such a petition as that contained in the text.*

▶ *Some of the ways in which God answers requests of this kind.*

What is implied in the sincere and acceptable offering of such a petition as that contained in the text.

It must imply the realization of the omniscience of God. When David penned this psalm, he deeply realized the omnipotence of God and the searchings of His eye. He begins the psalm by saying, "O Lord, thou hast searched me, and known me. Thou knowest my downsitting and mine uprising, thou understandest my thought afar off. Thou compassest my path and my lying down, and art acquainted with all my ways. For there is not a word in my tongue, but, lo, O Lord, thou knowest it altogether. Thou hast beset me behind and before, and laid thine hand upon me. Such knowledge is too wonderful for me; it is high, I cannot attain unto it. Whither shall I go from thy spirit? or whither shall I flee from thy presence? If I ascend up into heaven, thou art there; if I make my bed in hell, behold, thou art there. If I take the wings of the morning, and dwell in the uttermost parts of the sea; even there shall thy hand lead me, and thy right hand shall hold me. If I say, Surely the darkness shall cover me; even the night shall be light about me. Yea, the darkness hideth not from thee; but the night shineth as the day: the darkness and the light are both alike to thee."

I have read these verses to show that the Psalmist, at the time of offering this petition, was under a deep impression of the omnipotence and omniscience of God, and the searching blaze of His eye throughout his whole being. And I suppose that this is always the state of mind of every individual when he asks God to search him. The very request implies the belief that God understands his real heart and is able to search him.

An acceptable offering of such a request also implies a sense of the moral purity or holiness of God. Observe, he prays to be searched—that his whole being may be exposed to see if there was any iniquity within him, and that he might be led in the way everlasting. It is plainly implied that he had such a sense of the purity of God as to be convinced that God was infinitely opposed to all iniquity.

It implies in the next place the necessity of being perfectly pure himself. An individual who offers such a petition does not, and cannot, offer it without this conviction.

An acceptable offering of this petition must imply a thorough wakefulness of mind to one's moral or spiritual state. It must be that he is in a very honest, searching, state of mind himself—thoroughly in earnest to know all about himself. He is wide awake to his own spiritual condition and heartily desires that all his errors may be rectified.

It implies an intense anxiety to be perfect as God would have him to be—conformed to the holy will of God. Observe, he prays that his heart may be searched to see if there is anything wicked within, and to be led in the way everlasting, which plainly implies that he was willing to be led to abandon all iniquity. An individual who makes such a request as this must have an intense longing to be entirely delivered from the dominion of iniquity.

To be acceptable, this request must also imply, I suppose, that the individual offering it is not at the time conscious of living in sin—conscious of indulging in any known sin. Now, the Psalmist would not have made such a request as this if he had been at the time indulging in sin. He would surely not have asked God to search him to see if there was any wickedness in him if he was at the same time conscious of indulging in known sin. Had this been the case he could not have made such a request without downright hypocrisy.

The acceptable offering of such a petition as this implies the assumption, on the part of the petitioner, that he needs to be deeply tried—penetrated with the light of truth to the deepest recesses of his soul. When an individual offers such a petition, he assumes there may be something he has overlooked, and he asks for the scrutiny of God's eye to search it out, and to apply such texts so that he may see it.

The acceptable offering of such a petition implies a willingness to be subjected to any process of searching God may see to be needful. He does not point out any particular way in which he desires to be searched, and tried, but he leaves that to the divine discretion. He only asks that it may be done, without attempting to dictate how it shall be done. When we ask to be searched, without any real design to be searched, there is an inclination to dictate the way in which it shall be done, but this is not an acceptable way of offering such a petition. The time and manner of the searching must be left entirely to the divine discretion. Let the thing be done! Let God do as it seems good to Him! This is the commitment in which the prayer must be offered.

An acceptable offering of such a petition implies of course that the petitioner is really willing to have the petition answered, and will not resist any process through which God causes him to pass as the means by which he is answered.

Some of the ways in which God answers requests of this kind.

God often searches us by His *Spirit* and by the application of His *Truth*. By these means light often shines into the mind and gives individuals a view of themselves they could never have had without this searching. But while it is true that God often searches the human mind in this way, and has done so in all ages, yet it is by no means the *only* way. He much more frequently searches individuals in other ways.

Observe: God's object in searching is not to inform himself regarding us, but to reveal us to ourselves. He knows all about the state of our minds, our spiritual latitude and longitude: what we are in our present state, and what sort of characters we should develop under any and all circumstances. Consequently, in bringing us out to our own view, God must apply such tests to us as shall assist in this development to let us see ourselves as He himself sees us.

In order to do this, to make us understand ourselves and those around understand us, God answers such petitions as these by means of His *providence without*, and by His *Spirit within*; and observe, these never contradict one another. God is working without by His providence, bringing us into various states and circumstances for the development of character, and then comes by His Spirit and presents it to our minds when it is developed. Notice some of the *ways* in which God answers these petitions.

Ordinary Encounters

He often allows things to occur that really will show to us, and to those around us, what sort of *tempers* we have. For instance, people speak against us, and the way in which we bear their accusations shows what our tempers are. Now when we pray to be searched, God often allows us to be defamed and spoken against in order to try the state of our minds and show whether we possess the virtue of meekness, or whether we will say that we have a right to be angry.

Now, perhaps some of you have had such a test as this applied to you this very day. Someone has said or written something of you of a disagreeable and injurious tendency. What state of mind did it develop? Did it develop the meekness and gentleness of Christ, or did it make you angry? Perhaps you had been praying that you might be searched, and God caused your character to be displayed so you, and those around you, might see it. And what sort of character was it?

God often arranges matters so that we are treated with neglect—perhaps sinfully so—by those about us. Now God does not prevent this, but allows it to be done. He could have interposed to prevent it, but did not. Well, how does this affect us? It developed the state of mind that we were in. And what was the real state of mind that it brought out? Did it make us angry and manifest an unholy temper, or otherwise? Perhaps God allows us to be treated with injustice, and when thus tried, do we manifest the Spirit of Christ? Do we find working in us the temper that was manifested by Christ on such occasions? Remember, it is written, "If any man have not the Spirit of Christ, he is none of his."

Now we would be exceedingly ignorant of ourselves if none of these tests were applied. When people have nothing to try them, they are in great danger of deceiving themselves; but when people are tried, then their real disposition and the temper of their minds are developed. Let me ask, has anybody cheated you? Has someone taken advantage of you—treated you unjustly, refused you honest wages, or repudiated a just debt? Well, under these painful circumstances, what spirit did you manifest? Did you find the Spirit of Christ within you? Mark! These are providences occurring to search you that you might understand yourselves, and that those around you might understand you. Perhaps you have been misunderstood and misrepresented; well, how have you borne it? Perhaps you have been treated disrespectfully by those who are under particular obligation to you; well, how did you bear it? Did your indignation rise—did you manifest an un-Christlike spirit? Or did you find the Spirit of Christ was in you? You prayed to be searched, and in answer to your prayer your children or employees, or those related to you, and who were under particular obligations to you, treated you in a very improper manner—directly the reverse to what you had a right to expect from them. Perhaps your employees have done that which is exceedingly wrong. Now admit that all this was very wrong and exceedingly provoking. But, what has been the effect upon you? What has it taught you? And what has it taught those who witnessed the development? Has it brought out your state of mind? Doubtless, it has: and if it was not outwardly manifest, what were the feelings within?

Again, perhaps someone has contradicted you! Can you bear the contradiction? Do you bear it well? Were you patient under it? Do you act as Christ would have acted under the circumstances, or did you behave un-Christlike? Perhaps, in your business this day, some of those whom you employ have not attended to their duty, or have destroyed your property; and all this might have been exceedingly wrong and highly provoking. What spirit did you manifest to them who had done the wrong? Such a spirit as Christ would have manifested? What has been the result of such an occurrence?

Observe, these things never occur by accident. God designs that every one of them should develop our character. They should try us and prove what there is in us, and bring it to our own consciences and reveal to us the springs of action within us. Now, when these tests of your character and disposition have been applied, what has been the result? Did you find that you were still the same old sinner? That instead of finding Christ within you, and His temper developing itself, you found the old man with his deceitful lusts!

Opportunities For Gain

Often, when individuals pray to be searched and tried, God gives them opportunities in their business to prove if they love their neighbors as themselves, or whether they will speculate with a view to make all they can out of their neighbors, adopting any means to this end that will not subject them to any criminal charge or ruin them in a business point of view. God tries them to see if they will really consult their brother's interest as well as their own, to see if they will share the profits where there is money to be made; or whether they will be disposed to dip their hands as deeply in their neighbor's pockets as they can without losing their character for honesty.

God often tries people in this way. He will give them opportunities to take some unfair advantage in the way of trade. For example, a man who needs a loan comes to an individual that professes to be a Christian, and who is quite able to lend it, but he pretends that to agree to the request and oblige his friend, he shall have to make great sacrifices, when, at the same time, he really means that his friend shall have the money if he will but give an exorbitant interest rate and good security. Or, he finds a neighbor in trouble; how does he act? Does he come right out like a Christian and help his neighbor, as Christ and the apostles would have done had they been placed in similar circumstances?

Now, whenever cases of this kind occur, they are golden opportunities for us to know ourselves, and are designed to search us to the bottom of our hearts.

Oftentimes, God so arranges it that individuals can take advantage of others without danger to their own reputations. They are very cautious not to take advantage when there is danger of public knowledge; they have no design to ruin themselves. But, sometimes, there is little or no danger to their business reputation by being dishonest, so now is the time of trial, when an individual has no other selfish reasons to keep him honest. A person may be naturally dishonest, but he will not take advantage when it is likely to hurt himself. But when this is not the case, when he can be honest or dishonest without injury to his business reputation, then is the time for a person to try himself and see whether it is the love of God or the fear of man that actuates him.

Suppose someone has bought something at your store, paid too much for it, but is never likely to find out. Or, suppose you have found something in the street and you can keep it or restore it to its owner. These are searchings from God and are designed to show people their true character for honesty. The honest person would no more take and appropriate the mistaken change than he would cut his own throat; nor keep the articles found in the street any more than he would leap into the fire.

Now suppose that instead of finding the Spirit of Christ manifesting itself, he developed the opposite spirit, and has to resort to some selfish reasonings to quiet his conscience and make himself appear as an honest man. Well, it is written upon him, "Mene, Mene, Tekel—weighed in the balance and found wanting."

God will reveal our temper to us and enable us to see whether we are impatient or otherwise. He will show us whether we are ambitious—whether we desire to climb and scramble up some height from which we can look down with scorn or contempt upon our fellows.

God often gives us opportunities of self-display to see whether we will display self. On the other hand, He often denies us such opportunities, to see if we will murmur and be envious of those who have. Many people will be found speaking against display when they have not the means to indulge in it. They will be very loud in their censures upon other professing Christians who furnish their houses in a superior style; but give these people the means of doing the same, and see what they will do—see if they will not imitate, and perhaps act more extravagantly, than those whom they before condemned. A little while ago they were very piously complaining of display, but now they have the means of doing the same thing and they do it, showing it was not principle that caused them to speak as they did, but simply because they could not indulge in those things themselves. They pretended to be greatly grieved with others for doing so.

God often allows people to accumulate property so they may have an opportunity to extend the cause of truth and righteousness in the earth. He tries them to see if they will do it or not. Professing Christians acknowledge themselves to be but stewards for God, that everything they possess is His; consequently, their possessions are at His disposal. Now, is it a fact that these people act in harmony with what they profess? Well, God often tries them to see if they are hypocrites or not.

Denying Treasures

God in His providence often causes us to suffer losses by bad debts, by fire, or by some such means, just to see whether we will think and speak of these losses as being *our* losses—whether we regard these losses as God's or our own. As Christians, we profess that everything is God's, and that we are only stewards. Well, look at a professing Christian who once had large property to manage. By some means he has lost it all, and he goes about saying that *he* has sustained such and such great losses. He proves by such conduct that he acted hypocritically in professing that he believed it to be God's property and that he was only the steward of it. Suppose a clerk, whose master had sustained heavy losses, should go about and complain that *he* had sustained the losses. How absurd and untrue it would be. When we are in possession of property, we may profess that it belongs to God, even deceive ourselves into believing that we are sincere in our professions. But when a loss occurs, it often shows to us that we did not regard it as God's but our own.

Sometimes God will deny individuals many things, to see if they will be satisfied with the providence of God. Do they bear poverty well, or are they envious of the rich? Are they in their poverty what Christ would have been in their circumstances? Thus riches and poverty, sickness and health, and a thousand other things, are sent to try people and prove to them and to those around them what their real state is.

God quite regularly tries us to see if we are self-willed, to see if our wills are ready to submit to His will, or whether we shall make ourselves unhappy and wretched because God so wills respecting us. Often, individuals do not know whether they are self-willed. So long as the providence of God seems to pet them, they are very pious and can talk about submission with the greatest apparent sincerity. But let God just drive across their path, lay His hand upon them, blow their schemes to the winds of heaven, and see whether they will talk of submission then. See whether they are self-willed, or whether as little children they will instantly submit. Can they say with the Psalmist, "O Lord, thou knowest that I am not haughty; surely, I have behaved myself as a child weaned of its mother: my soul is even as a weaned child"? Blessed man! When he was tried, he said, "Surely I have behaved as a child that is weaned of its mother."

Probably, most of you have had opportunities of knowing by actual observation what this means. Perhaps you have seen a self-willed child ready to wrestle with everybody, but what a great change comes over him, when his will is subdued. God often in His providence tries individuals, but instead of being a weaned child, they have been as an unweaned child. They are unable to say as the Psalmist did, but are obliged to confess, " 'I have been as a bullock unaccustomed to the yoke,' restive, self-willed, domineering, and ready to make war upon God." Most of the people to whom I address myself have doubtless passed through such scenes as these. Now let me ask, how have they affected you? What state of mind did you discover in yourselves? God was searching you, applying the texts that should infallibly show what was the working in your minds.

It is frequently of the greatest importance for God to introduce measures to show if we are disappointed at any course He adopts toward us. When a person is devoted to God, he is willing that everything he possesses, and his own life also, should be devoted in any way that God should choose. If he is in a right state of mind, he will not be disappointed at any providence, believing that everything occurs by the will of God; and this being the case, all must be right and contribute to their real good. Now when circumstances occur to disappoint us, if we will not allow ourselves to be disappointed, we may understand and conclude that our will is such as it ought to be.

Again, God often tries us to see if we idolize our friends. He visits us with affliction, or the loss of property, to try whether our affections and love are set as much upon God as upon our friends. Remember the case of Eli, when he was informed of what had occurred to his family, he said, "It is the Lord: let him do what seemeth him good." Now, it is a great thing for individuals to have opportunities occur in the providence of God to try them. There is, no doubt, a meaning in the things God is perpetually bestowing upon us. And the very things we are apt to regard as evil things, when we are in a bad state of mind, are working for our good. But let a man be in a right state of mind and he will not object to being thoroughly tried, for he knows the grace of God will be given to assist him to bear the trial. He can say with Paul, "I can do all things through Christ who strengthens me." And how much good the trial does him. It is good for him to be searched and tried and stripped; if need be, of property, health, friends, and all else—no matter what. These individuals have the satisfaction of feeling the grace of God spring up in their hearts, and it shines forth on all around them.

My design is, as you perceive, to pass very rapidly over an outline which I beg you to fill up by looking back from time to time at what is occurring around you. What has occurred today to try you? How did it affect you? Keep an eye upon this tomorrow, and remember that God is searching you to try your temper and state of mind. Perhaps you are a Christian mother and your child is unruly and unreasonable. How does this affect you? Do you know that God is allowing this to see whether you will be patient or not?

How often will God try us to see whether we are really willing to lose the good opinion of the world, to lose the respect and confidence of our friends, and to lose status in society for truth's sake. Some man, perhaps, has been cast down from the heights of society, and has become poor and loses friends and reputation. How now is he affected? Does this trial cause him to shine as a holy man, caring but little how men regard him? If so, the event is for his own spiritual good and the honor of God. Indeed, everything that passes in society—new fashions, new styles of dress, new colors—are constantly developing the state of our minds. Are our minds intent upon these things? Or to what extent do they affect us? It is often interesting to see how much such things will affect professing Christians and others. The design of God in this dispensation is to make all classes of men understand themselves—whether they be professedly religious or not. Thus He says of the Church in ancient days: "Forty years have I led thee in the wilderness to humble thee and to prove thee, to know what was in thine heart, whether thou wouldst keep his commandments or no."

Again, let me say that many times God will introduce dispensations that may severely test professing Christians to prove whether they love Him supremely. Now, I have observed that there are many who profess to love God supremely, who will stand by in silence while God's name is blasphemed by men who seek to bring dishonor upon His name and to subvert His kingdom. But these same people, if any word is spoken against themselves, are in the greatest excitement. They can see contempt and abuse heaped upon God without exhibiting, or even feeling, much grief; or being able to sympathize with the Psalmist when he said, "I beheld the transgressors, and was grieved." "Rivers of waters run down mine eyes, because they keep not thy law." Now, do they think the Psalmist expressed himself in a manner that was not true? No surely! When wickedness took place before his eyes, how did it affect him? Why, he tells us, and tells God himself how it affected him: "I beheld the transgressors and was grieved." Now nothing is more common than for God to allow wickedness to occur before the eyes of professing Christians to see what state of mind it will develop, whether they are more devoted to their own characters than the honor of God. Whenever these things occur the fact is revealed whether we love God or ourselves supremely.

REMARKS

People do not always realize what is implied in the prayers which they offer to God. They offer requests to God without seeming to realize what is implied in their requests. For example, they pray to be searched, but they do not understand what is implied in such a request. Do they know what they are asking? In making requests, people ought to understand their petitions, and what may be necessary as a condition for receiving an answer.

People often receive answers to their prayers without recognizing the answers. They are praying, but are looking in another direction. They have their own thoughts about the manner in which they expect God to answer. For example, how many people have offered the prayer which is contained in our text. They have an idea in their minds that the searching would take place when they were in their closets—not thinking that it was really impossible for God to do this. Now when people pray with this idea, they do not recognize the answer to their prayers because it comes from a different direction than they were looking. Perhaps some of you have received answers to your prayers that have wholly confounded you. You have prayed to be searched, but instead of having the inward light you expected, you feel as if the spirit of Satan were developing itself within you.

Let me say again that people frequently resist the answers to their prayers. It is no doubt true that God frequently answers petitions, in a certain sense, even when they are not offered in a right spirit, and perhaps the answers are intended expressly to show that they were not offered rightly. For example, an individual prays to be searched, and God searches him to show that he is not able to be searched. Professing Christians pray that they may be searched, and the minister comes forward with their portraits drawn full length and holds them out to view. Now just look at them! They cannot bear it! What is the matter with them? They prayed but a few days before that they might be searched, and now see the effect of this searching!

I am reminded of an incident that once occurred under my own notice. A Presbyterian church, in the center of New York, had existed for many years without a revival of religion till it was in danger of becoming extinct. I went there for the purpose of merely spending a night. The members of the church were holding a prayer meeting. I declined to take the lead in the meeting, being a stranger, so one of the elders led the meeting. He began by reading a long psalm, or hymn, then they sang it. Then he read a passage of Scripture and did what he called a prayer. He doled out a long talk to God, in which he said a great many things about their state and condition; how long they had been so, and that they had met there every week for many years to pray, etc. Another hymn was sung, and another leader did the same as the first. They had about three such prayers, when one of the elders desired that I would make some remarks before the meeting closed. I complied with the request, and took their prayers as my text.

I began by asking them plainly if it was understood that the meeting was called to mock God? They had met together once a week for many years and had confessed their sins, but they had never forsaken them. What was that but mockery? I took up each man's prayers separately and pointed to him while I remarked that if what that man said is true, he is a hypocrite! I then took another one's prayer and told him that he certainly was a hypocrite, too, if what he said in his prayer was true: that is self-evident.

Well, they looked so angry that I thought they would get up and leave the house, yet I did not spare them. I just threw their prayers back in their faces, and charged them with holding a prayer meeting to mock God. They turned and twisted about in their seats for some time, and were most uneasy, till at length one of the elders fell forward in tears, saying, "It's all true! It's all true!" This was a commencement of a revival, which in a few weeks spread throughout the neighborhood. These men had not understood that they mocked God while they pretended to hold a prayer meeting. They asked to be searched, and God searched them in a way they did not expect.

As I said, people will often pray to be searched without understanding what is included in the answer. Just take up their own confessions sometimes, and ask them if they mean what they say. Tell them, "If you are guilty of what you say you are, what wicked men you are. You will certainly be lost unless you repent immediately." Just adopt this course and you will soon see whether they are willing to be searched, whether they are in earnest.

All the trials of saints are in answer to their prayers—are sent to try them. Sometimes this fact is not recognized, and sometimes when people do recognize this, they are really afraid to be searched. I have known people afraid to have spiritual blessings bestowed upon them, lest the trial attending the bestowal be too severe.

A woman said to me once, "I am afraid to ask the Lord to sanctify me, for if He does I am fully persuaded that He will take my husband away from me." Well now, although it is not often the case that people understand so distinctly the state of their minds in this respect, yet there is no doubt that people often really fear that God should introduce some sanctifying dispensation, lest He should deeply wound them in some tender part—perhaps deprive them of friends, of children, or perhaps even of their own characters.

These things which try the unregenerated part of mankind

are often in answer to the prayers of the saints. The saints pray that God will convert sinners, and God adopts the means that are needed to this end, but the means that are adopted perhaps were little anticipated, and are not always recognized as answers to prayer. It comes to pass many times that individuals need to lose their character, their friends, or their property. They are so hedged in that God must adopt some stringent measures in order to bring them into a right state of mind and cause His truth to operate upon them.

Saints who ask to be searched must be willing to suffer anything which God sees fit to lay upon them. They must make up their minds to submit to any dispensations of His providence.

Saints should be prepared to receive answers to their prayers in their own persons. Perhaps God lays them on a bed of sickness just when they had some very great object in view. Well, it is intended for their good: therefore they ought not to complain nor murmur, but receive with thankfulness the good that is intended for them.

It is necessary for these trials to come to us, for it is not good that God should always feed His children on candy. We need severe discipline: it makes us good soldiers. A mere silken religion that passes through no trials has little efficiency in it. These providential trials take away the dross and tin, and make us strong in the Lord. How lovely is the character of the Christian who has patiently endured the trials through which he has had to pass. He becomes like a weaned child, and quiets himself under all the dispensations of providence. He receives everything as bestowed upon him from his Father.

The more Christians really become holy, the more sincere and earnest they are to have their whole character and being completely searched, developed and cleansed. The more they find it needful to lay their whole heart before Him, asking Him for His providence to search and purify on every side, the more He will work until He is satisfied.

Christian, are you in the habit of asking the Lord to satisfy himself to do that which shall bring you into a condition pleasing to Him? Do you not long for the pruning knife to be applied, to be purged of all your selfishness and everything offensive to God, so that you may stand before Him as a young child in meekness and love, while He looks upon you and says, "This is my handiwork, and it is very good"? Ask God to search you then, and do not be afraid to have it done. Look upon the trials of life as coming from your heavenly Father, so that if you are really self-deceived you may know it, and if you are not, that you may grow up into the likeness of the Son of God.

6

ON BEING SEARCHED OF GOD*

"Search me, O God, and know my heart: try me, and know my thoughts: and see if there be any wicked way in me, and lead me in the way everlasting" (Psalm 139:23, 24).

These words occur at the close of that wonderful psalm written under a vivid sense of God's omniscience and omnipresence, and which begins: "O Lord, thou hast searched me and known me."

In treating my text, I propose to show:

▶ *When this prayer, always appropriate, is especially and peculiarly so.*
▶ *Why people need divine searching.*
▶ *The manner in which God answers prayer to be searched.*

When this prayer, always appropriate, is especially and peculiarly so.

This prayer is especially pertinent when people are in spiritual darkness and have low and faint conceptions of spiritual things. Then they have great reason to suspect something is wrong and should search for the cause that it may be set right. It must be that something separates your soul from God, and you should set yourself to pray this prayer unceasingly.

In a state of spiritual insensitivity people should cry to God to be searched. When you do not *feel* the power of Truth, you may be assured something is wrong and you should search for

---

The Oberlin Evangelist, July 4, 1855.

the cause, giving yourself no rest until it is discerned. Those who allow themselves to remain without inquiry for the cause do wrong to their own souls.

If your mind is oppressed with a sense of guilt, but you do not clearly see where the guilt lies, you should not remain at ease till the whole matter is searched to the bottom. Often people carry a sense of guilt in their souls a long time, yet do not see the particular cause. Probably they will not see it unless the Spirit of God searches them thoroughly. Hence, they should cry mightily unto Him for His searching power.

Whenever you attempt to approach God and find access denied to you, when you try to pray, but cannot find God, when your prayer seems to be shut off and fails and never rises toward God, then you should inquire why your Father's door is shut against you, and why, when you try to come to the throne of grace, you can get no access to it. Ask God to search you.

When you have no spirit of prayer, you should ask God to search your heart for the cause. When you have no inclination to go to God, when you know you need blessings but do not feel inclined to go to God and seek them in earnest prayer, then is the time to cry to God for the searching grace of His Spirit.

When prayer, instead of being spontaneous, costs you *effort*, and it seems a hard labor to bring your mind to prayer, then you should know that your heart does not *pray*. It is only your lips that pray at best. Alarmed at such a state, you should fall back upon this preliminary prayer and earnestly implore grace from God to search you and show you all the fearful wrong of your heart or life.

Some of you may be in this state. Will you ask yourselves how this can be and why?

Equally so, if your prayers do not prevail with God, then you should by all means inquire what can be hindering your prayers before God. You may safely assume that there is something wrong in yourself. There is nothing wrong in God, nor has He forgotten His promises.

Another reason for this prayer is when you are not successful in your efforts to do good. When God does not animate your efforts and crown them with His blessing, then let not your soul rest but arise and cry mightily to God that you may know why His grace is withheld from your endeavors.

The searching prayer should be made when the Bible, religious truth and the gospel means are not enjoyed. When you can neglect the Bible and not find it precious to your soul, and your soul is not deeply in earnest, then something is in the way. The Spirit of God is grieved, and you should awake to a most earnest search for this cause. This is an unnatural state of things for a Christian.

Indeed, whenever you are not filled with the Spirit, you should inquire *why not?* There is surely some valid reason why you are not, and it behooves you to search for that reason.

When the path between our souls and God is not clear; when, instead of standing in His sunlight, there is plainly some thick cloud between God and your soul, and you cannot commune freely with Him, then you need to be alive to your danger. If you are weak in faith and your heart does not take hold of the great things of God and of salvation with earnest power, then something is wrong and you should by no means allow it to remain unsearched and still undermining your spiritual life.

Why people need divine searching.

Many have supposed that they need the Spirit, not because they are not well disposed, but because there is some defect beyond and beneath their own activities, and which therefore they *cannot* reach, and none but God *can.* Their need of divine aid is of such a nature that they can excuse themselves if they do not have it. Now in fact, if Christians examine themselves, they will see that the very reason they need it lies wholly in themselves. This will appear as I proceed to show what these reasons are.

Another reason for divine searching is the influence of prejudice or errors in judgment. People take up a one-sided view of a case. They even do this under the influence of a *dishonest* prejudice, for if they were thoroughly honest, they would be careful about forming opinions and would more often avoid serious mistakes. We are prone, under temptations, to adopt opinions with only a partial and one-sided view of the case, and yet may not be aware of the fact. The mind acts under its present views, but the reason these views and no others are present is due to prejudice. The mind is not thoroughly honest. So opinions are formed of *people* under prejudice. Those who form them do not know better, but they *ought* to know better. In such cases men should pray earnestly that God would reveal to them their prejudices, casting themselves on God for His aid.

People need the Spirit because they are prone to justify themselves on a false standard. Not having before their minds the love required in both the Law and the Gospel, they judge themselves not by God's rule but by some other rule. Whereas, if they would bring themselves under the light of the Golden Rule and require of themselves the same love everywhere in all relations they bear toward wives and children, brothers and sisters, they would soon see their mistake.

But people are not inclined to use the Golden Rule in honest application. When you see a difficulty spring up between two people, each wrong, perhaps, yet each justifying himself, you will find they have a false standard of gospel love. You will readily see that all is wrong.

I have often been shocked at my own mistakes in judging myself from a false point of view, neglecting and forgetting Christ's spirit in which He could even die for an enemy. Instead of looking at it in that light, I found myself inclined to take quite another view and therein I learned my great need of the Holy Spirit.

We are often blinded by our feelings also. These have a surprising influence on our opinions. Feelings are allowed to control the intellect, and this acts toward the control of the will. Hence we fall into errors because we are blinded by excited feelings.

People sometimes say, "We have been so tried and abused we have good reason for feeling excited." Yet, after all, they cannot be satisfied in a course which conscience condemns. Still, they manage to keep themselves blind, while really their excuse is no excuse at all. It avails nothing that people try to justify themselves in wrongdoing because others have done wrong first, arguing that we may rightly injure those who have injured us. Such a state of self-satisfaction needs to be thoroughly searched out by the Spirit of God.

One peculiarity is often overlooked. It often happens that people, finding themselves the subject of abuse, bear it firmly, being on their guard. But when another person is abused, then they think it *noble* to resist and repel the wrong, and often go into this with a spirit which they would at once condemn if it were aimed to repel a wrong done themselves. The devil gets great advantage over them. They think they are standing up in defense of truth and right, but do it with a wrong spirit. Many a person has pled for the slave in a spirit that shuts him off from God. Seeing despotism lording it over his fellowman, he lets his indignation loose and steps into the place of him who has said, "Vengeance is mine." God wants no such advocacy even of the oppressed. Let no person assume that God neglects His duty of avenging the wrongs of earth!

Often in this way people are unknowingly led into a wrong spirit. They find themselves shut out from God and begin to inquire for the reason. They say, "In such a case, I recollect I became greatly excited, but I had good reason, for that poor man was shamefully abused." Take care; you must not become uncharitable and grieve the heart of God!

We often need God's searching Spirit because we tend to forget. We cultivate the habit of forgetting what we do not wish to remember. Under some influence leading in that direction, we do not care to remember. God says, "They do not consider that I remember all their sins." Hence, it behooves you to cry, "O Lord, what is it?" We need some special providence, or some form of divine utterance that shall wake us up to remember our deeds.

People often shield themselves under some false principle or some supposed fact, either of which they admit to be true without sufficient care. Having once adopted the principle or the fact, the mind becomes incapable of seeing things as they are. This incapability is a great sin because the will has had an influence in producing it. Thus blinded, people pass on till they plunge into an ocean of errors, all growing out of their self-will.

Often people are blinded by self-esteem. They have a much better opinion of themselves than they ought to have. Hence, they underestimate their wrong deeds and overestimate their right ones. By this means they must, of course, fall into darkness. Indeed, the spirit of egotism amounts sometimes to a sort of insanity. There is a species of egotistical insanity in which the mind forever resorts to itself and never sees anything pertaining to self in a just light. Let me not be understood to imply that this insanity is a misfortune and not a crime, for it certainly is a great crime growing out of a blameworthy and sinfully indulged self-esteem. This egotism is one of the most difficult things to root out from the mind. There is little hope for such a one unless God interposes to open his eyes and reveal his heart to himself in its just light.

Many times people are also blinded by self-interest. You are aware that courts of law will not allow a person to either witness or juror if he has any self-interest in the case. A judge will not even allow himself to sit and hear a case if he has any personal interest in it. I knew of a man who had been consulted as a lawyer upon a case, and gave his opinion upon it; subsequently coming upon the bench, the same case was brought before him in the court of appeals, and he refused to hear it on the grounds that he might be biased by his previously formed and expressed opinion. People often overlook this danger and get deeply involved in some sin and allow themselves to justify their own course under the obvious influence of self-interest. In such a case, how earnestly should people cry out to God: "Oh, my God, open my heart, and let thy light in! Draw me out lest I die in my sin!"

We often need God's light because we are blinded by the fear or the love of man. The fear or the love of the creature more than the Creator leads us astray. I think I could name ministers who have lost their power with God and with man by means of being led astray by the fear or the love of some of their congregation. Their prayers are cold as death, and their position on great moral questions plainly shows that they do not stand in God's counsels.

People often fall into the habit of professing more in their prayers than is strictly true. Sometimes they continue professing to be Christians when they know they ought not to, for they have no heart in it. They may excuse themselves by pleading that they are about as good as their neighbors are, yet they know this excuse can avail nothing before God. Such people must fall into great darkness. Oh, how many ministers have continued on in all the forms of religion, but with hearts hard as a stone, their very declarations of orthodoxy altogether hypocrisy and deceit before God!

In this spirit, people sometimes fill the office of deacon, holding it solemnly before God and the church, yet with none of the spirit of a true deacon. Some hold on in this way year after year and completely destroy their own souls. Sanctimonious, selfish, fast asleep, they never find that when they open their mouths, there is a bursting out of feeling from the living fire in their souls. Cold, formal, speculative, dead, the heart with no fellowship with God—how plainly such people ought to cry out to God, "Oh, my Strength, cast me not off; there must be something wrong in me. Oh, tell me what it is! Search me till all is revealed."

We need this divine searching because we are so prone to attend to others' sins more than our own. We are in great danger of this, especially if we feel annoyed by others' sins, and get into a bad state of mind ourselves. Indeed, we are in more danger precisely as we get further away from God. Often this becomes a habit because people hear preaching that is not applied to them personally. They do not allow the truth to reveal their own hearts, but look at others. Now, unless God comes down to search such people, they will never return to life and love again.

People are exceedingly apt to rest in the letter without the spirit, satisfied with holding the truth without obeying it. The Jews of old stumbled on this rock. Such people are not aware of their danger; for those truths which they hold may be truly valuable, yet if this truth does not affect and even arouse them, it is all bad.

People need God's searching Spirit because they are so liable to sear their conscience if they abuse its guidance. They see nothing on the field of consciousness, and therefore think all must be right. Surely they will go to destruction unless God arouses and searches them thoroughly! By conscience, such people understand a feeling of remorse; and hence, not feeling this, they think all is well. It is not strange, therefore, that they should live in great sin a long time without seeing their real condition, and because of their blindness, they lose their communion with God. There is little hope in their case unless they arouse themselves to cry mightily unto God for His searching Spirit.

People are apt to overlook the sin of unbelief, perhaps confounding it with *disbelief*; hence, not being conscious of denying the truth in disbelief, they assume they are not guilty of resisting its power in unbelief. Really, they do not give God credit for truthfulness, and much less still do they earnestly trust Him according to all their needs and to His grace to supply them. Only by God's searching Spirit are they likely to be recovered from this snare.

Often people mistake the will for the conscience. They think their conscience is seared and the will is *up* in its strength, and has assumed more than all the functions of conscience. If their conscience were in a healthy state, they would readily distinguish between the two; but now, having only a will in action, they must have their eyes thoroughly opened by the divine Spirit, or they will not discriminate between the will and the conscience.

Many people also confound memory with imagination. Having passed through a course of doubtful conduct, they conceive what would excuse them, and then bring themselves to think it was so. The circumstances are suggested by the imagination, and are then supposed to be held as by simple memory. Such people are very probably not aware of this deception, but go on sinning and covering up their sin as they go. Unless God convinces them of their sins, they wax worse and worse. They get fearfully far away from God, even while assuming that all is right. While plainly, if they were to apply honestly even the simplest tests of Christian experience, they would find the bottom of their piety altogether fallen out.

People are prone to take credit for what is of little or no real value. Often they do things only in the *letter of the law* with not a particle of the spirit which God requires, and which only makes the outward doing real obedience. Thus people will attend religious meetings, right to the letter, but with no heart for worship and no regard to pleasing God; hence, all is lacking in the *spirit* of the deed. Or, they give their money for a benevolent object, yet give it most grudgingly or selfishly, and therefore in a spirit which God abhors. Now, if people take credit to themselves for such services, they are under a most radical mistake and need God's Spirit to open their eyes to see it.

Often people overlook a multitude of dishonesties and hypocrisies. They go on in a course of prayers toward God which being empty are unutterably loathesome to Him. Who can save them from this delusion but God himself?

People are apt to resist and grieve away the Holy Spirit without remembering when and how they did it. They were walking with God up to a certain point; then they parted from Him, but they did not at once notice the fact and do not subsequently recall the circumstances so as to see the reason why God left them. The truth, doubtless, was that the Holy Spirit urged some point of duty, but they resisted. So they lost their life and peace, and passed on, so much interested in something else that they failed to notice that God had departed from them. In such a state man's only help is to cry to God for His searching Spirit.

We are apt to fail in fulfilling the conditions of prayer, and hence begin to doubt and become greatly discouraged. Parents praying for children fail to fulfill the conditions, and hence make no real use of the promises. Such people greatly need God's searching Spirit to show them their own case.

Some people are at issue with God because they make excuses for their sins. How many have been in a terrible state of commotion, agonized, distressed, anxious to know why they feel this way, when really the fact is they are excusing some sin.

People sometimes suppose themselves fully consecrated to God when they are not so. Some little idols are hidden among them, as in the case of Rachel. No matter how small, a ring or a pin, if reserved as our own and not heartily laid on God's altar, it mars your consecration to God. You are not a fruitful branch, just a dry stalk. You can have no hold on God in prayer. In real consecration, the heart is full of God, and this full heart breaks forth in appropriate emotions and reveals itself in a rich spiritual life. If your case lacks these evidences, you need to inquire, "Lord, is this all? Is Christianity a powerless religion?" You need to cry out, "Tell me, Oh, my Father, am I really consecrated to you or am I deceived?"

People are in great danger in the line of covering up sin or refusing when convicted to confess it. These causes involve them in great spiritual darkness.

Sometimes people harbor resentment without being aware of it. They would not exactly like to inflict evil on another, but are more than willing it should befall him, no matter who does it. There is really an ill feeling. In this state of mind, you find yourself shut out from God and need to cry out for light.

The manner in which God answers prayer to be searched.

God will directly call our attention to the thing we need to see. He may do this by the direct agency of His Spirit, bringing up some truth of His Word with amazing power and applying it in a most searching manner to our hearts. It is not so much the Bible, as the Holy Spirit of God *in* the Bible and by means of the Bible, that brings such light.

A lady, having made a profession of faith and entered upon a Christian life, subsequently found herself so greatly tried that she at length said, "I must give up all profession of piety and all attempt to live a Christian life unless I can succeed better." At that time she had not been taught that she might find deliverance through Christ. But at this juncture, the doctrine of sanctification was brought before her mind, and she felt her need of its provisions. She embraced it in theory hoping, and for the time assuming, that this would bring her the desired relief. But this failed, and she was about to abandon the theory when it was suggested that she had not faithfully put the doctrine into practice. One of her most besetting and powerful sins was in her temper. She began to see that she must have grace for a victory over this. Just at this crisis, her husband in family worship read the passage, "In the world ye shall have tribulation: but be of good cheer; I have overcome the world" (John 16:33). It thrilled her very soul. She cried out, "My temper is dead; through grace I have conquered, and my victory is complete." Many years afterward she said of herself, "Never since that hour have I felt any risings of unhallowed temper, and I no more expect to give way to that sin than I expect to cut my neighbor's throat."

Often God brings about the same result by the aid of His providence—providence acting from without and His Spirit working within. Together, they reveal to the mind what was not seen before. One man meets with losses of property, and the loss shows him that this property was held as *his*, not as God's.

Only last winter a lady told me she had fallen into a dreadful state of mind bordering on despair, so that her friends feared she would kill herself. At length, providence showed her what the matter was. Her husband had refused to perform the duty of family worship, and she had gotten angry about it. She was so full of zeal for God, as she thought, that she was not aware of her great sin. At length, God brought help by converting her husband. Then, seeing that she was parted from him and that she had been sinfully angry, her heart was broken down into penitence, and her soul restored to the joys of God's salvation.

REMARKS

Having made this prayer, be careful not to resist the divine searching. Whatever means God may use, let Him go on, unresisted on your part. When we most need to be searched, we are in greatest danger of resisting the process.

Having begun, be careful not to desist from praying and self-searching till the work has gone to the bottom. Cease not till you find your soul filled with peace and power, such as will reveal itself everywhere.

As fast as God reveals light, we should use it. Many begin well and pray well, but defer repentance and reform till they shall have seen the whole. They want everything revealed before they begin to repent and reform. Or they look for the blessing before they have fulfilled the conditions. They say, "Give me the blessing, and then I will repent." This is no way to deal with God. Let them rather deal honestly and put away all iniquity as fast as they discover it.

When people pray that God would search them, they should

use all fit means to search themselves. Not to do this shows that you are not really honest in desiring the blessing.

Some of you have lived a long time, and have passed through many scenes of refreshing, and many agencies of both providence and grace designed for your good. But now you seem to have thrown off a sense of responsibility, and to have wandered far from God. How greatly do you need to open your hearts before God and expose all to the light of His grace and truth. It would be sad if amid so much religious activity, some should be very far out of the way. We need a general awakening of mind in which each one shall fix his mind on his own sins. After such a sermon as this, someone will say, "That is the preaching we need. Do you think the Church needs such preaching?" And yet this very person who cares so benevolently for the Church needs the sermon more than any other. The thing most often needed is that each person should apply it to himself, asking, "In what respect do I need this sermon? For what do I need to be searched?" Pray for God to search you and try you and see if there be any evil way in you. Some of you, I am afraid, are in most perishing need of this personal treatment. Brethren, when shall your church be as holy as it professes to be, as it is supposed to be, and as its theory leads people to assume that it is? When will all our theories be practiced?

It often happens that people most in the fog about their own state are most tried with the bad state of others. This is sometimes a great and sore delusion! Beware of it!

How many of you are in the habit of taking your spiritual reckoning every week, or even every month, to see where you are and whether you may not be coasting along the shore, just off the rocks, heading toward them under wind and tide, the breakers roaring under your bow! Pray that God may search you all out, and leave nothing undisclosed! Pray that God will search everyone around you, each according to his need. This more than anything else is what the unrepentant need to see in every house and in every Christian—each of us an epistle of Christ, known and read by all. Then the gospel would be honored and its truth be enforced with resistless power.

7

THE LORD'S PRAYER*

"After this manner therefore pray" (Matthew 6:9).

Before I come to this text directly, I deem it important to make several remarks upon the general subject of prayer and of answers to prayer. I intend to show:

► *What the distinction is between answers to the letter of prayer and to the spirit of prayer.*
► *There are conditions of acceptable prayer.*
► *What condition is implied in this text.*

What the distinction is between answers to the letter of prayer and to the spirit of prayer.

The Bible most unequivocally asserts that all that is properly called *prayer* is heard and answered. "Everyone that asketh"—that is, in the scriptural sense of the term— "receiveth, and he that seeketh, findeth." This declaration is perfectly explicit and to the point.

Prayer is not always answered according to the letter, but often only according to the spirit.

---

*From Charles G. Finney, *Sermons On The Way Of Salvation* (Oberlin: Edward J. Goodrich, 1891), pp. 372–390. Formerly abridged and titled, "Conditions Of Prevailing Prayer," this sermon was the second in a series of three first printed in *The Oberlin Evangelist* each under that same title. This sermon has been edited here to include both the first and second sermons consecutively as one, published on May 26, 1847, and June 9, 1847, respectively. In this book, the third sermon in the series is number 19, "Principles Of Communion With God."

This is a very important distinction. It can be made plain by an example taken from Scripture. Paul informs us that he was afflicted with a thorn in the flesh. He has not told us precisely what this was. He calls it his "temptation that was in his flesh," and evidently implies that it was a snare and trouble to him, a thing which might naturally injure his influence as an apostle. For this latter reason, probably, he was led to "beseech the Lord thrice that it might depart from him." This prayer was obviously acceptable to God, and was graciously answered; answered, however, you will observe, not in the letter of it, but only its spirit.

The *letter* of the prayer specified the removal of this thorn in the flesh; and in this view of his prayer it was not answered. The *spirit* of the prayer was doubtless that his influence might not be injured, and that his "temptation" from this evil thing, whatever it was, might not overpower him and draw him into sin. Thus far, and in these respects, his prayer was answered. The Lord assured him, saying, "My grace is sufficient for thee; for my strength is made perfect in weakness." This was a real answer to Paul's prayer, although it did not follow the particular *way* of doing it that Paul had named in his prayer. Paul had asked that certain desired results might be secured to him in a particular manner. The results sought constituted the spirit of the prayer; the specified manner constituted its letter. The Lord secured to him the results, and perhaps even more fully than Paul expected or specifically asked; but He did it, not in Paul's specified way, but in His own.

So it often happens when we pray. The ways of the Lord are so much wiser than our own that He kindly and most benevolently declines to follow our way, and takes His own. The great *end*, however, which we seek if our prayer is acceptable to Him, He will certainly secure—perhaps more perfectly in *His* way than He could in ours.

If, therefore, we suppose that prayer must always be answered according to the letter, we shall find ourselves greatly mistaken. But the spirit of acceptable prayer God will always answer. If the letter and the spirit of prayer were in any case identical, the Lord would answer both; when they are not idenical, He may answer only according to its spirit.

Many things are really answers to prayer which are not recognized as such by those praying or by observers.

This may very easily happen in cases where the spirit and the letter of prayer are diverse from each other. An observer, of course, is not likely to notice anything but the letter of another's prayer. Consequently, if a prayer is answered only in the spirit of it, and not in the letter at all, he will fail to recognize the answer. And the same thing may occur with respect to the person praying. Unless he notices particularly the inner state of his own mind, he may not understand what constitutes the spirit of his own prayer. If his attention is chiefly turned toward the letter of it, he may receive an answer to its spirit, and may not notice it as a real answer to his prayer.

The acceptable prayer of any Christian may be quite a different thing from what others suppose it to be, and sometimes different from what he himself supposes. In such cases, the answer will often fail to be recognized as an answer. Hence, it is of vital importance that we should ourselves understand the real spirit of our own prayer.

All this applies yet more frequently in respect to others than to the petitioner himself. Usually they see only the letter of a prayer and not the spirit. Hence, if the latter is answered and not the former, they will naturally suppose that the prayer is not answered, when really it is answered and in the best possible way. Skeptics often stand by tauntingly, crying, "You Christians are always praying; but your prayers are never answered." Yet God may be really answering their prayers in the spirit of it, and in the most effectual and glorious manner. I think I could name many instances in which, while skeptics were triumphing as if God did not hear prayer, He was really hearing it in regard to the true spirit of it, and in such a way as most remarkably to glorify himself.

Much that is called prayer is not answered in any sense whatever, and *is not real prayer*. Much that goes under the name of prayer is offered merely for the form of it, with neither care nor expectation to be answered. Those who pray thus will not watch to see whether their prayers are answered in any sense whatever.

For example, there are some who pray as a matter of cold duty—only because they *must*, not because they feel their need of some specific blessing. Hence, their prayer is nothing but a form. Their heart is not set upon any particular object. They only care to do what they call a duty; they do not care with anxious heart for any object they may specify in their prayers. Hence, the thing they really care for is not the thing they pray for. In words, they pray for this thing; in heart, for quite another thing. And the evidence of this is that they never look for the thing they prayed for in words. If they prayed in heart for anything, they would certainly watch to see whether the blessing asked for was given.

Suppose a person petitioned for some appointment to office and sent his application to the president or to the appointing power. Probably his heart is greatly set on attaining it. If so, you will see him watching the mail for the reply to his communication. Every day you may see him at the post office ready to seize his letter at the earliest possible moment. But if, on the other hand, he applied only for form's sake and cares nothing about the office or does not at all expect it, you will see him about other business or pleasure which he does care for.

The latter case rarely occurs in human affairs, but in religious things nothing is more common. Multitudes are engaged from time to time in what they call praying; their object being often only to appease their consciences—not to obtain any desired blessing. Of course the quiet of their conscience is the only thing they really seek by prayer, and it would be absurd for them to look for any other answer than this. They are not inclined to be guilty of this absurdity. Of course those who pray in this way are not disappointed if their prayers are not heard.

A real Christian sometimes asks in the letter of prayer for what he finds God cannot give. In such a case he can be satisfied only with the consideration that God always exercises His own infinite wisdom and infinite *love*. The thing that is nearest his heart, if he is in the true spirit of prayer, will be granted—namely, that God may be honored in the exercise of His own wisdom and love. This God will surely do. And in this way, therefore, the spirit of his prayer will be granted.

It deserves special notice that those who pray as a matter of form only, and with no heart set upon the blessing named in the prayer, never inquire about the reasons why they are not answered. Their minds are entirely at ease on this point, because they feel no concern about the answer at all. They did not pray for the sake of an answer. Hence, they will never trouble themselves to inquire why the answer to the words of their prayer fails of being given.

Many of you may see in this the real reason why you so rarely look for any answer to your prayers; or the reason why you care so little about it, if your mind should chance to give attention to it at all.

There are conditions of acceptable prayer.

When our petitions are not answered either in letter or spirit, it is because we have not fulfilled the revealed conditions of acceptable prayer. Many people seem to overlook the fact that there are conditions of acceptable prayer revealed in the Bible. This is far too important to be overlooked. Every Christian should know not only that there are conditions, but also what those conditions are.

Let us fully understand that if our prayers are not answered, it is because we have failed to fulfill the revealed conditions. This must be why our prayers are not answered, for God has assured us in His Word that all real prayer is always answered.

Nothing can be more important than that we should thoroughly understand the conditions of prevailing prayer. If we fail to understand them, we shall probably fail to fulfill them, and of course fail to offer prevailing prayer. Alas, how ruinous a failure must this be to any soul!

There are those, I am aware, who do not expect to influence God by their prayers; they expect to produce effects only upon themselves, perhaps just psychologically. They only hope by means of prayer to bring themselves to a better state of mind, to change their attitude.

To all such I have two things to say. First, it may be that an individual not in a right state of mind may be benefited by giving himself to prayer. If the prayer is offered with sincerity and solemnity—with a real feeling of need, as it is sometimes in the case of a convicted sinner—it may have a very happy effect upon his own state of mind. When such a man gives himself to confession and supplication, spreading out his case before the Lord, it is usually a most important step toward his real conversion. It helps to bring the character and claims of God distinctly before his mind, and has a natural tendency to make his own soul realize more deeply its guilt, its need of pardon, and its duty of submission and of faith in Christ.

But if any person should suppose that a case of this sort involves all that is included in prevailing prayers, he is greatly mistaken. In prevailing prayer, a child of God comes before Him with real faith in His promises and asks for things agreeable to His will, assured of being heard according to the true intent of His promises. Thus coming to God he prevails with Him, and really influences God to do what otherwise He would not do by any means. That is, prayer truly secures from God the bestowment of the blessing sought. Nothing less than this corresponds either with the promises of Scripture, or with its recorded facts in respect to the answers made to prevailing prayer.

Secondly, God is unchangeable in the attitude of answering

prayer. This is true for the same reason that He is unchangeable in the attitude of being highly satisfied in holiness whenever He sees it. The reason in both cases lies in His infinitely benevolent nature. Because He is infinitely good, and for no other reason, He is evermore in the attitude of answering suitable prayer, and of being strongly satisfied toward all real holiness. As in the latter case, whenever a moral change takes place in a sinner of such a nature that God *can* love him with satisfaction in his character, His infinite love gushes forth instantaneously and without bounds. So in the former case, as soon as any petitioner places himself in such an attitude that God can wisely answer his prayer, then instantly He inclines to his petition, and the answer is freely given.

To illustrate this point, suppose that for a season some obstacle interposes to obstruct the sunbeams from the rosebush at your door; it fades and it looks sickly. But take away the obstacle, and instantly the sunbeams fall in their reviving power upon the rose. So sin casts its dark shadow upon the soul and obstructs the sunbeams of God's smiles. But take away the obstacle—the sin—and the smiles fall in of course, and *in their full blaze* on that penitent and morally changed heart. The sun of God's face shines always: shines in its own nature; and its beams fall on all objects which are not cast into some deep shade by interposing sin and unbelief. On all objects not thus shaded, its glorious beams forever fall in all their sweetness and beauty.

All real prayer moves God, not merely by benefiting the person praying through its reflex action, but really and in fact inducing Him to grant the blessing sought. The notion that the whole benefit of prayer is its reflex influence upon the petitioner, and not the obtaining of any blessing asked for, is both vain and preposterous. You might as well suppose that all the good you get by removing obstacles that cut off the sunbeams is the physical exercise attending the effort. You might as well deny that the sunbeams will actually reach every object as soon as you take away that which throws them into the shade.

God does truly hear and answer prayer, even as an earthly parent hears the petition of a dutiful child, and shapes His course to meet that petition. To deny this involves the denial of the very nature of God. It is equivalent to denying that God is benevolent. Nothing can be more plain than the fact that God promises to be influenced by prayer so as to bestow blessings to the person praying that are given to none others and on no other condition.

If God is pure and good, then it must follow that—the obstacle of sin being removed in the case of a fallen being—the divine love must flow out toward him as it did not and could not before. Good remains forever the same, just as the sun forever shines. God's love meets every object that lies open to His beams, just as the sun's rays cheer everything not shaded by positive obstructions.

God may hear the mere cry of distress and speedily send help. He "hears the young ravens when they cry," and the young lions too when they roar and seek their meat from God. The storm-tossed mariners also, "at their wit's end, cry unto the Lord in their trouble, and he bringeth them out of their distress." His benevolence leads Him to do all this wherever He can without detriment to the interest of His government. Yet this case seems not to come under the promises made to the believing prayer. These cases of distress often occur in the experience of wicked men. Yet sometimes God seems obviously to hear their cry. He has wise reasons for doing so; probably often His object is to open their eyes to see their own Father, and to touch their hearts with a sense of their ingratitude in their rebellion against such a God.

But whatever the reason, the fact cannot be disputed. Cases frequently occur in which nonbelievers are afflicted by the dangerous illness of near friends or relatives, and lift their imploring cry of distress to the Lord and He hears them. It is even said in Scripture that Christ heard the prayer of devils when they "besought him much that he would not send them away out of the country," and said, "Send us into the swine, that we may enter into them."

Manifestly the Lord often hears this kind of prayer whenever no special reason exists for refusing to hear it. Yet this is far from being that special kind of prayer to which the specific promises of hearing and answering prayer are made.

It is however both interesting and instructive to see how often the Lord *does* hear even such prayer as these cries of distress. When the cattle moan in the fields because there is no water, and because the grass is withered, there is One on high who listens to their moans. Why should He not? Has He not a compassionate heart? Does not His ear bend under the quick impulse of spontaneous affection, when any of His creatures cry unto Him as their Father, and when no great moral considerations forbid His showing favor?

It is striking to see how much the parental character of God the Father is developed in the course of His providence by His hearing this kind of prayer. A great multitude of facts are exhibited both in the Bible and in history that set this subject in a strong light. I once knew a wicked man, who, under deep affliction from the dangerous illness of his child, set himself to pray that God would spare and restore the dear one; and God appeared to answer his prayer in a most remarkable manner.

Those of you who have read the "Bank of Faith" know that Mr. Huntington, before his conversion, in many instances seemed to experience the same kind of remarkable answers to his prayers. Another anecdote was told me once. A wicked man who had perhaps never prayed since he was a child was out with a hunting party in Iowa hunting wild buffalo. Mounted on trained horses, lasso in hand, they came up to a herd of buffalo, and this man encountered a fierce buffalo bull. The animal rushed upon him, and at his first push unseated him. But quick as a flash the man seized his own horse's neck, swung upon the underside of the neck, and there held on in the utmost peril of his life, his horse being at full gallop, pursued by a ferocious wild bull. To break his hold and fall was almost certain death, and he was every moment in the utmost danger of falling under the flying feet of his rushing horse. In this predicament he reminded himself of prayer; but the only words he could think of were, "Now I lay me down to sleep, I pray the Lord my soul to keep."

Perhaps he had never heard much other prayer than this. This lay embalmed among the recollections of his childhood days. Yet even this prayer the Lord in His infinite mercy seemed to hear and answer by rescuing the man unhurt from this perilous condition. The case affords us a striking exemplification not only of the fact that God hears the cry of mere distress, sometimes even when made by wicked men, but also of another fact, namely, that the spirit of a prayer may be a very different thing from its letter. In this case, the letter and the spirit had no very close resemblance. The spirit of the prayer was for deliverance from imminent peril. This the Lord seemed to have heard.

But it should be continually borne in mind that these are not the prayers which God has pledged himself by promise to hear and answer. The latter are evermore the believing prayers of His own children.

Let us now consider those prayers that God has solemnly promised to answer. Attached to the promises made respecting this class of prayers are certain *conditions*. These being fulfilled, God holds himself bound to answer the prayer according to the letter and spirit both. If they both correspond, or if they do not correspond, then He will answer according to the spirit of the prayer. This is always the meaning of His promise. His promise to answer prayer on certain conditions is a pledge at least to meet it in its true spirit, and do or give what the spirit of the prayer implies.

Now let us consider the conditions of prevailing prayer.

What condition is implied in this text.

The first condition is *a state of mind in which you could offer the Lord's Prayer sincerely and acceptably.*

Christ at their request taught His disciples how to pray. In doing so, He gave them an example of the appropriate subjects of prayer, and also threw a most important light upon the *spirit* with which all prayer should be offered. This form is exceedingly comprehensive. Every word is full of meaning. It would seem very obvious, however, that our Lord did not intend here to specify all the particular things we may pray for, but only to group together some of the subjects which are appropriate to be sought in prayer, and also to show us what attitude and spirit we should have before the Lord.

The Lord's Prayer is evidently not designed as a mere form, to be used always and without variation. It cannot be that Christ intended we should always use these words in prayer, and no others; for He never again used these words himself, so far as we know, but did often use other and very different words, as the Scriptures abundantly testify.

But this form answers a most admirable purpose if we understand it to be given us to teach us these two most important things; namely, what sort of blessings we may pray for and in what spirit we should pray for them.

Most surely, then, we cannot hope to pray acceptably unless we can offer this prayer in its real *spirit*: our own hearts deeply sympathizing with the spirit of this prayer. If we cannot pray the Lord's Prayer sincerely, we cannot offer any acceptable prayer at all.

Hence, it becomes us to examine carefully the words of this recorded form of prayer. Yet remember, it is not these words, as mere words, that God regards or that we should value. Words themselves, apart from their meaning, and from their meaning *as used by us*, would neither please nor displease God. He looks on the heart.

Let us now refer to the Lord's Prayer and to the context in which it stands.

"When ye pray," says our Lord, "use not vain repetitions, as the heathen do: for they think that they shall be heard for their much speaking."

Hence, there is no need that you continue to clamor unceasingly, "O Baal, hear us; O Baal, hear us." Those were indeed vain repetitions—just such as the heathen use. It is a most notable fact that even some Christian churches have fallen into the practice here condemned. Like the priests of Baal, in Elijah's time, they demand and practice everlasting repetitions of the same words, estimating the merit of prayer by the quantity, and not the quality, of their prayers. They believe the more repetitious, the greater the value. This principle, and the practice founded upon it, our Savior most pointedly condemns. How God must be bored or angered at such a mechanical and impersonal way of coming to Him!

Many people seem to lay much more stress upon the *amount* of prayer than upon its character and quality. They think if there can only be prayer enough, that is, repetitions enough of the same or similar words, the prayer will be effective and prevail with God. No mistake can be greater. The entire Word of God rebukes this view of the subject in the most pointed manner.

Yet, be it well considered, the precept "use not vain repetitions" should by no means be construed to discourage the utmost perseverance and fervency of spirit in prayer. The passage does not forbid our renewing our requests from great earnestness of spirit. Our Lord himself did this in the garden, repeating His supplication "in the same words." *Vain* repetitions are what is forbidden, not repetitions which gush from a burdened spirit.

Our Father

This form of prayer invites us, first of all, to address the great God as "*Our Father which art in heaven*." This authorizes us to come as children and address the Most High, feeling that He is a *Father to us*.

Hallowed

The first petition follows, "*hallowed be thy name*." What is the exact idea of this language? To hallow is to sanctify; to deem and render *sacred*.

There is a passage in Peter's epistle which may throw light on this. He says, "Sanctify the Lord God in your hearts." The meaning seems plainly to be this: Set apart the Lord God in your hearts as the only true object of supreme, eternal adoration, worship and praise. Place Him alone on the throne of your hearts. Let Him be the only hallowed object there.

So here, in the first petition of the Lord's Prayer, we pray that both ourselves and all intelligent beings may in this sense hallow the name of the Lord God and sanctify Him in their hearts. Our prayer is: Let all sanctify thee, the infinite Father, as the only object of universal adoration, praise, worship and love.

This prayer implies a desire that the hallowing of God's name be universal. We must concur heartily in this sentiment. Our inmost souls cry out: Let God be honored, adored, loved, worshiped and revered by all on earth and all in heaven. Of course, praying in this spirit, we shall have the highest reverence for God. Beginning our prayer in this manner, it will be thus far acceptable to God. Without such reverence for God's name, no prayer can possibly be acceptable. All irreverent praying is mockery, most abhorrent to the pure and exalted Father in heaven.

Thy kingdom come

This language implies a desire for God's kingdom to be set up in the world and all men to become holy. The will is set upon this as the highest and most to be desired of all objects whatever. It becomes the supreme desire of the soul, and all other things sink into comparative insignificance before it. The mind and the judgment approve and delight in the kingdom of God as in itself infinitely excellent, and then the will harmonizes most perfectly with this decision of intelligence.

Let it be well observed that our Lord, in giving this form of prayer, assumes throughout that we shall use all this language with most profound sincerity. If any man were to use these words and reject their spirit from his heart, his prayer would be an utter abomination before God. Whoever would pray at all should consider that God looks on the heart and He is a *holy* God.

This petition implies that the suppliant *does* what he can to establish God's kingdom. He is actually doing all he can to promote this great end for which he prays. Otherwise he utterly fails to show his sincerity. For nothing can be more sure than that every man who prays sincerely for the coming of God's kingdom, truly desires and wills that it may come; and if so, he will neglect no means in his power to promote and hasten its coming. Hence, every man who sincerely offers this petition will lay himself out to promote the object. He will seek by every means to make the truth of God universally prevalent and triumphant.

I might also say that the sincere offering of this petition implies a resistance of everything inconsistent with the coming of this kingdom. This you cannot fail to understand.

Thy will

We now advance to the next petition, *"Thy will be done in earth as it is in heaven."*

This petition implies that we desire to have God's will done, and that this desire is supreme. It implies also a delight in having the will of God done. There is implied a state of the will in harmony with this desire. A person whose will is averse to having his own desires granted is insincere, even though his desires are real. Such a one is not honest and consistent with himself.

In general, if this petition is offered sincerely, the following things must be true.

The petitioner is willing that God should require all He does and *as* He does. His heart will agree both in the things required and in the manner in which God requires them. It would indeed be strange for a person to pray sincerely that God's will might be done and yet not be willing himself that God should give law or carry His will into effect. Such inconsistencies never can happen where the heart is truly sincere and honest before God. No, never. The honest-hearted petitioner is as willing that God's will should be done as the saints in heaven are. He delights in having it done—more than in all riches—more than in his highest earthly joy.

When a person offers this petition sincerely, he implies that he is really doing all the known will of God. For if he is acting contrary to his actual knowledge of God's will, it is most certain that he is not sincere in praying that God's will may be done. If he sincerely desires and is willing that God's will should be done, why does he not do it himself?

He implies a willingness that God should use His own discretion in the affairs of the universe—and just as really and fully in this world as in heaven itself. You all admit that in heaven God exercises a holy sovereignty. I do not mean by this, an arbitrary, unreasonable sovereignty; but I mean a control of all things according to His own infinite wisdom and love—always exercising His own discretion, and depending on the counsel of none but himself. Thus God reigns in heaven.

You also see that in heaven all created beings exercise the most perfect submission and confidence in God. They all allow Him to carry out His own plans, framed in wisdom and love, and they even rejoice with exceeding joy that He does. It is their highest blessedness. Such is the state of feeling toward God unanimously in heaven. And such it should be on earth. If you offer this petition sincerely, you will have the same attitude of those in heaven. You will rejoice that God appoints all things as He pleases, and that all beings should be, and do, and suffer as God ordains. If a man has not such confidence in God as to be willing that He should control all events respecting his own family, his friends, all his interests—in short, for time and eternity—then certainly his heart is not submissive to God, and it is hypocrisy for him to pray that God's will may be done on earth as in heaven. It must be hypocrisy in him, because his own heart rebels against the sentiment of his own words.

This petition offered honestly implies nothing less than universal, unqualified submission to God. The heart really submits and delights in its submission. No thought is so truly pleasing as that of always having God's will done. A sincere offering of this prayer, or indeed of any prayer whatever, involves the fullest possible submission of all events for time and for eternity to the hands of God. All real prayer puts God on the throne of the universe, and the person praying low before Him at his footstool.

To offer this petition sincerely implies conformity of life to this state of will. You will readily see that this must be the case, because the will governs the outward life by a law of necessity. The action of this law must be universal so long as man remains a voluntary moral agent. Therefore, the ultimate purpose of the will must control the outward life.

Hence, one who offers this prayer acceptably must live *as he prays*, must live according to his own prayers. It would be a strange and most unaccountable thing, indeed, if one's heart should offer this prayer sincerely, yet in life act directly contrary to his own expressed and supreme preference and purpose. Such a case is impossible. The very supposition involves the absurdity of assuming that a person's supreme preference shall not control his outward life.

In saying this, however, I do not deny that a person's state of mind may change so as to differ from one hour to the next. He may in one hour offer this prayer acceptably, and the next may act in a manner directly against his prayer. But if in this latter hour you could know the state of his will, you would find that it is not such that he can pray acceptably, "Thy will be done." No; his will is so changed as to conform to what you see in his outward life. Hence, a person's state of heart may be to some extent known from his external actions. You may at least know that his heart does not sincerely offer this prayer if his life does not conform to the known will of God.

Daily bread

We proceed to the next petition, *"Give us this day our daily bread."*

Plainly, this petition implies dependence on God for all the favors and mercies we either possess or need. The petition is remarkably comprehensive. It names only bread, and only bread for *"this day"*; yet none can doubt that it was designed to include also our water and our needed clothing—whatever we really need for our highest health, usefulness, and enjoyment on earth. For all these we look to God.

Our Savior doubtless meant to give us in general the *subjects* of prayer, showing us what is proper to pray for and also the spirit with which we should pray. These are plainly the two great points which He aimed chiefly to illustrate in this remarkable form of prayer. Whoever offers this petition sincerely is in a state of mind to recognize and gratefully acknowledge the providence of God. He sees the hand of God in all the circumstances that affect his earthly state—the rain and the sunshine, the winds and the frosts. Hence, he looks up in the spirit of a child, saying, "Give me this day my daily bread."

But there are those who philosophize and speculate themselves entirely out of this filial dependence on God. They arrive at such ideas of the magnitude of the universe that it becomes in their view too great for God to govern by a minute attention to particular events. Hence, they see no God other than an unknowing nature in the ordinary processes of vegetation, or in the laws that control animal life. A certain indefinable but unintelligent power, which they call nature, does it all. Hence, they do not expect God to hear their prayers or notice their needs. Nature will move on in its own determined channel whether they pray or not.

Now, people who hold such opinions cannot pray the Lord's Prayer without the most glaring hypocrisy. How can they offer this prayer and mean anything by it if they truly believe everything is nailed down to a fixed chain of events, in which no regard is had or can be had to the prayers or needs of people? Surely, nothing is more plain than that this prayer recognizes most fully the universal providence of that same infinite Father who gives us the promises, and who invites us to plead them for obtaining all the blessings we can ever need. It recognizes God as ruler over all in very practical ways.

What if a man should offer this prayer and then add to it an appendix of this sort: "Lord, although we ask of Thee our daily bread, yet Thou knowest we do not believe Thou hast anything at all to do with giving us each day our daily bread; for we believe Thou art too high, and Thy universe too large, to admit of our supposing that Thou canst attend to so small a matter as supplying our daily food. We believe that Thou art so unchangeable, and the laws of nature are so fixed, that no regard can possibly be had to our prayer or our wants." Now, would this style of prayer correspond with the petitions given us by Christ or with their obvious spirit?

Plainly, this prayer dictated by our Lord for us implies a state of heart that leans upon God for everything, for even the most minute things that can possibly affect our happiness or be to us objects of desire. The mind looks up to the great God, expecting from Him, and from Him alone, every good and perfect gift. For everything we need, our eye turns naturally and spontaneously toward our great Father. And this is a *daily* dependence. This state of mind which it implies is habitual.

As we forgive

We must pass now to the next petition: *"Forgive us our debts, as we forgive our debtors."*

In this immediate context, the Savior says, "For if ye forgive men their trespasses, your heavenly Father will also forgive you: but if ye forgive not men their trespasses, neither will your Father forgive your trespasses." The word "trespasses," therefore, doubtless explains what is meant by debts in the Lord's Prayer. Luke, in reciting this Lord's Prayer, has it, "Forgive us our sins; for we also forgive every one that is indebted to us."

These various forms of expression serve to make the meaning quite plain.

It may often happen that in such a world as this some of my fellowmen may wrong or at least offend me—in some such way as I wrong and displease God. In such cases this petition of the Lord's Prayer implies that I forgive those who injure me even as I pray to be forgiven myself. The phraseology in Matthew makes the fact that we forgive others either the measure or the condition of our being forgiven; while, as given by Luke, it seems to be at least a condition, if not a ground or reason of the request for personal forgiveness. The former reads, "Forgive us AS we forgive," etc., and the latter, "Forgive us, FOR we also forgive every one indebted to us."

This request cannot possibly imply that God will forgive us our sins *while we are still committing them.* Suppose one should use this form of petition: "Lord, forgive me for having injured Thee as Thou knowest that I do most freely forgive all men who injure me" while it is perfectly apparent to the person himself and to everybody else that he is still injuring and abusing God as much as ever. Would not such a course be equivalent to saying, "Lord, I am very careful, Thou seest, not to injure my fellowmen, and I freely forgive their wrongs against me; but I care not how much I abuse and wrong Thee"? This would be horrible! Yet this shocking prayer is virtually invoked whenever people ask of God forgiveness with the spirit of sin and rebellion in their hearts.

This petition never reads thus, "Forgive us our sins and *enable* us to forgive others also." This would be a most abominable prayer to offer to God; if it implies that we cannot forgive others unless we are especially enabled to do so by power given us in answer to prayer; and worse still, if this inability to forgive is imputed to God as its Author. However, the phraseology is explained, and whatever it is understood to imply, it is common enough in the mouths of men, but nowhere found in the Bible.

Christ, on the other hand, says, Forgive us as we forgive others. "We have often injured, abused and wronged Thee. Our fellowmen have also often injured us, but Thou knowest we have freely forgiven them. Now, therefore, forgive us as Thou seest we have forgiven others. If Thou seest that we do forgive others, then do indeed forgive us, and not otherwise." We cannot ask to be forgiven on any other condition.

Many seem to consider themselves quite pious if they can put up with it when they are injured or slighted, if they can possibly control themselves so as not to break out into a passion. If, however, they are really wronged, they imagine they do well to be angry. It may be true that somebody has wronged them. Shall they not then resent it and study how to get revenge, or, at least, redress? But remember that the Apostle Peter says, "If when ye do well and suffer for it, ye take it patiently, this is acceptable with God." "For even hereunto were ye called," as if all Christians had received a special call to this holy example. Oh, how such an example would rebuke the spirit of the world!

One vital condition of being answered in prayer is that we harbor no ill-will to any human being. We must forgive all who wrong us, forgiving them *from the heart*. God requires us to love our enemies as we love our friends, to forgive others as we ask forgiveness for ourselves. Do we always bear this in mind? Are you, beloved, always careful to see to it that your state of mind toward all who may possibly have wronged you is one of real forgiveness, and do you never think of coming to God in prayer until you are sure you have a forgiving spirit yourself?

Plainly, this is one of the ways in which we may test our fitness of heart to prevail with God in prayer. "When ye stand praying, forgive, if ye have aught against any." Do not imagine you can gain audience before God unless you have most fully and heartily forgiven all who may be thought to have wronged you.

Sometimes people of a peculiar temperament lay up grudges against others. They have enemies against whom they not only speak evil but also do not know how to speak well of. Now, people who harbor such grudges in their hearts can no more prevail with God in prayer than the devil can. God would as soon hear the devil pray and answer his prayer as hear and answer them!

How many times have I had occasion to rebuke this unforgiving spirit! Often, while in a place laboring to promote a revival, I have seen the workings of this jealous, unforgiving spirit, and I have felt like saying, "Take these things hence! Why do you have a prayer meeting and think to pray to God when you know that you hate your brother, and know moreover that I know you do? Away with it!" Let such professing Christians repent, break down, get into the dust at the feet of God, and men too, before they think to pray acceptably! Until they do thus repent, all their prayers are only a "smoke in the nose" before God.

Lead us not

Our next petition is, *"Lead us not into temptation."*
And what is implied in this? A fear and dread of sin, a watchfulness against temptation, an anxious solicitude lest by any means we should be overcome and fall into sin. On this point Christ often warned His disciples, and not them only, but what He said to them, He said to all, *"Watch."*

A man not afraid of sin and temptation cannot present this petition in a manner acceptable to God. You will observe, moreover, that this petition does not by any means imply that God leads men into temptation in order to make them sin, so that we need to implore Him not to lead us thus, lest He should do it. No, the spirit of the petition is this, "O Lord, Thou knowest how weak I am, and how prone to sin; therefore, let Thy providence guard and keep me that I may not indulge in anything whatever that may prove to me a temptation to sin. Deliver me from all iniquity, from all the stratagems of the devil. Throw around me all Thy precious guardianship that I may be kept from sinning against Thee." How needful this protection is, and how fit that we should pray for it without ceasing!

Thine is the kingdom

This form of prayer concludes, *"For thine is the kingdom, the power, and the glory forever. Amen."*
Here is an acknowledgment of the universal government of God. The petitioner recognizes God's supremacy and rejoices in it. Thus it is when the mind is in the attitude of prevailing prayer. It is most perfectly natural then for us to regard the character, attributes, and kingdom of God as infinitely sacred and glorious.

How perfectly spontaneous is this feeling in the heart of all who really pray, "I ask all this because Thou art a powerful, universal and holy Sovereign. Thou art the infinite Source of all blessings. Unto Thee, therefore, do I look for all needed good, either for myself or my fellow beings!"

How deeply does the praying heart realize and rejoice in the universal supremacy of the great Jehovah! "All power, and glory, and dominion are Thine, and Thine only, forever and ever. Amen and amen. Let my whole soul re-echo, Amen. Let the power and the glory be the Lord's alone forevermore. Let my soul forever feel and utter this sentiment with its deepest and most fervent emphasis. Let God reign supreme and adored through all earth and all heaven, henceforth and forever."

REMARKS

The state of mind involved in this prayer must be connected with a holy life. It can never co-exist with a sinning life. If you allow yourself in sin, you certainly cannot have access to God in prayer; you cannot enter into the spirit of the Lord's Prayer and appropriately utter its petitions.

The appropriate offering of this prayer involves a corresponding sensibility, a state of feeling in harmony with it. The mind of the petitioner must sympathize with the spirit of this form of prayer. Otherwise he does, by no means, make this prayer his own.

It is nothing more than mockery to use the Lord's Prayer as a mere form. So multitudes do use it, especially when public worship is conducted by the use of forms of prayer. Often you may hear this form of prayer repeated, over and over, in such a way as seems to testify that the mind takes no cognizance of the sentiments which the words should express. The chattering of a parrot could scarcely be more senseless and void of impression on the speaker's mind. How shocking to hear the Lord's Prayer chattered repeatedly in this way! Instead of spreading out before God what they really need, they run over the words of this form, and perhaps of some other set forms as if the utterance of the right words served to constitute acceptable prayer!

If they had gone into the streets and cursed by the hour, every one of them would be horribly shocked and would feel that now assuredly the curse of God would fall upon them. But in their senseless chattering of the Lord's Prayer by the hour together, they as truly blaspheme God as if they had taken His name in vain in any other way. People may mock God in pretending to pray as truly as in cursing. God looks on the heart, and He considers nothing to be real prayer into which the heart does not enter. For many reasons it must be especially provoking to God to have the forms of prayer spoken often, and yet have no heart of prayer attending them.

Prayer is a privilege too sacred to be trifled with. The pernicious effects of trifling with prayer are certainly not less than the evils of any other form of profanity. Hence, God must abhor all public desecration of this solemn exercise.

Now, brethren, in closing my remarks on this one great condition of prevailing prayer, let me beseech you never to suppose that you pray acceptably unless your heart sympathizes deeply with the sentiments expressed in the Lord's Prayer.* Your state of mind must be such that these words will most aptly express it. Your heart must run into the very words, into all the sentiments of this form of prayer. Our Savior meant here to teach us *how* to pray; and here you may come and learn how. Here you may see a map of the things to pray for, and a picture of the spirit in which acceptable prayer is offered.

---

*The theme of "Conditions of Acceptable Prayer" is continued in Finney's three sermon series in chapter 19 on James 4:3.

8

ACCEPTABLE PRAYER*

"Thy will be done in earth, as it is in heaven" (Matthew 6:10).

These words are part of what is commonly called "The Lord's Prayer," and it is one of the petitions which our Lord Jesus Christ taught His disciples to present to God. I must assume that certain things are admitted by my readers, among them, that you admit that the will of God is perfectly done in heaven, that God is perfectly obeyed there, and that everything is done there perfectly in accordance with His will. This I shall not attempt to prove, but shall take for granted that it is admitted by all my readers. In speaking from the words of our text, I design to call to your attention:

- ► *Some of the principal relations in which the will of God may be contemplated.*
- ► *What is implied in an acceptable offering of this petition to God.*
- ► *That to be in this state of mind is a present and universal duty.*
- ► *The guilt of not being in this state of mind.*
- ► *This state of mind is a condition of salvation.*

---

*From *The Penny Pulpit*, delivered May 12, 1850, at the Tabernacle, Moorfields, and at the Borough Road Chapel, Southwark, in November 1849. No. 1,518. From the collection: "Miscellaneous Sermons," 6 713 F6, and published by the courtesy of the Burke Library, Union Theological Seminary, New York, New York.

Some of the principal relations in which the will of God may be contemplated.

Now, observe that God must be a moral agent if He is a virtuous being. This I take to be a universally known truth and conceded—that God's virtue must be voluntary, that it must consist, substantially, in the same thing in which all virtue consists. If, then, God is a moral agent and a virtuous being, and has an intelligent will, He must live for some good and desirable end. He must exercise His will for some good purpose, and not act at random and without discretion or aim; but that wherever He exercises His agency, it is for some good purpose or end.

We say then, first, that God's will may be contemplated in relation to the *end* upon which it is fastened and which it is endeavoring to realize. In this must the virtue of God, and all other moral agents, substantially consist. If God has chosen a worthy and good end, He is a worthy and good being; but if He has chosen an unworthy end, He cannot be called a good being; for goodness cannot consist in divine substance, irrespective of divine action and will. God's virtue, then, consists in the attitude of His will.

Now, if I see that God has proposed to himself some great and good end, upon which His heart is set—upon which it was set from all eternity—and that this design and aim is really what it ought to be—what the divine intelligence would point out as an end worthy of being chosen and realized, then I can understand the relation of God's will and character thus far: that He is pursuing an end well worthy of himself. We are told in His Word that this end is to secure His own glory and the good of the entire universe.

In the second place, the will of God may be contemplated in respect to the *means* which He uses in order to secure this end. I refer to the government of God: as all that is implied in the movements of the universe that secure the end at which He aims. We may contemplate the will of God as it relates to both physical and moral government: as it relates to the arrangements and order of nature—the physical universe which He has created; and as it relates also to the moral government—rewarding the good, and punishing the guilty.

The will of God also may be contemplated as the will of a sovereign, who exercises sovereignty over His people; not arbitrarily, for which there is no reason, but in that He acts according to His own will without consulting any other being. God's will, then, may be contemplated in relation to His character, His government, the exercise of His providential government in the physical creation; and in respect to all moral agents, prescribing the law and showing how it was to be obeyed, and then punishing those who refuse to obey and rewarding those who do obey. God's will may be regarded as the law of the sovereign, acting according to His own discretion, and aiming at those things which to himself shall seem wise.

What is implied in an acceptable offering of this petition to God.

"Thy will be done in earth, as it is in heaven." Now, doubtless, when our Lord Jesus Christ taught His disciples to pray this prayer, He meant something more than that they should just repeat these words. They were intelligent beings and moral agents, and doubtless He intended that they should express the state of their own minds. He would not, therefore, have them understand that they would be regarded as offering acceptable prayer *because* they offered this mere form. He intended that they should use this language in sincerity of heart, understanding and meaning what they said. I suppose this will not be doubted. Then the question which we have to answer is, "What is the state of mind required in an individual, and which must be implied in his offering such a petition as this to God?"

The acceptable offering of this petition must imply that the petitioner understands what God's will is. I mean this, he must have some knowledge of the true character and will of God. If he has not a true conception of this, he may fall into grievous errors. Suppose an individual should conceive of God as a selfish being. Suppose that he should conceive of God's will as being neither wise nor good; and if with this state of mind, he should pray for God's will to be done in the earth, would he offer an acceptable petition to God? By no means. Then, to be acceptable, he must conceive rightly of what God's will is. He must regard God as a wise and good being. For if God's will was neither wise nor good, people ought not to do His will. Suppose that God's will was neither wise nor good, and yet He should require us to offer this petition, "Thy will be done in earth, as it is in heaven"—and that there was nothing, neither wise nor good, done in heaven, it could not be our duty, as moral agents, to offer such a petition. The offering of this petition, then, implies that we understand God's will as perfect, both as to its wisdom and goodness.

An acceptable offering of this petition must imply that we have implicit confidence in His will, as being perfectly wise and perfectly good; for if we have not this confidence, we cannot honestly and intelligently pray this prayer.

The acceptable offering of such a petition as this implies sincerity of heart. If an individual asks anything of God, he is required to ask it in sincerity. But what is implied in an individual being sincere in asking this of God? It must imply that he really desires God's will should be done, that this petition is in accordance with His will and expressive of the true state of His heart. If it is not so, then the offering of such a petition would be hypocrisy. Of course it follows, secondly, that the state of mind which can sincerely offer this petition to God must be in entire harmony with the will of God, so far as God's will is known. If there is anything in which his will is not conformed to the will of God, he cannot offer this petition without base hypocrisy.

The acceptable offering of this petition implies, of course, that we understand and embrace the same end that God embraces; that is, that we really consecrate ourselves to the end for which God lives, and that we sympathize with Him in the end for which He consecrates and exercises all His attributes. If we have not the same end in view that God has, how can we say, "Thy will be done"?

Unless we sympathize with Him in the means that He uses, how can we say, "Thy will be done"?

An acceptable offering of this petition to God also implies a willingness to say and do just what He tells us. If we are not satisfied with the divine conduct in all respects, how can we say, "Thy will be done"? If we are not willing for Him to require of us just what He does; if we have in our hearts any objections to what He does; if we regard His will as exacting and unjust to us, we can never offer this petition acceptably. But suppose that intellectually we admit that His will is not grievous. That is not enough if the heart does not fully consent, for observe this prayer is to be the prayer of the *heart*.

The acceptable offering of this petition not only implies that we are willing that He should require just what He does, but that He should require it on the condition of all the pains and penalties upon which He does require it.

It implies an entire willingness on our part to obey Him.

How can a person sincerely pray, "Thy will be done in earth, as it is in heaven," who himself is not willing to do the will of God? If he is not truly and really obedient, to God's will as they are in heaven, so far as he knows His will, how can he offer such a petition as this? If he is resisting God's will on any point and in any form, he cannot without gross hypocrisy offer this petition. The offering of this petition implies that we sympathize with the spirit of heaven, that our hearts are really yielded up in most solemn and earnest devotedness to God. For how can people whose wills are not yielded up to the will of God, without being hypocrites, say to God, "Thy will be done in earth, as it is in heaven"? In heaven, the will of God is perfectly done, universally done; and shall a person acceptably offer such a petition as this if he is not in a state of mind to go the full length of God's will and subscribe heartily to it? It cannot be.

Observe, then, that the acceptable offering of this petition must imply present obedience in the heart to God. The will of the petitioner must have been given up to the control of the will of God. His will must be the expression of God's will so far as he knows it, or he cannot honestly offer such a petition as this to God. I say that the acceptable petitioner must do the whole of the will of God, so far as it is expressed, in whatever way it is made known: whether through Christ, through the Spirit, through providential arrangements and occurrences, through the Word of God, through the workings of his own heart and mind, or in whatever other way this will is made known.

The heart that is sincere in offering this petition must really embrace and express the whole of God's will as really and truly as it is embraced and expressed in heaven itself. By this I do not mean to affirm that the will of God is known to the same extent in earth as it is in heaven; but so far as it is known, the petitioner must as really and truly embrace it and obey it as they do in heaven. It is not to be supposed that God's will is fully known upon earth; undoubtedly many things concerning the will of God have not been fully revealed to us, so that we cannot understand all the details of His will; but, in so far as we understand it, there will be a willingness to obey it entirely.

The acceptable offering of this petition implies the absence of all selfishness in the mind that offers it. God is not selfish; selfishness is the will set upon itself, regardless of all else. The person who offers this petition cannot be selfish. The very petition implies the present absence of selfishness.

An acceptable offering of this petition implies that we really hold ourselves at the divine disposal as honestly and truly as we suppose they do in heaven. Who does not suppose that every being in heaven holds himself at the divine disposal? It must be that every being there considers himself as belonging to God—that to God all his powers are consecrated; and that any indication of the divine will as to how these powers are to be disposed is to be readily adopted and carried out by the agent himself. Who can conceive that there is any hesitation to do the known will of God in any particular?

To sincerely offer such a petition as this to God, there must be an entire consecration of the will and the whole being to Him. A person who offers this petition acceptably must be in such a state of mind as to consider that he has no right to the disposal of himself. He must lay his whole being upon God's altar and hold himself entirely at the divine disposal. The same is true of all he possesses. Who doubts that everything in heaven is held as belonging to God? We know not what things the inhabitants of heaven have in possession, or what their employments are—what they may be employed about, and what instruments they may use to promote the great end that God is intending to realize. But this we know, that whatever they have influence over is all held at the divine disposal. No one in heaven thinks of disposing of anything to promote any selfish interests of his own. Who can believe that anyone there has a separate private interest?

Now, how should we regard our possessions if we are to offer this petition acceptably to God? Why, God's will respects the release of our possessions, our time, our talents, our influence, our character and everything to Him. These must be held at the divine disposal, given to the divine discretion, laid on His altar and left there. No one can offer this petition acceptably to God without doing this. If he would be selfish, and selfishly use anything in the whole world, he is in no state of mind to offer this petition to God. If he is endeavoring to promote his own will, do you suppose he is fit for heaven? Do the inhabitants of the heavenly world act without consulting God, without reference to His will? No, indeed! When people say, "Thy will be done in earth, as it is in heaven," does not this imply that everything on earth is to be done at the divine disposal, and to be as truly disposed of for God as they are disposed of in heaven? Let it be understood, then, that he who offers this petition to God must as really design to obey Him, use all his powers and everything that he possesses for His glory, just as they do in heaven. If he has not this deliberate and solemn purpose in his mind, what does he mean by such a petition as this?

The offering of this petition implies that the petitioner is really and truly willing to make sacrifices of any personal ease and comfort for the promotion of God's glory, so far as he understands that he ought. Who doubts that in heaven they are willing to be sent to any part of the universe, or to give up personal ease or anything else for the promotion of the great end for which God is aiming? We are informed in the Bible that "angels are ministering spirits sent forth to minister to them who are heirs of salvation." Any moment they may be called to self-denial and arduous labor. Doubtless they are often called, but do they hesitate, do they consider it a hardship? No; because they sympathize with God and with Christ in this great work. They do not hesitate to make any personal sacrifices that are demanded of them. They are perfectly cheerful and happy in it. Now, a person who would say, "Thy will be done in earth, as it is in heaven," must be willing to make any sacrifice that he knows is to be in accordance with the will of God. If it is plainly a matter of duty for him to do this or that, to go here or there, he must be perfectly willing to comply, or how can he offer this petition?

The state of mind in which this petition can be acceptably offered implies that there is an opposition to sin as real as there is in heaven. I suppose not to the same degree, because we have not the same appreciation of its character that they have; but, insofar as it is understood here, the individual that offers this petition is as really opposed to sin as they are in heaven.

An individual who offers this petition acceptably to God must have as real a sympathy with all that God has as they have in heaven. In heaven they doubtless sympathize with all that is good, so the individual who offers sincerely this prayer must have intense hatred to all that is wicked, and must deeply sympathize with all that is good. There must be as true a renunciation of self and all selfishness, and as genuine a disposition to please God in every heart that offers this petition, as there is in heaven. I speak not of degree, because I suppose we do not apprehend these things so clearly as they do; but, insofar as we understand what God loves, our sympathy must be as real as it is in heaven.

That to be in this state of mind is a present and universal duty.

Every person is bound, *now*, to be in this state of mind. I say *every* man; not merely Christian ministers and professing Christians, but every moral agent is bound to be in this state.

It is demanded by the nature of things. How can people be released from this obligation? Every person knows that he ought to obey God; he affirms it by an affirmation that is irresistible. Everyone knows that God's will is wise and good. Who ever heard this called in question by anyone who had a true idea of God developed in his mind? Every moral agent admits he is bound to consent that God's will should be done, and that he ought himself to do it.

Every moral agent knows, too, that it is not his duty merely to do this sometime or other, but it is his *present* duty. He has no right for a moment to resist the divine will. I need not, of course, enlarge upon this part of the subject, because I suppose that these truths need only to be stated to be universally recognized and affirmed to be true, as seen in the light of their own evidence. Are not men so constituted as to have it confirmed by a law of their own nature that they ought to conform to the will of God? They would not be moral agents if they were under no obligation to obey the will of God.

The guilt of not being in this state of mind.

If an individual is not in this state of mind, he refuses to sympathize with God. If he knows that all God's aims are directed toward an end worthy of the pursuit of God, worthy of the Creator of the universe, and yet he refuses to agree with God in this end, he sets it at naught, he turns his back upon it, though he knows it is good.

If an individual is not in this state of mind, he is unwilling that God should govern the universe, not only in relation to the end that He seeks, but also in the means that He uses. He refuses his consent that God should govern the universe in any shape. The man who will not obey God's law, really rebels against the will of the lawgiver; he actually refuses to consent that God should govern.

Let me say that the individual who is not in this state of mind really refuses in his heart to consent that God should be good. He would not have God do what He is doing. He is unwilling to obey Him. He would rather that God did not require

what He does; that He would not do what He does do; and yet
these things are implied in the goodness of God and are essential to His goodness. God would not be a good being if He did
not require and do just as He does. The individual who is not
in this state of mind, then, refuses to consent that God should
be a good being—that God should do that which He knows is
proper to do. Now just think of this, he rebels against that which
constitutes the very goodness of God.

The individual who is not in this state of mind really refuses
that God should comply with the necessary conditions of His
own happiness; for the necessary conditions of God's happiness
must be His virtue. An individual who is unwilling to obey God
is unwilling that God should comply with the necessary conditions of His own happiness. The individual who is in this state
of mind cannot say, "Thy will be done," for he is really at war
with the holiness and happiness of God—he is arrayed against
both. He is unwilling that God should will as He does. And
since holiness belongs to His will and consists in willing as He
does will, all God's actions are included in the actions of His
will. The individual who is not in harmony with God not only
refuses to sympathize with Him, but he also refuses to consecrate himself to the end for which God is consecrated. He arrays
himself against God. Yes, he virtually says, *"Let God cease to
be.* Let Him not require what He does. Let Him not pursue the
end that He does. Let Him not govern the universe; let not His
will be universal law!" He may just as well go one step further
and say, "Let God not be happy; *let Him be infinitely and eternally miserable."* For if God were not holy, who does not know
that He would be infinitely unholy? And I tremble to say it, but
who does not know that if God were a wicked being, instead of
a good being, the workings of His own infinite nature would fill
His mind with infinite agony?

Now, observe, what does a man mean when he takes this
attitude—that he will not consent to have God's will done, that
he will not obey Him, that he is virtually opposed to His being
good? Why, if God is not good, what must be the consequences?
If He may not will as He does, and require as He does, and do
as He does, He must do the opposite! And does not sin imply
this—that the sinner really takes this attitude? Yes, it does!
People who refuse sincerely to offer this petition are opposed to
the holiness and the happiness of God, and would consent to
the eternal overthrow and total ruin of God and His whole em-
pire! This is certainly implied in resistance to the will of God.

Let it be understood that no moral agent can be indifferent to the will of God: he must either subscribe to it, or resist it: he must yield himself to it, or array himself against it! And if against it, no thanks to him if there is any particle of good in God's universe; no thanks to any moral agent who cannot honestly and sincerely subscribe to this petition. It matters not to him if any being in the universe is either holy or happy! He is opposed to it all! The state of his mind is perfectly opposed to it all, and, were he to have his will, he would annihilate the whole of it, and introduce sin and misery into every part of the universe. How great, then, must be the guilt of an individual who has his will opposed to the will of God. I could expand upon this at large, but must now proceed to my next point.

This state of mind is a condition of salvation.

By a condition of salvation, I don't mean that it is the ground upon which sinners will be saved, that they will be saved because of universal and perfect obedience. But I affirm this, that it is a condition in this sense, that without being in this state, salvation is both naturally and governmentally impossible.

It is naturally impossible. Heaven is no place for the person whose will is not in harmony with the will of God. Suppose that he entered there, he would introduce a jarring note. He would introduce discord; heaven would be no place for him.

It is governmentally impossible for him to possess heaven, whose will is not in harmony with the will of God. God is the Governor of the universe. God's will is infinite, and where God is, His will must be the law. In every community there must be some one mind that sways every other, or there will be discord. Some will must give law to the universe. There must be someone whose will is universally confided in as perfect, and that will must be universally performed or there will be jarring, there will be clashing. God, therefore, as Governor of the universe, must be obeyed. The indication of His will must carry all minds with it. Now, to the person who hates God's will, this would be intolerable; therefore, governmentally it is impossible for any person to enter heaven who cannot sincerely say, "Thy will be done in earth, as it is in heaven."

REMARKS

I must now conclude by making a few observations.

How shocking it must be for people to use the Lord's Prayer

as a mere form. Just think of it! While he is living in known sin, an individual offers such a petition to God! What can he mean? What profanity! What blasphemy is involved in it! It makes one's hair stand on end to hear an individual pray in that manner to Jehovah, the heart-searching God.

How shocking it is for some congregations (many of whom, perhaps, are unconverted, ungodly men and women) to make use of such petitions as this, pretending to worship God. Yet how common it is to repeat this prayer as a mere form; and it is often introduced into the nursery, and the children repeat it without being told what is implied in it. Why, no wonder their hearts become hardened. But perhaps someone will say, "If this be so, I will not offer this petition at all." But what petition, I ask, will you offer? For remember that you can offer no petition acceptably unless you offer it sincerely!

For example, let us read over these very petitions. "After this manner, therefore, pray ye: Our Father which art in heaven." What does this imply? Why, the recognition of God's relation as our Father. "Hallowed be thy name." What is implied in that? Why, a similar state of mind as that which I have just pointed out. "Thy kingdom come." What is implied in the offering of that petition? Why, that you have set your heart upon the same end that God has, that your will is to obey His will, that you are consecrated to the interests of His kingdom.

Then follows the petition contained in the text, "Thy will be done in earth, as it is in heaven."

"Give us this day our daily bread." What is implied in that? Why, the recognition of the universal providence of God. "And forgive us our debts as we forgive our debtors"; not, as some say, "forgive us our trespasses, and *enable* us to forgive them which trespass against us"; but "*as* we forgive them which trespass against us." If you do not forgive the trespasses of others, you pray to God not to forgive you yours. It implies, then, a most forgiving state of mind on your part. I have often been acquainted with the state of mind of certain individuals in respect to others, and I have wondered, when they attempted to pray the Lord's Prayer, that this petition did not choke them. How many people, when they pray this prayer, really pray to God that He would not forgive them at all? For they don't forgive their enemies.

But let us proceed a step. "And lead us not into temptation, but deliver us from evil." What state of mind does this imply? Why, a dread of sin, and an opposition of the heart to it; and a most sincere yearning of soul to be conformed to everything that is good. "For thine is the kingdom, and the power, and the glory, for ever. Amen."

Now, suppose that any should say, "Why, if this is a true exposition of the Lord's Prayer, I shall never dare to offer it again." And what prayer will you offer? Take any other petition, and does not an acceptable offering of it by you imply that you agree with God, and that you will submit to all His will? Can you expect Him to hear and answer you unless you are in an obedient state of mind? Why, if you expect Him to hear and answer you while you refuse to obey Him, you do not regard the plain declaration of His Word, which says, "He that turneth away his ear from hearing the law, even his prayer shall be abomination."

"Well," some of you say, "if this be true, it is no use for a sinner to pray." What do you mean by that? Of no use for a sinner to pray! Well, of what use can it be for a sinner to lie to God and mock Him? Do you ask me if I mean to prohibit sinners praying? I say, no! But I want to prevent their being hypocrites. Let them pray, but let them cease to be sinners, and submit themselves to the will of God. They should consecrate themselves to God at once. It is their present duty. They need not say, "I will not pray because I am a sinner!" What business have you to be a sinner? "My will is not in a right state," you say. But why is it not in a right state? The sinner is bound to pray on pain of eternal death, but he has no right to tell lies to God. He is bound to be sincere and honest with God. And is it difficult for people to be honest and sincere? Is it an impossible thing? For my right hand, I would not discourage any individual from praying; and neither, for my right hand, would I encourage him to pray with a heart wicked and rebellious against God. The truth is, men ought to know that they are shut up by the divine requirements and the affirmations of their own minds to unqualified submission to the will of God upon pain of eternal death.

It is easy to see, from what has been said, that a great many individuals offer the Lord's Prayer and other prayers, and leave it for others to do the will of God. They pray, "Thy will be done" but they leave it to others to perform this will.

It is easy to see what it is to be truly religious; it is to have the will entirely given up to God. It implies, of course, faith in our Lord Jesus Christ, and much more of which it is not now my design to discuss, as I must confine my attention to the point before us.

Many people will say that this *ought* to be the state of their minds, that they ought to offer this prayer in sincerity without solemnly inquiring, "Am I really willing that God's will should be done? Do I really do it?" But this is implied in an acceptable offering of this petition, that, for the time being, we are in a state in which we really do all we know of our duty. By a necessary law, if the will is right, the outward life will correspond.

There is an amazing degree of carelessness among many people as to what they really say in prayer. They begin, and talk right on, without considering that God requires truth in the inward parts. They often say many things that are not true. They verify what the Lord says, "They did flatter him with their mouths, and they lied unto him with their tongues."

While individuals are not in this state of mind, there is no true peace. While their wills are not under the control of God's will, and while they are not devoted to him, what multitudes of things are continually occurring to agonize them and destroy their peace of mind! But when individuals yield up their wills to the will of God, they breathe an atmosphere of love, and live in profound peace and tranquillity.

When people are in this state of mind, and regard everything as an expression in some sense of God's will, how easily God's will sits upon them!

Much that is called prayer is really an expression of self-will. I would here refer to a case that occurred some years ago in the western part of the State of New York. A gentleman of high standing, intelligent and influential, became very annoyed by the minister of the congregation where he usually attended, pressing upon his hearers the fact that they were not willing to be Christians. The man to whom I refer insisted that he was willing—had long been willing—to become a Christian. His wife remarked that she had never seen him so irritated before upon any subject.

The minister kept turning that over, and pressing it upon the people that they were not Christians because they were not willing to become Christians. But this man was obstinate in affirming that he knew, for his own part, that he was willing to become a Christian, and would anybody deny that he knew the state of his own conscience? He went home in this state of mind one evening, and in the morning his mind was so weighed down that he sought relief by going in a place alone to pray. He kneeled down to pray, but found that he could not pray; he could not think of anything that he really wished to say. It occurred to him to say the Lord's Prayer. The moment he opened his mouth to say, "Our Father," he stopped to consider, Do I recognize God as my Father? He hesitated and trembled to say it. "Hallowed be thy name." No, that is not the expression of my heart. "Thy kingdom come" was the next petition, and he said he was conscious he never wanted the kingdom of God to come, that he had never lived to promote it, and was not living now to promote it. Then he came to the next petition, "Thy will be done in earth, as it is in heaven." He paused for a moment, and the inquiry rushed upon him, How is God's will done in heaven? Am I willing that it should be done in earth? Am I willing to do it myself? As these inquiries came over him, he perceived for the first time what was included in being a Christian. He now saw that to be a Christian implied that the heart should be consecrated to God, that he should fully obey God's will. He felt that he did not do that; that he never had done that; that never, by his own will, had the will of God governed him.

He continued upon his knees, and the perspiration poured down him, because he was in such agony of mind. He now felt what the minister had said was true, and the question came up, Why am I not willing to be a Christian? He felt there was no reason why he should not, and no excuse that he could make for refusing any longer. If he was not willing to do as he ought, he felt he ought to go to hell, and be willing to go and take the consequences—that he ought to be sent there and have no disposition to open his mouth by way of objecting. He himself said, "I gathered up all my soul and energies, and rose up in my strength, and cried at the top of my voice, *Thy will be done.*' I know that my will went with my words; and then so great a calmness came over me that I can never express it, so deep a peace instantly took possession of me. It seemed as if all was changed; my whole soul justified God and took part against itself."

I need not enter into this further; but let me say, dearly beloved, when you go away, can you kneel before your Maker and say, "O my God, let Thy will be done in earth as it is in heaven, require just what Thou doest, require of me just what Thou doest; O God, my whole being cries out, Let Thy will be universally done in earth as it is in heaven"? Or can you not say that? You ought to be able to say it, and to be honest in saying it; but if you never have yet, let me ask you to do so at this very moment. If you have never found peace before, you shall know what it is to go to bed in peace for once. You shall know what that peace of God is that passes understanding, and drink of the river of His pleasures. Do not rest until the attitude of your mind is to do all the will of God.

9

THE KINGDOM OF GOD UPON EARTH*

"Thy kingdom come" (Matthew 6:10).

You will instantly recognize this petition as being one of those contained in what is generally called "The Lord's Prayer." In considering these words, I propose briefly to explain:

▶ *What is meant by the kingdom of God.*
▶ *What is implied in an acceptable offering of this petition to God.*
▶ *That the state of mind that can acceptably offer this petition to God is universally binding upon all people.*
▶ *This state of mind is a condition of salvation.*

What is meant by the kingdom of God.

In some respects there are two ideas concerning the kingdom of God. One class of theologians supposes that the kingdom of God is purely spiritual; others suppose that the Lord Jesus Christ will reign personally upon the earth, that when He comes a second time, it will be to set up His kingdom in this world and reign here in His visible presence. These two classes, however, agree in this: that His kingdom must be spiritual, whether outward and visible or not. In either case He can reign over man no further than He reigns in their hearts.

A spiritual kingdom must be set up in the soul: the divine law must be written in the heart. If the Lord Jesus Christ

---

The Penny Pulpit, delivered May 12, 1850, at the Tabernacle, Moorfields. No. 1,517.

should come and dwell visibly in your city, walk in its streets, and mix with its people, and be here as truly as the mayor is; what would the people gain unless they were converted and truth prevailed in their hearts? Unless the laws of His kingdom were written in their hearts by the Holy Spirit, the people of your city would be none the better for the Lord Jesus Christ's living among them. Therefore, whether the Lord Jesus Christ comes and reigns personally or not, His kingdom will be established and His dominion extended by the same means that it is now.

When people pray, therefore, "thy kingdom come," if they pray sincerely, they pray that there may be universal holiness in the earth—that this kingdom of grace may be set up in all hearts, and that Christ should exercise universal influence over the minds of men.

What is implied in an acceptable offering of this petition to God.

It was no part of the design of our Lord Jesus to give His disciples merely a form of prayer, the words of which they might repeat without knowing or caring what they meant or said. He did not give this prayer merely to be repeated as a ceremony, without significance or interest. There is no greater profanity in the universe than to jabber it over in such a manner as it is frequently used. The Lord Jesus gave this prayer to be understood, so the petition should be offered with sincerity and with faith and in a certain state of mind. Who can doubt this? Did He intend to teach His disciples and His people in later ages to be hypocrites? No, indeed! Did He intend them to offer insincere worship? No, indeed! Then He must have designed that they should offer these petitions with sincerity. Now, the question is, what is implied in sincerity? When is a man sincere in offering this petition to God? What are the characteristics and elements of sincerity? What is implied in being sincere?

A sincere and acceptable offering of this petition implies repentance of past sins, for sin rejects God and tramples down His laws. No one who lives in sin can offer this prayer without gross hypocrisy. The person who rejects Christ and tramples on His laws lives in sin and cannot offer such a prayer as this acceptably. It implies, then, repentance and renunciation of all sin.

It also implies confidence in God. It is a petition to God that

His kingdom may come. If an individual does not have implicit confidence in the character and wisdom of God, in the perfection of His government, and in all the provisions of His kingdom, why should He pray it may come?

It is not enough for a person to believe as a mere speculation that God is good, that His law is good, that His kingdom is what it should be. The devil knows this as well as anybody else. It is not enough that a man should admit intellectually that these things are so; he must confide in God with his whole heart. To offer this petition acceptably, he must really have heart-confidence in God's existence, in His wisdom, in His universal right to legislate for the world, and in the perfection and wisdom of His government. He must have full confidence in God before he can offer this petition acceptably.

Another thing implied in the acceptable offering of his petition is that his heart obeys the law of God. An individual, for example, who does not in his heart submit to God's law cannot pray that His kingdom may come. For what would he mean by that: that others may obey it, that others may submit to Christ's authority, that God's law may be set up in others' hearts, but not in his own? He cannot pray acceptably thus. The petitioner must have the law of God set up in his own heart, and his own life must be governed by it.

Inasmuch as a person's outward life is always of necessity, by a law of his nature, *as his heart is*, it implies an obedient life as well as an obedient heart. The term "heart" is used in various senses in the Scriptures; but whenever it is used in the sense that implies virtue, it means the "will." We say of those whose will is devoted to God that their hearts are right; they are devoted to God, consecrated to Him. Now, if we consider the heart as the will—and that is the sense in which I now use the term—the will governs the outward life. If this will, or heart, devotes itself to the will of God, and yields itself up to obedience to the law of God, the outward life must be in conformity with the law of God, so far as it is understood. Let no man say, then, that his heart is better than his life. Let no man say that his heart has received the kingdom of God, while his outward life disobeys it.

Sincerity in offering this petition implies universal sympathy with God. By this I mean, first, that the petitioner really does sympathize with the great end which God is endeavoring to secure through the instrumentality of His law and by the government of His kingdom.

Now, government, remember, is not an end but a means. God's government is not an end but a means. He proposes to insure certain great ends by means of His government and His kingdom. When a person prays that God's kingdom may come, to be sincere in his petition he must fully sympathize with the end which is sought to be accomplished and on which God has set His heart, which is His own glory and the interests of His kingdom. To offer this petition, "thy kingdom come," acceptably, a person must understand this to be the great end, and set his heart upon it. To this end he must consecrate his being, as the end on which God has set His heart.

But it also implies sympathy with God in reference to the means by which He is endeavoring to secure this great and glorious end. Again, sympathy with God implies a real and hearty aversion to all that stands in the way of the progress of His kingdom—all sin in every form and in every shape. The individual that is not deeply and thoroughly opposed to sin does not want God's kingdom to come; for God's kingdom would destroy all the works of the devil, would destroy sin in every form and degree. Those who offer this petition in sincerity virtually pray that all sin may cease. Now, how can a man who does not cease from sin himself present such a petition as this? How can he pray for God's kingdom to come while he is violating the known laws of that kingdom? If a man be not opposed to all sin, he cannot offer this petition acceptably.

Sincerity in offering this petition must imply supreme attachment to the King, His law and government. Observe, the petition does not express a *partial* attachment to the kingdom of God, but is an expression of *entire* agreement with God in reference to His kingdom—a universal submission, a universal attachment to the King and His entire administration. I think everyone will say that no man is or can be sincere in offering this petition if he is not heartily and devotedly attached to the King and His government—to every principle and precept of His holy Law and Gospel, to His entire administration.

A sincere offering of this petition implies a sympathy with all the means that are used to establish this kingdom in the earth—to establish it in the hearts and souls of all people. If an individual prays that this kingdom may come, he prays that people may be made holy, as the condition of their being made happy and of their being saved. Now, the person who does not truly love the souls of others, and desire their salvation, never offers this petition in sincerity. He must care for people.

It implies a supreme desire that God's kingdom may come. It is one thing for an individual to say "thy kingdom come" and another thing for him supremely to desire that it may come. It is common for a person to ask in words for what he does not deeply and sincerely desire; but I said that for a person to offer this prayer acceptably, he must deeply and sincerely and supremely desire that God's kingdom may come. But if a person is in bondage to his own lusts, and desires their gratification supremely, he cannot offer this petition acceptably. Now, I suppose that to offer this petition acceptably there must be a supreme desire for the object prayed for, that no desire shall be allowed to prevail over this, that no merely selfish enjoyment or selfish indulgence shall have a chief place in the heart.

Let me ask you this question, "Suppose you should see a man on his knees offering this petition, and if you knew at the same time that he was a self-indulgent man, not willing to make any sacrifices, or hardly any, to promote the interests of this kingdom, spending ten times more on his own lusts than he gave to the cause of Christ, how could any of you believe that such a man was sincere in offering such a prayer?" Such a man, if he uses this petition, virtually says, "Lord, let Thy kingdom come without my exercising any self-denial; let Providence enrich me, but let me keep all I get: let Thy kingdom come, but let me seek my own gratifications." Now, if a man should pray in this way, you would say it is little less than blasphemy! But he might not say this in words for very shame. Yet, suppose he *said*, "let thy kingdom come," and *acted* quite the opposite to any such desire, would his prayer be any the better?

But not only does an acceptable offering of this petition imply supreme desire—that is, without more influence than other desires—but it implies also that the mind is supremely devoted to the end for which it prays. It implies that the voluntary power of the will devotes itself, and devotes the whole being, to the promotion of this end.

Suppose we should hear a man pray in this way, "Lord, let Thy kingdom come if it can come without my being devoted to its interests. Let Thy kingdom come if it can come without my ever giving my heart, time, energies, property, possessions, sympathies and prayers to promote it. I will say let Thy kingdom come, but I will go on in my own way and do nothing to promote it or hasten its approach." You would say that this is not an acceptable offering of this petition. I suppose that none of you are disposed to deny that an acceptable offering of this petition really does imply that the heart is truly and sincerely devoted to the kingdom of God.

An acceptable offering of this petition must imply self-denial. Now please understand what I mean by self-denial. Remember, self-denial is not forsaking the gratification of one thing for another. It sometimes happens that people forsake the gratification of one appetite in order that they may gratify another. People may deny themselves in a great many respects, yet be guilty of much selfishness.

Suppose a man is avaricious and loves money, his heart is supremely set upon acquiring it and hoarding it. That man may be very frugal in his expenditure. He may be very disgusted with many who spend money for their own gratification. This avaricious man may deny himself many things. He may go so far as to deny himself the comforts of life, as misers do, and berate everyone who does otherwise. But the man is selfish nevertheless. The love of money prevails over the love of everything else—his heart is set upon that.

What people call self-denial is often no self-denial at all. Self-love is very frequently at the bottom, after all. But real self-denial consists in this: an individual's refusing to live to please himself, to promote his own profit and interests as distinguished from God's kingdom. Real self-denial means refusing to do anything simply and entirely for self. It implies that an individual ceases from self and consecrates himself to God, lives to please God and not himself, and sympathizes with nothing whose ultimate end is not to serve and glorify God. Now, when a man who does not deny himself offers this petition to God, what does he mean? He is a rebel against God, opposed to His law. Why does he want God's kingdom to come? Let no selfish man, then—no man who lives in any form of self-pleasing, suppose that he can offer this prayer acceptably.

It implies, on the part of those who offer this prayer, a real and wholehearted launching of their all with God in this great enterprise. If we offer it sincerely, it implies that we have come into such sympathy with Him as to embark ourselves, body and soul, for time and eternity, our characters and affections, our all, in making common cause with God in the advancement of the interests of His kingdom. All this is included in a sincere offering of the prayer, "thy kingdom come."

Take the case of an earthly prince desiring to establish a kingdom. True patriotism consists in sincerely seeking the promotion of the aim of the prince. The fact is plain, the acceptable offering of this petition must imply that those who offer it have given themselves up to the promotion of this object; that they have committed their all in this great enterprise; that for this end they live, move, and have their being.

It implies an aversion toward whatever would be calculated to retard the progress of this kingdom. People in a right state of mind hate everything that would hinder the advancement of this kingdom, because they have set their hearts on its establishment. Sin and every form of evil is loathsome to them, because it retards the establishment of the kingdom of God on earth. It is a law of man's being which makes him quiveringly, tremblingly alive to any interests on which he has set his heart, and causes him to be eagle-eyed, and ever on the watch to remove anything that stands in the way of the progress of that upon which his hopes are so deeply set. Now, be it remembered that this law of mind invariably shows itself in religious as well as in worldly matters. It does do so, and must.

Those who offer this petition sincerely manifest grief and indignation at whatever is contrary to God's will. If they see an error that does not involve sin, they are grieved. But if an error involves sin, they feel indignation. I do not mean malicious indignation, but a benevolent, a holy, a compassionate indignation.

Lastly, I observe that a right offering of this petition implies the joyful exercise of an economy in our lives, whether of time, talents, influence, or whatever else we possess. There is a joyful economizing of everything for the promotion of this end. Now, who does not know that when people set their hearts upon any great object, that just in proportion to their attachment to that object will be their devotedness to it—just in that proportion are they cheerful, eager, and ready in using every economy for the promotion of this object. They conserve everything for the promotion of that end.

As an illustration of this, let me notice an affecting circumstance that occurred within my own experience. A woman, who was a slave in one of the southern states of America, had escaped from her bondage, but she had left her husband and children in slavery. The master of these individuals offered to sell them their time, and let them go free. This poor woman gave herself up to earn the money to redeem them; and it was very affecting to see how she toiled, and denied herself even the necessaries of life, in order to secure their liberty. Nothing daunted her; no hardship discouraged her. In the cold, when the snow was on the ground, you might see her working with very little clothing on and bare feet. If you gave her a pair of shoes or a garment, she would soon sell them to get money to increase the fund which was to secure the liberation of her husband and children. Now, this poor creature practiced economy for the promotion of the great end she had in view. I do not say that was wise economy in her case, for she nearly sacrificed her own life to it. Now, you mothers can understand and appreciate this woman's conduct. If you had husbands, sons or daughters in slavery, would you not do as she did? This woman had no love for money, or for anything, only as it sustained a relation to the one great end on which her heart was set. This circumstance illustrates most powerfully this great principle, that whenever our hearts are supremely set upon any object, we count everything dear as it sustains a relation to and secures that object. He therefore, who prays sincerely, "thy kingdom come," must have his heart so set upon the object, as to exercise a joyful and perpetual economy with a special reference to that end.

That the state of mind that can acceptably offer this petition to God is universally binding upon all people.

The heathen themselves, by virtue of their own nature, know there is a God and that this God is good. They know they ought to love their neighbors as themselves and God supremely. The Bible teaches us that the light of nature, which they possess, leaves them wholly without excuse if they do not love and obey their Creator. To believe and embrace the Gospel, then, is a universal duty.

This state of mind is a condition of salvation.

Understand me, I do not mean that it is a *ground* of acceptance with God. I do not mean that men are saved by their own righteousness, that on this ground they will be accepted of God. I know, and you know, that people are to be saved by the righteousness of Christ, and not by their own righteousness; therefore, when I say that this state of mind is a *condition of salvation*, I mean what I say. It is a *condition* as distinct from a *ground*: a *condition* in the sense that a man cannot be saved without being in this state of mind, but this state of mind is not the *ground* of salvation. "All have sinned, and" therefore "come short of the glory of God."

To be in this state of mind is a *natural* condition of salvation. Could anybody that cannot offer this petition be happy in heaven? What would such a person do in heaven? God has perfect dominion there. Now, unless an individual is in a state of mind that he can sincerely, acceptably, and prevailingly offer this petition to God, unless it be the natural expression of his heart, what possible enjoyment could he have in heaven? None whatever.

It is *governmentally* a condition of salvation. Every attribute of God in His moral government of the universe forbids any person to enter heaven who cannot present this petition acceptably to God.

REMARKS

This state of mind is not only a condition of salvation in the sense in which I have mentioned, but it is also a state of mind that must always be a condition of prevailing with God in prayer. Now, let me ask, "Can anyone expect to prevail with God if he is in a state of opposition to Him, or not in the state of mind I have already described? While in a state of rebellion, while resisting God's authority, not having the heart in sympathy with God, not desiring the kingdom of God to come, how can an individual expect to have his prayer answered?" No, neither this nor any other petition—that is very plain.

It is true that God hears the young ravens when they cry, a mere cry of distress. And even when Satan himself prayed to the Lord Jesus Christ that he might not be sent out of the country, but that he might go into the herd of swine, his petition was granted; but the devil was not in a state of mind for prevailing, in the sense of offering prevailing prayer to God. I speak now of a state of mind that can secure the things promised, and this must be the state of mind in which a petitioner can acceptably offer the Lord's prayer. He must be within the meaning of the injunction of Christ's promise, as a condition upon which He has promised to hear and answer.

We can see from this subject why it is that prayer is so often repeated by the petitioner, and is so seldom answered. God is "the hearer of prayer," not of hypocritical utterances in which the heart does not unite. Such prayers are not heard, because, in truth, they are not prayers at all. Individuals may repeat the Lord's Prayer every day, ten times a day, and the more frequently they repeat it the more they grieve the Spirit of God and expose themselves to God's righteous indignation.

Those who offer this prayer acceptably are universal and very liberal contributors to the great cause of missions, and zealous supporters of all those various societies whose aim is to extend Christ's kingdom in the earth. By this I do not mean to say that these persons are always in a condition to give large amounts; but they will be cheerful and large contributors according to their means. And why? For the same reason that the slave mother was a cheerful and large contributor to that upon which she had set her heart, because their hearts are set upon the coming of Christ's kingdom in all its fullness, power and blessedness. I know that some may not be able to contribute more than their two mites, but I know also that they can give even this little with a full heart and a liberal hand.

In a congregation to which I preached several years, in the city of New York, there was a woman named Dina, who had been brought up a slave, and continued a slave until she was forty years old and incapable of work. But although so poor, she always gave a quarter of a dollar every Sabbath to assist in meeting the current expenses of the congregation, and other things to which the money was applied. This was a free church: all the seats were free to everyone. When Dina was asked how she could afford to give so much, she replied that the first quarter of a dollar which was given her in the week she laid by till the next Sabbath for the purposes of the sanctuary. "I live upon God every day," she said, "and I know He will give me what I need." At the monthly missionary meeting also, a box was carried round and individuals put in their money, wrapped up in a piece of paper with their names written upon it. Constantly among the rest was Dina's name written on a paper, enclosing a dollar. One of the collectors asked her if she really meant to put in so much as a dollar, and with some surprise she replied, "Why, it's only a dollar—it's only a dollar; can't I give a dollar a month?" This poor woman seemed to have no interest in anything, only as it bore upon the advancement and interests of the Redeemer's kingdom. Now, it must be that individuals who can really offer the Lord's Prayer, and mean it, will prayerfully do everything they can toward promoting His kingdom.

This leads me to say again, "The end for which a person lives will always reveal itself in his life; his sympathies will lie in the direction in which his efforts tend, and the reverse. If a man sincerely offers this petition, he will do everything in his power to spread a knowledge of the Gospel among men, and so extend the Savior's reign upon earth."

The true Christian finds it "more blessed to give than to receive." For example, the slave mother never felt so happy as when she was paying the price of her husband's and children's release. When she gave that money to the master, she felt it much more blessed to give than to receive; a great deal more blessed than to have spent it to please herself, to gratify her own appetites.

Unrepentant people are greatly deceived when they profess that Christians feel it a great sacrifice, a great trial, to be asked to contribute of their substance for the promotion of religion. I have known sinners, even professing Christians, to keep away from God's house because they felt it would be a hardship to give to a collection. Some do not want to be "dunned," as they call offerings for the Lord's work. Now, what sort of a conception have such people of religion? Why, they know nothing about it!

Suppose a number of men were to meet together to originate and carry out some object of business or benevolence, which they professed to have deeply at heart, and when they came together, they found that money must be contributed by each of them, and they were to say that it was a great and intense abomination to be called upon to give money! What would you think of their sincerity? But would they act thus? Why, no! They would be anxious to give of their substance in order that the object which they had at heart might be realized.

The real Christian never gives grudgingly, but thankfully and joyfully. When you have dropped your contribution into the box, Christian, doesn't your heart go away echoing, "God bless it! God bless it!" And if you have nothing to give, you will pray for a blessing on the contributions of others.

10

THE CONDITIONS OF PREVAILING PRAYER*

"Ask, and it shall be given you; seek, and ye shall find; knock, and it shall be opened unto you; for every one that asketh receiveth; and he that seeketh findeth; and to him that knocketh it shall be opened" (Matthew 7:7, 8).

In discussing what is intended by these verses, I shall point out:

▶ *The two common misunderstandings about unanswered prayer.*

▶ *Some conditions for answered prayer.*

The two common misunderstandings about unanswered prayer.

Matthew affirms that all prayer is heard and answered: "Every one that asketh receiveth; and he that seeketh findeth; and to him that knocketh it shall be opened." James says that some ask and do not receive, and gives the reason why: "They ask amiss" (James 4:3). Yet, these scriptures do not contradict each other by any means. When it says that "every one that asketh receiveth," we are to understand, of course, that there is a right asking and a wrong asking. What James says will compel us to this conclusion. "Ye ask, and receive not, because

*The Penny Pulpit, No. 1,559, May 21, 1850, delivered at the Tabernacle, Moorfields. The first of a series of three lectures on "The Conditions of Prevailing Prayer."

ye ask amiss"; which informs us that there are certain conditions for right asking, and that there is such a thing as asking amiss.

There are few people who have not some time or other been perplexed by these passages. So much is said in the Scriptures about God's answering, yet so much is prayed for that is not answered that it is a sore trial to many. For some time I could not understand how it could be that such unqualified assertions as those which are made by Matthew were consistent with so much unanswered prayer.

My mistake was twofold. First, I expected *all prayer to be answered literally.* Overlooking the fact that God often answers prayer according to the spirit when He does not answer it precisely according to the letter.

We have an illustration of this when Paul prayed to be delivered from the thorn in his flesh. This "thorn in the flesh was a messenger of Satan sent to buffet him, lest he should be exalted above measure," because of the abundance of the revelations which had been committed unto him. Christ had a particular object in giving him this thorn in the flesh, whatever it might have been. It appeared that Paul was distressed about it, and he besought Christ to remove it. His object was not selfish. It would interfere with his usefulness, he thought. Now, Christ did not grant the letter of this petition, yet He granted the spirit of it. He said, "My grace is sufficient for thee," informing him that he had this thorn in the flesh for a good purpose; that it should not prove an injury, or stand in the way of his influence, but that His grace should be "sufficient" for him. Paul now says, he "gloried in his infirmities"; in short, instead of persisting in desiring to have the thorn removed, he rather gloried in it that the power of Christ might rest upon him, assured that the thing he feared should not come upon him. This was all he wanted. He did not want the thorn removed if it would not injure his usefulness. Let this illustrate what I mean.

I said I stumbled, and many others have done so, because they did not understand that prayer is frequently answered not according to the letter but according to the true spirit: the substance and essence is granted, though not in the way which was expected.

The second mistake I fell into, and which I suppose is common among intelligent people, was that I overlooked the fact that *there are certain conditions expressed in the Bible upon which prayer may be expected to be answered,* and that there is a distinction between that which is commonly regarded as prayer and that which God regards as such. As soon as my attention was directed to that question, I was satisfied that the difficulty lay not in the Bible not being true. The difficulty was not that God was a hearer but not an answerer of prayer, but that He himself had pointed out certain conditions upon which He would answer it—expressly in some instances, always impliedly, and that we need not expect an answer except upon those conditions.

No doubt God often listens to the cry of distress without regard to the character of the petitioner, or whether he has any character at all. In other words, I suppose He often hears the moanings of animals in distress and comes to their assistance. He hears the young ravens when they cry. He even hears human beings; that is, He can do it, and He is disposed to do it, when He can do so consistently with His relations to the universe. This, however, is not prayer. It is merely the cry of anguish. God comes to the relief of such whenever He can properly do it. I would not throw a stumbling block in the way of those who have this in their minds. No doubt there is a cry of distress, but I have to speak of that prayer which is heard and answered. In hearing the cry of distress without regard to the character, motives, or designs of the petitioners, it is a mere breaking forth of God's benevolence without having given any pledge that He would hear and answer such petitions.

Some conditions for answered prayer.

There is a kind of prayer that God has pledged to answer. I desire especially to consider some of the *conditions* for answering prayer that God has revealed to us in the Scriptures.

You Must Keep A Clear Conscience

Let me quote a passage to illustrate what I mean: "Beloved, if our heart condemn us not, then have we confidence toward God. And whatsoever we ask, we receive of him, because we keep his commandments, and do those things that are pleasing in his sight" (1 John 3:21, 22). By the term "heart," we understand to mean conscience; for it is our conscience that condemns us or approves us. If our conscience condemns us not, we can expect answers to our prayers. If we violate our conscience by sins of omission and sins of commission God cannot be pleased with us; therefore, we cannot expect an answer to our supplications. This is plainly implied in our text: "If the heart condemns us, God much more condemns us." If our hearts condemn us not, *then* we may expect an answer to prayer. But if our hearts do condemn us, we cannot and we ought not to expect an answer to our petitions.

Obviously, a clear conscience—a conscience void of offense—is a revealed condition for prevailing prayer. Where people allow themselves to do anything their consciences do not approve, or where they live in any neglect or commission of sin, in any state of mind for which their conscience condemns them, and God all the more condemns them, how can they expect to prevail with God? Why, they are living in such a manner that their own consciences affirm they are not devoted to God!

The Psalmist says, "If I regard iniquity in my heart, the Lord will not hear me" (Psalm 66:18). Here we have the fact clearly stated: the rejection not only of sins of the outward life, but the rejection of heart sins is an indispensable condition of prevailing prayer. In the first passage I have read, it is merely implied that even if we do keep a conscience void of offense, if we do not reject the sins both of our heart and life, we cannot expect Him to hear us. In the second passage, this is plainly affirmed, "If I regard iniquity in my heart, the Lord will not hear me." What is this? Why, if you *have* iniquity in your hearts? What are heart sins? Every form of selfishness belongs to the heart, as does all sin, or properly speaking, every type of self-seeking. God plainly says, in some cases He will not hear you. Will not this account for the fact that many do that which they call "praying," without prevailing with God.

You Must Be Obedient

But again, a spirit of universal obedience is another revealed condition of prevailing prayer. It is said, "He that turneth away his ear from hearing the law, even his prayer shall be abomination" (Proverbs 28:9). The term "law" is here used to include the whole of the revealed will of God, and is inclusive of whatever God reveals as His will to men. "Turning away" here implies unwillingness to obey, a spirit of disobedience. Now, here we are informed that whosoever is in that state of mind, unwilling to obey God, "his prayer shall be an abomination."

But we also do well in such cases to inquire, what is it to turn away the ear, as the term is used here? All neglect to attend to what God says is turning away the ear. All refusal or neglect to obey what God requires is turning away the ear. Everything of this idea is implied in turning away the ear. Wherever people pretend in some things to obey God, while in other things they disobey Him, this is turning away the ear. Universal obedience, a state of mind desirous of doing whatever God's known law requires, is therefore a necessary condition of prevailing prayer.

You Must Abide In Christ

Being and abiding in Christ is another revealed condition of prevailing prayer. "If ye abide in me, and my words abide in you, ye shall ask what ye will, and it shall be done unto you" (John 15:7). It is also said that, "if a man abide not in me," that is, in Christ, "he is cast forth as a branch, and is withered; and men gather them, and cast them into the fire, and they are burned" (John 15:6). Surely a man who abides not in Christ cannot be expected to be in a state of mind to prevail with God. It cannot be doubted, therefore, that unless you abide in Christ, you cannot prevail in prayer with God.

What is it, then, to abide in Christ? It is to live and walk in the Spirit, to have Christ dwelling in us, and we so dwelling in Him that His Spirit shall influence us. In other words, it is yielding ourselves completely to Him in confidence, embracing Him in faith, and so completely abiding in and committing ourselves to Him as to be brought under His influence. Now, unless we are thus united to Christ by faith so that God regards us as being *in* Christ, and as receiving things *for* Christ's sake, and *through* Christ, we cannot expect to prevail with Him. This is abundantly taught in the Bible. We must be so united to Him by faith as really to walk in the Spirit of Christ. He says that if we are in this state, whatever we ask He will give us. How is this? He must mean a good deal by being in Him, if, when we are in Him and His Word abides in us, we shall have whatsoever we ask; for this is certainly a very extensive promise. "If ye abide in me, and my words abide in you, ye shall ask what ye will, and it shall be done unto you."

Now, again, "Ye shall ask what ye will." This plainly implies that people who are in Christ, in the sense here meant, are in such a state of mind as never to ask anything of Christ, the true spirit of which is not proper for Him to grant. He would not dare to make such a promise unless He knew that if a person really abode in Him, in this sense, he would only ask what could be consistently granted. It is of great importance that we should understand what is really implied in this.

What striking passages are these! He says, "If ye abide in me, and my words abide in you, ye shall ask what ye will, and it shall be done unto you." Does He mean that the person being and abiding in Him should ask anything whatever and it should be granted? Or does He mean that you would always ask according to His will—that you would, in that state of mind, never ask anything contrary to the revealed will of God—that the true spirit of your petitions would always be in precise accordance with His will. If He did not mean this, He could not make such a promise. He leaves the promise without any limitation, "Ask what ye will"; this must imply that they will not have the will to ask anything contrary to the revealed will of Christ, and that those who are really in Christ, abiding in Christ, are taught by the Spirit of God to pray in a much higher sense than people generally suppose.

"Likewise the Spirit also helpeth our infirmities; for we know not what we should pray for as we ought: but the Spirit itself maketh intercession for us with groanings which cannot be uttered. And he that searcheth the hearts knoweth what is the mind of the Spirit, because he maketh intercession for the saints according to the will of God" (Romans 8:26, 27). Here, then, we have it revealed that the saints are led to pray. Those that abide in Christ walk and live in His Spirit: we are informed and led to pray for things according to the will of God. In other words, they are led to pray for those things God would grant.

Now, if we really are in Christ and abide in Him and His words abide in us in the sense He must mean, the spirit of our prayers will always be in accordance with His will. He may therefore, with the utmost safety, promise to grant all that such people would ask.

Christ did not mean to say that every such petition would be granted to the letter, but that their hearts would be in such a state, living in the spirit of prayer, they would be so led that the spirit of their petitions would always be granted. But this implies plainly that there are some people who are *not* in such a state that they can expect an answer to their petitions. If a man does not abide in Christ, and Christ's words do not abide in him, his prayer is not in the spirit that Christ himself would pray; therefore, it cannot be expected to prevail.

In previous sermons I preached upon two petitions of the Lord's Prayer. There I clearly set forth the state of mind in which we could sincerely offer the Lord's Prayer.* Now, this state of mind is undoubtedly a condition of prevailing prayer. But as I explained then at large, I now will only say, to be in a state of mind in which you can sincerely offer the Lord's Prayer is a condition of prevailing prayer.

You Must Have Ardent Desire

Ardent desire is a condition of prevailing prayer. It is one thing to say a prayer, but quite another thing to be exercised with a strong desire. Prayer, when prevalent, is a strong desire of the heart to have a certain blessing. What would be thought of an individual who should petition the government of this country for a certain thing, and immediately become careless about it, and even almost forget what he had been seeking? Yet does not this resemble the prayer of some people? Those who pray in the spirit of prayer pray with a strong desire. The Holy Spirit himself is said to make intercession for the saints in groanings that cannot be uttered.

A willingness to have our prayers answered is an indispensable condition of prevailing prayer. People often pray when they would be very unwilling to have their prayers answered. They often ask things of God which they want only on certain conditions of their own. They want God *to take their way* of answering them, not willing that He should take His own way. Now, unless they are willing that God should answer them in His own way, that He should use the essential means and fulfill the essential conditions of answering them, why, of course, their prayer cannot be expected to prevail.

People often ask for things which cannot be done without strong measures, which would greatly agonize, distress and, as far as this world's goods are concerned, ruin the fortunes of those who pray for them. If we seek things of God, we must be willing to submit the *manner* of the answer to Him in any way that shall seem good to Him. If we ask for more faith, or to be perfected in love, we must of course be willing that God should take His own method—that He should remove whatever stands in the way of it, that He should take away whatever idol we have, that He should do what is necessary to be done in order to answer our requests.

Sometimes when people pray in their hearts they interpose conditions. They want God to humble them if He can do it with-

*The Penny Pulpit, No. 1,518 and 1,522. Chapters 8 and 9 in this book.

out disgracing them, or without destroying their property. They would have God sanctify them, if it can be done without breaking off their self-indulgences. Things, however, cannot be granted without the removal of obstacles; and to pray acceptably, we must be willing to part with a right hand or to put out a right eye, if these things stand in the way of God's granting our request.

For example, suppose a person prays to be made holy, he must be willing to be made holy. And if there is any stumbling block in the way, any besetting sin, any unmortified appetite, any passion, any propensity, he must be willing to give it up. If he is unwilling and insists that the blessing must be granted in his own way, then he cannot be said to pray acceptably.

Again, the man who would pray to God acceptably to be made holy must love his enemies. The man who would pray to God to be holy and yet continue in the practice of certain forms of sin is tempting God, because he is unwilling to give up his idols to be crucified to the world. People must be willing to be, to do, to suffer—whatever is implied in or indispensable to having their prayers answered—or they do not pray acceptably. Were they to examine the matter, they would often find the difficulty in themselves. They are praying for things which they know they need, but are making such conditions and reservations that their prayer cannot be accepted. I could relate many other cases which have come under my observations of people who have begun to question whether God was really willing to hear prayer and whether prayer had any such prevalence as it is represented to have in the Bible; but by and by they come to understand that the difficulty was not in God, but that *they* were really *unwilling* that God should give them what they sought on those terms on which He alone could do so.

Many people pray that they may be Christians, but all the time are unwilling to be Christians, and when they come to conceive rightly of what it is to be a Christian, they perceive that they are entirely unwilling to have their prayers answered. I remember the case of a young lady who professed to have an intense willingness to become a Christian. She had prayed a great deal, and had done all she supposed she possibly could. And finally, after making these pretenses, after a long time during which her mind was strongly exercised about her soul, one day she retired to her chamber to pray. She knelt down, but before she opened her mouth it was shown her what was implied in becoming a Christian—living a holy life. Certain things came so strongly before her as to what was necessary to be, to do, and to suffer in order to be a Christian that she said it seemed as if God himself had asked her, "Are you willing that every obstacle shall be removed?" Furthermore, it seemed clear that if she would ask sincerely, her prayer would be granted. But as soon as she saw what was really implied, she rose up and went away, and would not ask. She saw she had not heart to attempt it. So it often is where people continue praying until they doubt whether God is willing to answer prayer and are ready to accuse Him of being unfaithful. At length they see that within themselves they are not really willing to receive the true spirit of the thing which they seek.

You Must Not Be Selfish

I may remark again, disinterestedness is a condition of prevailing prayer. James says, "Ye ask and receive not because ye ask amiss, that ye may consume it upon your lusts." I do not mean by disinterestedness "absence of interest," that nothing should be sought, but directly opposite. We should desire, but it should be for a right reason.

Suppose an individual prays for his own sanctification. Why does he desire it? Is it merely for the pleasure or the honor of being sanctified? Why does he want to be sanctified? Is it not to effect a removal of the trouble and disgrace attending on sin? Is it not that he may enter the perpetual sunshine, and happiness, and joy of God's peace? Is this the reason? Does he seek it for his own particular benefit, for some selfish reason? No wonder, then, if he asks in this way, that he is not answered. He asks selfishly.

Suppose you are wounded to the heart at a world around you living in sin. If your object is to glorify God, your eye is single to this. If you hold up the true light of the Gospel that men may understand what it is, that their souls may be enlightened, saved, then you are sympathizing with God and you are asking the blessing for the same reason that God would give it to you.

Again, do you agree with God's motives, plans and designs? If people ask for blessings, they must agree with God in this respect. They must give God a good reason so He can give consistent with His character. It must not be such a reason that God would blush to acknowledge to have influenced His conduct. On the contrary, it must be such as to justify Him in the sight of every moral agent in the universe. A selfish petition, therefore, will have no influence with God. It would disgrace Him if it did.

Petitions must be free from selfishness. We must rise above mere selfish considerations and take into view the great reason for which God answers prayer. If people would pray, for example, for their own holiness and sanctification, it should be because they agree with God's view of sin. They must be willing to be holy, whatever fiery trials the attainment and maintenance of holiness may lead them through. People often take a wrong view of this matter, supposing sanctification has no trials, whereas it often tests and tries people in order that they and everyone else may see what God has done for them.

When God gives great blessings, He does not intend that they should be hidden under a bushel. When He gives people great grace, He always places them in a position to try them. If they do not pass through seasons to try them, how would anybody know that God had given them great grace? Now, are you willing to be sanctified, cost what it may? Are you willing to give up all iniquity in every form, let the consequence be what it may, so that God may be glorified?

You must have right motives, too, for praying for others as well as when praying for yourselves. For instance, consider when you are interceding for your children, your husbands, your wives. I recollect the case of a woman who had a husband who was impenitent. I questioned her as to the manner in which she prayed, and she told me that she had prayed for a long time, that she had not given up and did not mean to give up, but that she did not know why it was she was never answered. I then asked her why she prayed at all? She said, "Oh, because I could *enjoy myself* so much better. It would be altogether much more comfortable for *me.*" Everything she said clearly showed that it was for her own comfort she wanted her husband converted. I could get nothing else out of her but this. I told her, therefore, that it was no wonder her prayers were not answered while she was so perfectly selfish and did not enter into God's reasons at all. Now, parents pray for their children in the same spirit. It is merely a selfish thing they have in view. They pray, not because they at all sympathize with God respecting them.

A circumstance was related to me at a place where there was a revival of religion. The minister was going out in the morning to visit some inquirers, and he called upon one of the principal people in the place, who said to him, "What would you think of a man praying for the Holy Spirit day after day and his prayer remaining unanswered?" "Why," said the minister, "I should fear he was praying from wrong motives." "What motives should he have?" "What motives do you have? Do you want to enjoy your money more and be happier? The devil might have such a reason as this." The minister then quoted the words of the Psalmist, "Restore unto me the joy of thy salvation, and uphold me with thy free spirit. Then will I teach transgressors thy ways, and sinners shall be converted unto thee." He turned away from the minister, and he said afterward that the first thought that arose in his mind was a hope that he might never see him again, he was so angry. But he saw at once that his prayer had always been selfish. He was struck with this. Yet, so great was his pride that when he discovered he had always been selfish, that he had never had a true idea of religion or prayer in his mind, that he was perfectly selfish and nothing less than a hollow-hearted professing Christian, he prayed for God to take his life. He felt that he would rather die, even should he go to hell, than, after holding such a position in the church as he had, the people should know that he had been deceiving and deceived. Soon afterward he was converted, and then he saw clearly where he had been. The fact that we ask and receive not may be because we ask amiss, that we "may consume it upon our lusts." This is a great truth which many people would do well to ponder, instead of accusing God as they do of not giving them what they ask.

You Must Have Faith

Faith is an indispensable condition of prevailing prayer. As you all very well know, this is affirmed plainly in the Bible: "Ye have lived in pleasure on the earth, and been wanton; ye have nourished your hearts, as in a day of slaughter. Ye have condemned and killed the just; and he doth not resist you. Be patient, therefore, brethren, unto the coming of the Lord. Behold, the husbandman waiteth for the precious fruit of the earth, and hath long patience for it, until he receive the early and latter rain" (James 5:5–7). In other words, faith is often affirmed and everywhere always implied.

You Must Pray in His Name

We are to pray in the name of Christ. This is so often implied in the Bible that I need not quote any passages. Let us inquire what is meant by praying in the name of Christ. *How are we* *to use Christ's name?* Perhaps I had better not enlarge under this heading here. It is too extensive for the few remarks I shall now be able to give it. At a future time I will enlarge upon this more than I can at present.* There is a great mistake among professing Christians in this respect. Many do not understand what is meant. They do not, therefore, make such use of Christ's name as to prevail. Christ's name, properly used, is as prevalent in the mouth of His people as in His own. If used, as He intended it should be used, *it is just as prevalent in their hands as in His own.*

Suppose Baron Rothschild were to lend a man in this city his name, and suppose that such an individual were to go to the bank and stumble at his own poverty! If he had Baron Rothschild's signature, which is well known at the bank, how does he go? Does he go as if poor, too poor to have such a name prevail for him? No, indeed. He can get any amount of money he pleases. His own poverty is no stumbling block at all in his way. I will not enlarge; nevertheless, this is a condition of prevailing prayer.

You Must Persevere

Perseverance is another condition of prevailing prayer. To be in the spirit of prevailing prayer, we must have perseverance. We have some striking instances of this in the Bible. For instance, take the cases of Jacob, Moses, Elijah, Daniel, and the Syrophoenician woman. I cannot develop each of these here. I must defer this also to another time. Your spirit, though distressed, should not be at all disheartened. When individuals really have the spirit of prayer and set themselves to prevail with God, they are not disheartened because they do not at once prevail, but follow up petition with request, turning them over and over.

Take the case of Jacob, for example. How very affecting were the circumstances under which he is represented as prevailing with God! He wrestled all night. It must have appeared to him as if God was determined not to answer him. God seemed rather to *resist* him. The circumstances were these. Jacob, on account of his conduct toward his brother, had fled from his country and remained absent for a long time until God promised him that He would go with him and bless him. On his way, he was informed that Esau was coming with large hosts, and Jacob had

---

*See chapter 16, "The Use And Prevalence Of Christ's Name."

every reason to believe that his brother would take vengeance upon him for his past misconduct. This, of course, greatly distressed him. He made every arrangement which a prudent man would naturally make in order, if possible, to propitiate Esau. He sent on people before him, and then he retired alone to pray. Doubtless, Jacob had a great weight on his mind. He remembered, most likely, how he had injured Esau, how he became possessed of his birthright, and, therefore, he feared that Esau would take vengeance. He had God's promise, and he went aside to plead with God. For a time the Almighty *seemed* to resist him. He struggled, but he could not overcome. He continued to struggle and to pray throughout the night. God seemed to take every way to try him. He had many confessions to make, and a great deal of breaking down to undergo.

Some of you can cite from your own experience, when you have set your heart upon obtaining a blessing, and believe some point is not exactly clear between you and God. In such times you have felt yourselves in such agony that the perspiration has poured down you, and even if you have not obtained, yet you have not given up the struggle until you have finally humbled yourselves. Then you have prevailed. This was the case with Jacob. He needed to be humbled and broken down. Probably, till then, he never saw his conduct toward Esau exactly in the proper light. He struggled; God resisted. Yet he continued to struggle. God touched his thigh and made him a cripple to the end of his life. Nevertheless, when he could wrestle no longer, still he held on, exclaiming, "I will not let thee go," though God told him to do so. "I will not let thee go," he says, "except thou bless me." Had he a right to say this? Yes, he had. He had God's express promise; therefore, he would do it. It seemed as if God was not going to fulfill His promise. Doubtless, this delay, however, was of great importance. Jacob's mind was preparing to receive the blessing in such a manner as would do good. Jacob was determined not to be denied, as if he had said, "Thou hast promised, and I will not be denied." This is not impudence. He did not mean that Jacob should be disheartened, although severely tried, as was necessary.

He had not only much to confess, but much to promise. There was a great and a wonderful struggle within. Now consider this, suppose he had not held on—what then? The fact is he did hold on till the very last. What a remarkable answer when he said, "I will not let thee go except thou bless me." God said, "What is thy name?" I suppose Jacob blushed when he answered that his name was Jacob, which means a supplanter, a person who takes another's place by force or plotting. He confessed his name was "a supplanter," and that he was a supplanter, because he had supplanted his brother Esau. "I am a supplanter! That's my name." What a significant circumstance was this. Jacob was so bold and so vehement that he said, "I will not let thee go, except thou bless me." "What is thy name," said the Almighty, "that thou shouldest presume thus?" "My name," said he, "is Jacob." God said, "Thy name shall be called no more Jacob, but Israel: for as a prince hast thou power with God and with men, and hast prevailed" (Genesis 32:28). "No more shalt thou be called Jacob"; the matter was settled. He was a supplanter all along. You will recollect from the circumstance of his birth, how he came to be named Jacob, how he cried out, and illustrated his name by taking the birthright of his brother. Jacob all along had proved himself to be rightly named. But after this mighty exercise of faith, this taking hold and keeping hold of God's promises under all those discouraging circumstances, God did well to alter his name that it might remind him no more of his having been a supplanter, and to give him one which should remind him of his having had power with God and prevailed.

Again, take the case of Moses. He stepped forward as it were and took hold of the uplifted hand of the Almighty. God promised Moses that a certain thing should be done for the people, but the people had sinned and gone into idolatry. Then He said, "Let me alone, that my wrath may wax hot against them, and that I may consume them in a moment" (Exodus 32:10). What a peculiar position he placed himself in. It might have been a temptation to a man of less grace to have given up. God had promised to make him a great nation. Some men might have said, "Well, if God will make of *me* a great nation, let *them* be consumed. They are rebels and have destroyed themselves." But Moses said, "What will the Egyptians say?" See his regard for God's honor, and his persevering spirit. God seemed to have anticipated his prayer and forbade it. He did not mean this (it might have seemed to mean this, however, to a man without Moses' confidence and grace). God said, "Let me alone, that my wrath may wax hot against them, and that I may consume them," for they are a rebellious people. But no: Moses must step right forward to reason with God. "What will the Egyptians say? What wilt thou do with thy great name?" Having asked, "What will the Egyptians say?" he says, "Forgive their sin—

and if not, blot me, I pray thee, out of thy book which thou hast written." How beautiful was Moses' simple heartedness and confidence—his determination to stand in the gap between God and the people!

11

HOW TO PREVAIL WITH GOD*

"Ask, and it shall be given you; seek, and ye shall find; knock, and it shall be opened unto you: for every one that asketh receiveth; and he that seeketh findeth; and to him that knocketh it shall be opened" (Matthew 7:7, 8).

Let us proceed on the subject of prevailing prayer to show:

▶ *What other examples the Bible records of persevering.*
▶ *What the Bible means by travail of soul.*
▶ *What are some further conditions of prevailing prayer.*

What other examples the Bible records of persevering.

Perseverance can be a condition of prevailing with God. Sometimes the circumstances are such that there is *no time* for perseverance in any sense as prolonged praying. If the prayers must necessarily be repeated over a long period, the object sought cannot be attained at all. But often there are very good reasons why the petitioner should be left to wrestle and persevere. God is anxious by this means to develop a certain state of mind, sometimes for the petitioner's benefit, sometimes for the benefit of others, or both of these.

Some cases of this kind are recorded in Scripture, where God declined to answer at once in order that He might develop a certain state of mind in the petitioner for the benefit of others.

The Penny Pulpit, No, 1,560. Delivered on May 22, 1850, at the Tabernacle, Moorfields. The second of a series of three lectures on the "Conditions of Prevailing Prayer." The third in the series is chapter 16 in this book.

I have pointed to Jacob as an example of perseverance in struggling—persisting in supplication until he prevailed. I also mentioned the case of Moses, and now I will speak of Elijah.

Elijah had the express promise of God that He would send rain upon the earth. When Elijah had built an altar and slain the prophets of Baal, he gave himself to prayer, and sent his servant to see if there were any clouds arising. Elijah commenced praying. The servant went, but saw nothing. Elijah said, "Go again." I suppose he meant to say, "Keep on going until you see the approach of rain, for I must not leave this place till the blessing comes." He had a strong desire for rain for the benefit of the people, but there were other reasons. God expressly promised it should come. Elijah was determined its delay in coming should be no stumbling block. He continued to press his suit until at length a little cloud about the size of a man's hand was discovered. He did not go and ask God and then get up and go away, as is customary with many who think that if God has promised anything, to be reminded once of His promise is sufficient. No, it was not so. The prophet had an urgent spirit, a spirit which would not let him leave the throne of grace. The servant went and came seven times, and the last time he said, "There is a little cloud rising, about the size of a man's hand." Observe the *perseverance*. Elijah refused to leave his position until the rain came.

Again, take the case of Daniel. We have in the tenth chapter of Daniel a very affecting instance of perseverance. "In those days I Daniel was mourning three full weeks. I ate no pleasant bread, neither came flesh nor wine in my mouth, neither did I anoint myself at all, till three whole weeks were fulfilled" (Daniel 10:2, 3). Then came the answer. "Then said he unto me, Fear not, Daniel: for from the first day that thou didst set thine heart to understand, and to chasten thyself before thy God, thy words were heard, and I am come for thy words." Here it appears that a messenger had been sent to answer Daniel, but that he had been withstood by some agency. Indeed, an infernal spirit, here called the Prince of Persia (for I think, if we read the connection, it is clear that it was an infernal agent) withstood the messenger sent to answer Daniel, until Michael, one of the chief princes, who was, some have supposed, the Messiah himself, came to help him. Daniel pressed his suit for twenty-one days. There was no staying him till he had the answer.

The case of the Syrophoenician woman is another striking and affecting instance. This is recorded in the fifteenth chapter of Matthew. You will recollect the circumstances. The woman was not Jewish, but her daughter was tormented by an infernal spirit, and she came to Christ to have it cast out. She fell down and worshiped Him and said, "Have mercy on me, O Lord, thou Son of David; my daughter is grievously vexed with a devil." Now, the disciples were with the Savior. She followed and made supplication and wept along the road after them. They seeing that He took no notice, concluded that He was not going to answer her, and said, "Send her away; for she crieth after us." He replied, "I am not sent but unto the lost sheep of the house of Israel." Now, as I have said, she was not Jewish but a Syrophoenician; however, she was not discouraged but continued crying. At length He addressed her, "It is not meet to take the children's bread, and to cast it to dogs." "Truth, Lord," she says. Then in essence, she continues, "I ask no such thing. I am willing to be compared to a dog. I do not resent this, nor do I ask the children's bread; but may not dogs eat of the crumbs which fall from their master's table!"

What a spirit was this! Christ turned and said, "O woman, great is thy faith: be it unto thee even as thou wilt!" He had developed her faith. The disciples saw the spirit of perseverance and faith and what confidence she had. With less confidence she might have been at first confounded or discouraged when He said He was not sent but to the lost sheep of the house of Israel. But she was not to be discouraged by that. Notwithstanding this apparent discouragement, she would believe that she could get the blessing. Therefore, she pressed it still, only increasing the importunity, and would not be discouraged. Then He said, as if to try the temper of the woman (as everyone can see what His words were calculated to do), "It is not meet to take the children's bread, and to cast it to the dogs," almost treating her contemptuously, but she never resented it. "If you are going to treat me in this way," she might have said, "I won't speak to you anymore." But she did say, "I did not come to seek the children's bread, but might I not have the crumbs which fall from the master's table?" Now, this is a beautiful instance, not only of perseverance, but of the *power and prevalence of this perseverance.*

In the eighteenth chapter of Luke, we have the case of the unjust judge, who neither feared God nor regarded man. There are two parables in Luke which are especially designed by the Savior to teach the necessity and the power of perseverance, and the prayer is very striking in both these parables. Take the case of the unjust judge. "There was in a city a judge, which feared not God, neither regarded man: and there was a widow in that city; and she came unto him, saying, Avenge me of mine adversary. And he would not for a while: but afterward he said within himself, Though I fear not God, nor regard man; yet because this widow troubleth me, I will avenge her." Now Christ did not intend here to compare God to the unjust judge, but He had to take a strong case, and therefore to give a strong illustration of the truth enforced. He says, "Perseverance in supplication overcomes even the unjust judge. She so persevered that to avoid her importunity, to avoid being continually troubled by the woman, he would avenge her of her adversary." Christ tells us here what the unjust judge says, who neither feared God nor regarded man. And "shall not God," who is not unjust, for this is the idea, "avenge his own elect, who cry day and night unto him?" Here was a judge who took no interest in the case, who cared not for the woman or her adversary, who "neither feared God nor regarded man," but who, to avoid her importunity, avenged her of her adversary.

Now, if importunity could do this with such an individual, what shall it do with God whose elect are dear to His heart, who cares for them and their cause, and when they importunately cry day and night unto Him, shall He not avenge them? When the unjust judge was overcome by importunity, and with neither interest in the person or the cause, was moved by importunity, shall not God avenge His own elect? Yes, "he will avenge them," and that "speedily."

A curious circumstance occurred when I was in Birmingham, England. A Christian man called to see me to relate a fact about himself. He had heard, from time to time, different things about prevailing prayer. He felt, he said, that it was his duty to state the fact to me to show me how great was the faithfulness of God. It was of so extraordinary a character, involving such a principle, that I have thought of it almost ever since. "Some time back," said the gentleman, "a neighbor of mine lost his wife. When she was ill and nigh unto death, my wife went to nurse her, and stayed with her until she breathed her last. After she returned home, I was not satisfied that all was right. Things kept showing themselves continually. Circumstances occurred to show me that all was not right between that man and my wife. I told her what I feared. She confessed her guilt, and not only so, but avowed her determination to leave me, and to live with him, whatever might come of it. 'What do you say?' I exclaimed. I could not say anything more to her; but I went to God and cried day and night unto Him, 'O God, wilt thou not avenge me of this mine adversary?' For two weeks I scarcely slept at all, but prayed and wept, sometimes in one position and sometimes in another. But for two weeks I gave God no rest, but prayed continually, 'O God, wilt thou not avenge me of this mine adversary?' At the same time, I let my wife understand that my arms and heart were open to receive her if she would return, and I would forgive her all the past. I kept myself in that position. I wept before God. I prayed, and I cried unto Him to avenge me. At the end of the two weeks, she came back heartbroken, confessing her sin, humbling herself, and doing all that I could wish her to do. And she has since been all that I could wish her to be." What a striking case is this! Instead of at once turning her away, he went to God, and said, "O Lord, thou seest that this man hath torn away my very wife from my bosom! O God, avenge me of this mine adversary." If in any one case more than another, a man would feel a disinclination to make a matter the subject of prayer, it would be in such a case as this. Yet he did, and prevailed in the extraordinary manner I have described.

Let me now present an instance of *importunity for others*, which is recorded in the eleventh chapter of Luke. The Syrophoenician prayed for a blessing for herself. Christ gives a parable illustrative of the power of importunity in praying for others. It was a case where an individual went to the house of a friend in the night and said, "Friend, lend me three loaves," but he would not do it. He and his children were in bed, and he could not rise to give him what he wanted. The man, however, continued knocking and knocking, resolved to keep knocking all night. The man in bed concluded he might as well get up now as later or make up his mind to be awake all night. So much was he set on providing for the necessities of his friend who called upon him that he would stand knocking like this. And though the individual would not get up because of his friend, yet because of the constant knocking, in that way, with such importunity, he got up and gave him as many as he pleased.

Here, then, is an illustration of the great value of importunity when seeking blessings for our friends—those upon whose salvation we set our hearts. Here was an individual who wanted a blessing for his friend, and who would not suffer his other friend, from whom he could not get this blessing, to rest till he obtained it. The fact is that cases often occur in which it appears as if God has kept silence, but has actually allowed individuals to importune with the greatest perseverance and solicitude until a state of mind was developed which is so striking as to be very edifying to all who see it, particularly so to the petitioner himself.

What the language of the Bible means by travail of soul.

Often a condition of prevailing seems to be a *great degree of solicitude,* amounting almost to unutterable agony of mind. Blessings very great, which are sought, do not come until we are so strongly excited in mind as to be thrown into great agony—to travail in soul before God. Many professing Christians do not understand what this "travail of soul" is. It is spoken of repeatedly in the Bible as a state of mind to which great blessings are promised. The apostle speaks of "travailing in birth for those to whom he preached at Galatia." He says, "My little children have backslidden." To reclaim them gave him such agony of mind. When the prophet speaks of seeing a man in a vision, he says, "Ask ye now, and see whether a man doth travail with child. Wherefore do I see every man with his hands on his loins as a woman in travail, and all faces are turned into paleness?"

Have you examined your Bible with marginal references or a concordance to see what that book really says on the subject? What is promised to the person who is in agony and travail of soul? This is a delicate subject, yet it is so often dwelt upon in the Bible that people should search not only what the Scriptures say but be willing just to empathize with God so deeply that their souls travail in birth until other souls are born to God. I do not say now, or suppose that in all instances, this spirit is indispensable to prevail. But it often is. In the early days of Christianity, travail of soul was so common that the apostle speaks of it as a thing well known to Christians. He says, "Likewise the Spirit also helpeth our infirmities; for we know not what we should pray for as we ought; but the Spirit itself also maketh intercession for us with groanings which cannot be uttered" (Romans 8:26).

Do you know what this is? In the great revivals that prevailed in America some years ago, some striking instances of the prevalence of prayer occurred, as also in the days of President Edwards. In various parts of Great Britain, too, where revivals prevailed, there was a remarkable spirit of prayer. I have witnessed much of this myself. An aged minister well known by name to many of you mentioned this fact to me. He had not at that time been in those revivals much, but two of his daughters had grown up in impenitence. He told me the great exercise of mind he had had previous to their conversion, and when I told him that it was a thing perfectly common to revivals, he felt surprised that he should have so long overlooked what the Bible says on this subject. The man was so exercised that he could not sleep. So great was the weight upon him that he struggled until he said he told the Lord that "he must die or his daughters must be converted." He felt that his soul was loaded with such an unutterable agony that he really must die unless that petition was granted. He was literally in *travail* of soul for them.

Often when I have seen Christians in this condition, in expressing the state of their minds to me, they have used the very language of Scripture. They have said again and again, "My soul travaileth day and night. I cannot live unless I see the salvation of God." Such people, when in such a state of mind, are generally not disposed to see company or to go anywhere more than they can help. They want to be with God as much as possible. They have deep seasons of sighing unawares, seeking to be alone with God. And could you but hear and see how they wrestle with God, you might, perhaps, feel astonished at the holy boldness and confidence such a soul would manifest in its intercourse with God. You would hear such expressions and see such a mighty wrestling as you would probably never forget.

I have known such things in places where I am a stranger, and have been afraid to tell of them lest the people should think them untrue. In revivals of religion, I have often witnessed things so extraordinary that I have often seen answers to prayer bordering so closely upon the miraculous, that I feel afraid to tell them where I am unknown. The fact is, the answers to prayer which have come under my notice have been most wonderful, both in America and in England, to the great astonishment of those who have not understood them.*

But, let me say again that the whole category of hindrances to prevailing prayer may be summed up under one heading, which is one of the greatest, if not the greatest, of the difficul-

---

*See especially Charles G. Finney, *Answers to Prayer* (Minneapolis: Bethany House Publishers, 1983).

ties. I refer to a *lack of sympathy with God*. How can people hope to prevail with God unless they sympathize with Him? When people really sympathize with Him in such a manner as not to recoil from self-denial; when they are vitalized with the spirit that led Christ to make the atonement, that led Christ to deny himself and to do all that He did, to have such a state of mind is a great difficulty. Christ needs His Church to sympathize with Him, and while they do not sympathize with Him, and are not in a state of mind to deny themselves of even trifling gratifications for the sake of doing good to the worldly-minded, how can they expect to prevail with God?

This leads me to say again, a state of mind which will not grieve the Spirit of God but will watch against everything which does grieve the Spirit of God is indispensable to the true spirit of prayer. No one can prevail with God who does not bridle his tongue. In these days people talk a great deal, too much to pray well. They grieve the Holy Spirit by their much talking and their bad talking. People speak harshly of their brethren. Now, such a state of mind is not congenial to prayer, and if you wish to prevail with God you must take care to keep yourselves in the love of God by praying in the Holy Spirit.

In order to prevail with God, Christians must have the spirit of love, and walk therein. They must have a spirit tender for the reputation of Christ, and live in such a state toward sinners as to be willing to make any sacrifices for them. My dear friends, I should have asked before what I now intend to ask, as I go along, do you fulfill these conditions? Are you living in such a sympathy with God and Christ that you are willing to deny yourselves and to walk before God in such a manner as to give yourselves up to the great work of saving souls? I don't mean by this that you should forsake your necessary employments, and go about to do nothing else but talk and pray. But are you in such a state of mind as not to recoil from self-denial? Are you willing to live and be used up, body, property and everything, for the promotion of the glory of God and the salvation of the world? Or, would you complain to keep some trifling gratification? Can a person offer prevailing prayer who is unwilling to make sacrifices for the sake of doing more good?

Who that has looked at this subject as it is has not been agonized often to see the lack of sympathy with God? What was the secret of Paul's usefulness? He says, "I say the truth in Christ, I lie not, my conscience also bearing me witness in the Holy Ghost, that I have great heaviness and continual sorrow in my heart. For I could wish that myself were accursed from Christ for my brethren, my kinsmen according to the flesh." He meant to say he could forego anything personally, he could make any personal sacrifice, if by so doing he could save his kindred according to the flesh. I know that there has been much speculation upon this passage. I have wondered at this. Paul's language is strong, but I have mentioned the essence of his intentions. He would make any sacrifice so far as his own happiness was concerned. He could give up anything they could name. No doubt he did not intend to say he was willing to go to hell, but that there was no *personal sacrifice* he would not make. He was willing to hang on the cross, or to suffer anything, so that the world might be saved.

Now, I myself know a man who said this, and finally went so far in his sympathy with Christ as to say, "O Lord Jesus, not only am I willing to hang upon the cross, but till the end of time, if necessary." Now, this is saying much, but it is only expressing the vehement, the agonizing feeling of a person ready to suffer any conceivable thing, if, by so doing, Christ could be honored and souls could be saved. Such is the spirit to prevail with God—a spirit willing to enter into His sympathies, a spirit which will not hesitate to make any necessary and personal sacrifice in order to save the souls of men.

But let me say again: *Prevailing prayer is, after all, a state of mind rather than a particular exercise. By this I mean that a person, to prevail, must live in a prescribed state of mind.* Prayer is not the mere going aside and praying, but a perpetual yearning of the mind, an habitual presenting of the mind in a spirit of importunity. This is the true idea of prevailing prayer.

Sometimes in this world's matters people have a great burden on their minds about their business. Men get into such a state of mind when they are intensely anxious, when they fear bankruptcy. The changes which they expect to come over them cause such anxiety that it becomes the burden of their life. They are quite loaded down by the continuance of this struggle in their minds. Sometimes people get into such a state of mind as this about religion. They see the churches are not prospering, that the hand of the Lord is not revealed, that the church does not understand its whereabouts, that the professing Christians are worldly minded and not aware of it, that they are getting into a spirit of justifying themselves rather than of confessing their sins. They see the difficulty and run to God literally besieging His throne, as Daniel did. Even in their dreams they pray; all their waking hours they pray until they are really borne down. Such is the state of mind in which Christians begin to mourn over the condition of Zion, to take pleasure in her stones, and to favor the dust thereof. You hear them confessing their sins and those of the people with much weeping. Then may you understand that the spirit of grace and supplication is poured out, that this spirit of grace and supplication will prevail and is always indispensable to prevailing prayer.

What are some further conditions of prevailing prayer.

Again, *clean hands* is another condition of prevailing prayer. The Psalmist says, "I will wash mine hands in innocency: so will I compass thine altar, O Lord!" Now, if this is not the case, you cannot prevail with God; and if a man has wronged his neighbor, whether in character, property, or person, if he has spoken against him in a manner injurious to his character, if he has wronged him in any way, he can expect no good to arise till this is set right. "If thou bring thy gift to the altar, and there rememberest that thy brother hath aught against thee; leave there thy gift before the altar, and go thy way; first be reconciled to thy brother, and then come and offer thy gift" (Matthew 5:23, 24). Don't offer it, and then say "Lord, remember I have spoken against such a one. Pray give me a heart to repent of it." No! Repent first, then you can prevail; your hands must be clean. You must be reconciled to your brother. Have you in any way unnecessarily in any unjustifiable manner injured the feelings, or injured in any respect, any of your brothers or neighbors? Go and be reconciled to the brother. Make peace with him, and then come and offer the gifts. When this is not the case, you can never expect to prevail.

But this leads me to say again: *the spirit of forgiveness* is another condition of prevailing prayer; the spirit of forgiveness where you have been wronged. Christ says in Matthew 6:15: "if ye forgive not men their trespasses, neither will your Father forgive your trespasses." My dear friends, are you sure your hands are so clean that when you come to God you can say, "Lord, thou knowest that I have taken no man's money, goods, or property, without an equivalent. Lord, thou knowest that I have wronged no man—that I have injured no man in character, in property, or in anything whatever"? Or if you have done so, can you say, "Thou knowest, O Lord, that I have made restitution—I have not suffered this iniquity to cleave to my hands and that, O Lord, thou knowest"? How is this? Perhaps you have offered many prayers, but you are not conscious of having prevailed. Perhaps you have prayed a multitude of times without ever really noting whether you are answered or not!

I was conversing with a brother in one of the great cities of America, some years ago. We were in the presence of a lady richly dressed, with many artificial and other ornaments common to ladies of her class. I sat talking with the brother on the subject of prayer. I talked for some considerable time. At length, the lady began to pay attention to my conversation. I said I believed the Christians of that day did not really expect to be answered when they prayed. I observed she began thinking this over. At length she became so uneasy that she finally broke out, "I do not believe people are so bad." "I do," said I. I tried to reply to her as mildly as I could. I asked her, "Do you obtain the things you ask for?" Yes, she did; if she did not, she would not pray. I went on, "Are you a married woman?" "Yes." "Is your husband a Christian?" "No, sir." "Are you the mother of children?" "I am." "Are they converted?" "No, sir." "Is there a revival in the church where you belong?" "No, sir." "Have you had any since your connection with it?" "We have not." "Then what *can* you have been praying for? You say you have received what you prayed for. Now, as you have a husband unconverted, children unconverted, no revival in your church, and have not had any since your connection with it, what *can* you have been praying for that you have received? Have you prayed for these golden chains and other ornaments? These are among the things that you really have, and perhaps they are what you have been praying for." Before we left the room, she burst into deep grief, confessing that she didn't think in reality she ever had prayed! She said she had often gone over certain forms of prayer, but now she felt confident that she had never been heard. She had prayed rather as a task or a duty. No man ever does his duty by praying in such a manner. It should be done in faith, with a full expectation of receiving what is prayed for, and not as a mere duty. I ask you, and include myself, have we, in this sense, clean hands, that we can compass God's altar, and that He can receive us honorably to himself?

Have we actually forgiven our enemies? Why, I have known individuals to keep up the forms of religion in the same church while in such a state of mind that they would not speak to each other. Abomination! Abomination! Why, such people deserve to be excommunicated, I would nearly say, for ever praying under such circumstances! They pray that God would forgive their trespasses as they forgive those that trespass against them, and in doing so they tempt God. People praying in such a state of mind that they can really rise above the injuries they have received and pray to God heartily to forgive them and exercise a forgiving spirit are in a proper state of mind to pray. If they are not in such a state of mind, how can they expect to prevail? With feelings of ill-will, and a spirit that cannot speak peacefully of certain individuals, if you feel so toward anyone, even wicked men, you are not in a proper state of mind to offer prayer.

Angels, the great archangel Michael, would not bring a railing accusation even against the devil. Angels have no right to exercise any other than benevolent feelings, even toward the wickedest beings. It is impossible to restore individuals to our confidence while they remain wicked. We are not expected to do this, but we are expected to be in such a state of mind as to have no disposition to retaliate. We are expected to be in such a state of mind as not to wish them evil, but to wish them all good, and pray for them honestly and earnestly—to pray God that He would bless them. We are to do this with all our hearts, as opposed to the spirit that would pray God to curse them. Unless we have this spirit, we have no sympathy with Christ, who, when we were His enemies, so great was His compassion that He hesitated not to die for us.

Some of you are harboring an improper state of mind toward your brethren. Can you go home tonight and pray God literally to forgive you your trespasses as you have forgiven those who have trespassed against you? You have no right to expect God to hear you or to answer you unless you can *honestly* say this, "O Lord, forgive me, as I have forgiven them"; no matter how much they have injured you—that is not the question. People have not done much who have only treated well those who have treated them well; but no man can prevail with God in such a spirit as that. He must be willing to pour out his heart in honest, earnest supplications for his very enemies. Without this, he does not sympathize with Christ. "Love your enemies," says Christ. "Bless them that curse you, do good to them that hate you, and pray for them which despitefully use you, and persecute you; that ye may be the children of your Father which is in heaven: for he maketh his sun to rise on the evil and on the good, and sendeth rain on the just and on the unjust. For if ye love them which love you, what reward have ye? Do not even the publicans the same?" To prevail with God, you must "love your enemies, bless them that curse you, and pray for them that despitefully use you, and persecute you." Unless you are in this state of mind, you need not expect to prevail with God. Oh! that we could see this spirit prevail, that Christians would really do this: bless them that curse them, pray for those that persecute them, and humble themselves before God. The prayer of the man who prays for his enemy has a mighty power with God.

Job's friends greatly abused him, misunderstood him, reviled him, and accused him of being a hypocrite. Job prayed for them. God turned his captivity and blessed him with a double portion. While Job prayed that they might be forgiven, God was pleased, and smiled upon them and upon him too.

12

PRAYER AND LABOR FOR THE GATHERING OF THE GREAT HARVEST*

"But when he saw the multitudes, he was moved with compassion on them, because they fainted, and were scattered abroad, as sheep having no shepherd. Then saith he unto his disciples, The harvest truly is plenteous, but the laborers are few. Pray ye therefore the Lord of the harvest, that he will send forth laborers into His harvest" (Matthew 9:36–38).

In discussing this subject, I propose to consider:

▶ *To whom this precept is addressed.*
▶ *What is really intended in this precept.*
▶ *What is implied in the prayer required.*
▶ *That this state of mind is an indispensable condition of salvation.*

To whom this precept is addressed.

Beyond question, the precept is addressed to all who are under obligation to be benevolent; therefore, to all classes and all beings upon whom the law of love is imposed. Consequently, it is addressed to all *human beings,* for all who are human bear moral responsibility. We *ought* to care for the souls of our fellows, and of course fall under the broad sweep of this requisition.

Note the occasion of Christ's remark. He was traveling

---

*Charles G. Finney, *Sermons of Gospel Themes* (New York: Fleming H. Revell, 1876), pp. 319–333. Also, *The Oberlin Evangelist,* January 5, 1853.

through the cities and villages of His country, "teaching in their synagogues and preaching the Gospel of the kingdom, and healing every sickness and every disease among the people." He saw multitudes before Him, mostly in great ignorance of God and salvation; and His deeply compassionate heart was moved, "because he saw them fainting and scattered abroad as sheep without a shepherd." Alas! They were perishing for lack of the bread of heaven, and who should go and break it to their needy souls?

His feelings were the more affected because He saw that they *felt* hungry. They not only were famishing for the bread of life, but they seemed to have some consciousness of the fact. They were just then in the condition of a harvest field, the white grain of which is ready for the sickle and waits the coming of the reapers. So the multitudes were ready to be gathered into the granary of the great Lord of the harvest. No wonder this sight should touch the deepest compassions of His benevolent heart.

What is really intended in this precept.

Every precept relating to external conduct has its spirit and also its letter—the letter referring to the *external*, but the spirit to the *internal*; yet both are involved in real obedience. In the present case, the letter of the precept requires prayer; but let no one suppose that merely using the words of prayer is real obedience. Besides the words, there must be a praying state of mind. The precept does not require us to lie and play the hypocrite before God. No one can for a moment suppose this to be the case. Therefore, it must be admitted that the precept requires the *spirit* of prayer as well as the letter. It requires first in value a *praying state of mind*, and then also its due expression in the forms of prayer.

What, then, is the true spirit of this precept? *Love for souls.* Certainly it does not require us to pray for men without any *heart* in our prayer; but that we should pray with a sincere heart, full of real love for human welfare—a love for immortal souls and a deep concern for their salvation. It doubtless requires the same compassion that Jesus himself had for souls. His heart was gushing with real compassion for dying souls, and He was conscious that His own was a right state of mind. Therefore, He could not do less than require the same state of mind of all His people. Hence, He requires that we should have real and deep compassion for souls, such compassion as really moves the heart, for such most obviously was His.

This involves a full committal of the soul to this object. Christ had committed His soul to the great labor of saving men. For this He labored and toiled; for this His heart agonized; for this His life was ready to be offered; therefore, He could do no less than require the same of His people.

Again, an honest offering of this prayer implies a willingness on our part that God should use us in His harvest field in any capacity He pleases. When the farmer gathers his harvest, many things are to be done, and often he needs many hands to do them. Some he sends in to cut the grain, others to bind it. Some gather into the barn, and others glean the field, that nothing is lost. So Christ will have a variety of labors for His servants in the great harvest field; and no one can be of real use to Him unless he is willing to work in any department of his Master's service, thankful for the privilege of doing the humblest service for *such* a Master and in such a cause.

Hence, it is implied in honest prayer for this object that we are really committed to the work, and that we have given ourselves up most sincerely and entirely to do all we can for Christ and His cause on earth. We are always on hand, ready for any labor or any suffering. For, plainly, if we have not this mind, we need not think to pray to any good purpose. It would be but a sorry and insulting prayer to say, "Lord, send somebody else to do all the hard work, and let me do little or nothing." Everybody knows that such a prayer would only affront God and curse the offerer. Hence, sincere prayer for Christ's cause implies that you are willing to do anything you can do to promote its interests, in actual and absolute devotion of all your powers and resources for this object. You may not withhold even your own children. Nothing shall be too dear for you to offer on God's altar.

Suppose a person should give nothing—should withhold all his means and suppress all efforts; he only says he will *pray*. He professes indeed to pray. But do you suppose that his prayer has any *heart* in it? Does he *mean* what he says? Does he love the object more than all things else? No, not in the true sense of the word. You never could say that a young man does all he can for Christ's harvest if he refuses to go into the field to work, nor that an aged but wealthy man is doing all he can if he refuses to give anything to help sustain the field's laborers.

What is implied in the prayer required.

A sense of personal responsibility in respect to the salvation of the world. No man ever begins to obey this command who does not feel a personal responsibility in this thing: to feel it in a sense that brings it home to his soul as *his own work*. He must really feel, "This is *my work for life*. For this I am to live and spend my strength." It matters not on this point whether you are young enough to go abroad into the foreign field, or whether you are qualified for the gospel ministry; you must feel such a sense of responsibility that you will cheerfully and most heartily do all you can. You can do the hewing of the wood or the drawing of the water even if you cannot fill the more responsible trusts. An honest and consecrated heart is willing to do any sort of toil—bear any sort of burden. Unless you are willing to do anything you can successfully and wisely do, you will not comply with the conditions of a prayerful state of mind.

Another element is a sense of the value of souls. You must see vividly that souls are precious—that their guilt while in unpardoned sin is fearful and their danger most appalling. Without such a sense of the value of the interests at stake, you will not pray with fervent, strong desire; and without a just apprehension of their guilt, danger, and remedy, you will not pray in faith for God's interposing grace. Indeed, you must have so much of the love of God—a love like God's love for sinners—in your soul that you are ready for any sacrifice or any labor. You need to feel as God feels. He so loved the world that He gave His only begotten Son, that whosoever should believe in Him might not perish. You need so to love the world that your love will draw you to make similar sacrifices and put forth similar labors. Each servant of God must have a love for souls, the same in kind as God had in giving up His Son to die, and as Christ had in coming cheerfully down to make himself the offering. Without such love, the servant's prayers for this object will have little heart and no power with God. This love for souls is always implied in acceptable prayer, that God would send forth laborers into His harvest. I have often thought that the reason so many pray only in form and not in heart for the salvation of souls is that they lack this love, like God's love, for the souls of the perishing.

Acceptable prayer for this object implies confidence in the ability, wisdom, and willingness of God to push forward this work. No man can pray for what he supposes may be opposed to God's will, or beyond His ability or too complicated for His wisdom. If you ask God to send forth laborers, the very prayer assumes that you confide in His ability to do the work well, and in His willingness, in answer to prayer, to press it forward.

The very idea of prayer implies that you understand this to be a part of the divine plan—that Christians should pray for God's interposing power and wisdom to carry forward this great work. You do not pray till you see that God gives you the privilege, enjoins the duty, and encourages it by assuring you that it is an essential means, an indispensable condition of His interposing His power to give success. You remember it is said, "I will yet for this be inquired of by the House of Israel to do it for them."

Again, no one complies with the spirit of this condition who does not pray *with his might*—fervently and with great perseverance and urgency for the blessing. He must feel the pressure of a great cause, and must feel, moreover, that it cannot prosper without God's interposing power. Pressed by these considerations, he will pour out his soul with intensely fervent supplications.

Unless the Church is filled with the spirit of prayer, God will not send forth the laborers into His harvest. Plainly the command to pray for such laborers implies that God expects prayer and will wait until it is made. The prayer comes into His plan as one of the appointed agencies, and can by no means be dispensed with. Doubtless it was in answer to prayer that God sent out such a multitude of strong men after the ascension. How obviously did prayer and the special hand of God bring in a Saul of Tarsus and send him forth to call in whole tribes and nations of the Gentile world! And along with him were a host of others. "The Lord gave the word: great was the company of those that published it."

That this prayer should be *in faith*, reposing in assurance on God's everlasting promise, is too obvious to need proof or illustration.

Honest, sincere prayer implies that we lay ourselves and all we have upon His altar. We must feel that this is our business and that our disposable strength and resources are to be appropriated for its completion. It is only, then, when we are given up to the work, that we can honestly ask God to raise up laborers and press the work forward. When a man's lips say, "Lord, send forth laborers"; but his life in an undertone proclaims, "I don't care whether a man goes or not; I'll not help on the work," you will, of course, know that he is only playing the hypocrite before God.

By this I do not imply that every honest servant of Christ must feel himself called to the ministry, and must enter it; by no means; for God does not call every pious person into this field, but has many other fields and labors which are essential parts of the great whole. The thing I have to say is that we must be ready for any part whatever which God's providence assigns us.

When we *can* go, and are in a situation to obtain the needful education, then the true spirit of prayer in our text implies that we pray that God would send *us*. If we are in a condition to go, then, plainly, this prayer implies that we have the heart to beg the privilege for ourselves that God would put us into His missionary work. Then we shall say with the ancient prophet, "Lord, here am I, send me." Do you not suppose Christ expected His disciples to go and to *desire* to go? Did He not assume that they would pray for the privilege of being put into this precious trust? How can we be in real sympathy with Christ unless we love the work of laboring in this gospel harvest, and long to be commissioned to go forth and put in our sickle with our own hand? Most certainly, if we were in Christ's spirit we should say, "I have a baptism to be baptized with, and how am I straitened till it be accomplished?" We should cry out, "Lord, let me go! Let me go! For dying millions are just now perishing in their sins." How can I pray God to send out others if I am in heart unwilling to go myself? I have heard many say, "Oh, that I were young! How I should rejoice to go myself." This seems like a state of mind that can honestly pray for God to send forth laborers.

The spirit of this prayer implies that we are willing to make any personal sacrifices in order to go. Are not men always willing to make personal sacrifices in order to gain the great object of their heart's desire? Did ever a merchant, seeking quality pearls, find one of great value that he was not quite willing to go and sell all that he had to buy it?

Moreover, an honest heart before God in this prayer implies that you are willing to do all you can to prepare yourselves to accomplish this work. Each young man or young woman should say, "God requires something of me in this work." It may be God wants you as a servant in some missionary family; if so, you are ready to go. No matter what the work may be, no labor done for God or for man is degrading. In the spirit of this prayer, you will say, "If I may but wash the feet of my Lord's servants, I shall richly enjoy it." All young persons especially, feeling that life is before them, should say, "I must devote myself, in the most effective way possible, to the promotion of my Savior's cause." Suppose a man bows his soul in earnest prayer before God, saying, "Lord, send out hosts of men into this harvest field," does this not imply that he prepares himself for this work with all his might? Does it not imply that he is ready to do the utmost he can in any way whatever?

Again, this prayer, made honestly, implies that we do all we can to prepare others to go out. Our prayer will be, "Lord, give us hearts to prepare others, and get as many ready as possible and as well prepared as possible for the gathering in of this great harvest."

Of course it is also implied that we abstain from whatever would hinder us, and make no arrangements that would tie our hands. Many young Christians do this, sometimes carelessly, often in a way which shows that they are by no means set on doing God's work before anything else.

When we honestly pray God to send out laborers, and our own circumstances allow us to go, we are to expect that He will send us. What! Does God need laborers of every description, and will he not send *us*? Depend on it, He *will* send out the man who prays right, and whose heart is deeply and fully with God. And we need not be suspicious lest God should lack the needful wisdom to manage His matters well. He will put all His men where they should be, into the fields they are best qualified to fill. The good reaper will be put into his post, sickle in hand; and if there are feeble ones who can only glean, He puts them there.

When youth have health and the means for obtaining an education, they must assume that God calls them to this work. They should assume that God expects them to enter the field. They will fix their eye upon this work as their own. Thinking of the masses of God's true children who are lifting up this prayer, "Lord, send forth laborers to gather in the nations to Thy Son," they will assuredly infer that the Lord will answer these prayers and send out all His faithful, fit, and true men into this field. Most assuredly, if God has given you the mind, the training, the tact, the heart, and the opportunity to get all needful preparation, you may know He will send you forth. What! Is it possible that I am prepared, ready, waiting, and the hosts of the Church praying that God would send laborers forth, and yet He will not send me! Impossible!

One indispensable part of this preparation is a *heart* for it. Most plainly so, for God wants no one in His harvest field whose hearts are not there. You would not want workmen in your field who have no heart for their work. Neither does God. But He expects us to have this preparation. And He will accept this excuse from service from no one: that he has no heart to engage in it. The want of a heart for this work is not your misfortune, but your fault, your great and damning sin!

This state of mind is an indispensable condition of salvation.

Many congregations are dreadfully in the dark about the conditions of salvation. I was once preaching on this subject, and urging that holiness is one condition of salvation, "without which no man can see the Lord," when I was confronted and strenuously opposed by a doctor of divinity. He said, "The Bible makes faith the sole and only condition of salvation. Paul preached that faith is *the* condition, and plainly meant to exclude every other condition." "But," I answer, "*Why* did Paul press so earnestly and hold up so prominently the doctrine of salvation by faith? Because he had to oppose the great Jewish error of *salvation by works*. Such preaching was greatly and especially needed *then*, and Paul pressed into the field to meet the emergency. But when Antinomianism developed itself, James was called out to uphold with equal decision the doctrine that faith without works is dead, and that good works are the legitimate fruit of living faith, and are essential to evince its life and genuineness. This at once raised a new question about the nature of gospel faith. James held that all true gospel faith must work by love. It must be an affectionate filial confidence, such as draws the soul into sympathy with Christ, and leads it forward powerfully to *do* all His will."

Many professing Christians hold that nothing is needful but simply faith and repentance, and that faith may exist without real benevolence, and consequently without good works. No mistake can be greater than this. The grand requisition which God makes upon man is that he become *truly benevolent*. This is the essence of all true religion, a state of mind that has compassion like God's compassion for human souls; that cries out in earnest prayer for their salvation, and that shrinks from no labor to effect this object. If, therefore, true religion is a condition of salvation, then the state of mind developed in our text is also a condition.

REMARKS

This state of mind is as obligatory upon sinners as upon saints. All people ought to feel this compassion for souls. Why not? Can any reason be named why a sinner should not feel as much compassion for souls as a Christian? Or why he ought not to love God and man as ardently?

Professing Christians who do not obey the true spirit of these precepts are hypocrites, without one exception. They profess to be truly religious, but *are* they? Certainly not, unless they are on the altar, devoted to God's work and in heart sincerely sympathizing in it. Without this, every one of them is a hypocrite. You profess to have the spirit of Christ; but when you see the multitudes as He sees them, perishing for lack of gospel light, do you cry out in mighty prayer with compassion for their souls? If you have not this spirit, write yourself down as a hypocrite.

Many do not pray that God would send forth laborers because they are afraid He will *send them*. I can recollect when religion was repulsive to me because I feared that if I should be converted, God would send me to preach the Gospel. But I thought further on this subject. God, I said, has a right to dispose of me as He pleases, and I have no right to resist. If I do resist, He will *put me in hell*. If God wants me to be a minister of His Gospel and I resist and rebel, He surely ought to put me in hell, and doubtless He will.

But there are many young people who never give themselves to prayer for the conversion of the world, lest God should send them into this work. You would blush to pray, "Lord, send forth laborers, but don't send me." If the reason you don't want to go is that you have no heart for it, you may write yourself down as a hypocrite, and make no mistake about it.

If you say, "I have a heart for the work, but I am not qualified to go," then you may consider that God will not call you unless you are or can be qualified. He does not want unfit men in the service.

The ministry for the last quarter of a century has fallen into disgrace because young men have entered it who never should have entered. Their hearts are not fixed, and they shrink from making sacrifices for Christ and His cause. Hence, they do not go straight forward, true to the right, firm for the oppressed, and strong for every good word and work. By whole platoons, they back out from the position which they have sworn to maintain. The hearts of multitudes of lay brothers and sisters are in great distress, crying out over this fearful defection. To a minister who was complaining of the public reproach cast on his order, a layman of Boston replied, "I am sorry there is so much occasion for it; God means to rebuke the ministry, and He ought to rebuke them since they so richly deserve it." Do not understand me to say that this vacillation of the ministry is universal; no, indeed; I am glad to know there are exceptions; but still the painful fact is that many have relapsed, and consequently, as a class, they have lost character, and this has discouraged many young men from entering the ministry.

Let this be so no longer. Let the young men now preparing for the ministry come up to the spirit of their Master and rush to the front rank of the battle. Let them toil for the good of souls, and love this toil as their great Lord has done before them. Thus by their fidelity let them redeem the character of this class of men from the reproach under which it now lies. Let them rally in their strength and lay themselves with one heart on the altar of God.

With sorrow I am compelled to say, many don't care whether the work is done or not. They are all swallowed up with ambitious aspirings. Not everyone will sympathize with Jesus Christ.

Beloved, let me ask you if you are honestly conscious of sympathizing with your great Leader? I can never read the passage before us without being affected by the manifestation it makes of Christ's tenderness and love. There were the thronging multitudes before Him. To the merely external eye, all might have been fair; but to one who thought of their spiritual state, there was enough to move the deep fountains of compassion. Christ saw them scattered abroad as sheep who had no shepherd. They had no teachers or guides in whom they could repose confidence. They were in darkness and moral death. Christ wept over them and called on His disciples to sympathize in their case, and unite with Him in mighty prayer to the Lord of the harvest that he would send forth laborers. Such was His spirit. And now, dear young people, do you care whether or not this work is done?

Many seem determined to shirk this labor and leave it all for others to do. Indeed, they will hardly entertain the question of what part God wants them to take and perform.

Now let me ask you, "Will such as they be welcomed and applauded at last by the herald of judgment destiny, crying out,

'Well done, good and faithful servants, enter ye into the joy of your Lord'?" Never; no *never*!

Many say, "I am not called," but really they are not devoted to this work so as to care whether they are called or not. They do not *want* to be called!

Now the very fact that you have the requisite qualifications, means, and facilities for preparation indicates God's call. These constitute the voice of His providence, saying, "Go forth, and prepare for labor in my vineyard!" There is your scholarship; use it. There are classes for you to enter; go in and occupy till you are ready to enter the great white fields of the Savior's harvest. If providential indications favor, you must strive to keep up with their summons. Pray for the baptisms of the Holy Spirit. Seek the divine anointing, and give yourself no rest till you are in all things furnished for the work God assigns you.

It is painful to see that many are committing themselves in some way or other against the work. They are putting themselves in a position which of itself forbids their engaging in it. But do let me ask you, can you expect ever to be saved if, when you have the power and the means to engage in this work, you have no heart for it? No, indeed! You knock in vain at the gate of the blessed! You may go there and knock, but what will be the answer? Are ye my faithful servants? Were ye among the few, faithful among the faithless, quick and ready at your Master's call? Oh, no, no you were not. You studied how you could *shun* the labor and *shirk* the self-denial! I know you not! Your portion lies without the city walls!

Let no one excuse himself as not called, for God calls *all* to some sort of labor in the great harvest field. You never need, therefore, to excuse yourself as one not called to some service for your Lord and Master. And let no one excuse himself from the ministry unless his *heart* is on the altar and he himself praying and longing to go, held back only by an obvious call of God, through His providence, to some other part of the great labor.

Many will be sent to hell at last for treating this subject as they have, with so much selfishness at heart! I know the young man who for a long time struggled between a strong conviction that God called him to the ministry and a great repulsion against engaging in this work. I know what this feeling is, for I felt it a long time myself. A long time I had a secret conviction that I should be a minister, though my heart repulsed it. In fact, my conversion turned very much upon my giving up this contest with God, and subduing this repulsion of feeling against God's call.

You can see what it is to be a Christian, and what God demands of men at conversion. The turning point is: *Will you really and honestly serve God!* With students especially the question is likely to be, "Will you abandon all your ambitious schemes and devote yourself to the humble, unambitious toil of preaching Christ's gospel to the poor?" Many in Bible colleges are ambitious and aspiring. They have schemes for promotion and advancement, which are a trial to renounce altogether. Hence with you, your being a Christian and being saved at last will turn much, perhaps altogether, on your giving yourself up to this work in the true self-denial of the gospel spirit.

Many have been called to this work, who afterward backslide and abandon it. They begin well, but backslide, get into a state of great perplexity about their duty. Perhaps, like Balaam, they are so unwilling to see their duty and so anxious to evade it that God will not struggle with them any longer, but gives them up to their coveteousness or their ambition.

Young person, are you earnestly crying out, "Lord, what wilt Thou have me do?" Be assured, God wants you in His field somewhere. He has not abandoned His harvest to perish. He wants you in it, but He wants you first to repent and prepare your heart for the gospel ministry. You need not enter it till you have done this.

Many are waiting for a miraculous call. This is a great mistake. God does not call men in any miraculous way. The finger of His providence points out the path, and the fitness He gives you indicates the work for you to do. You need not fear that God will call you wrong. He will point out the work He would have *you* do. Therefore, ask Him to guide you to the right spot in the great field. He will surely do it.

Young person, will you deal kindly and truly with my Master in this matter? Do you say, "O my God, I am on hand, ready for *any* part of the work Thou hast for me to do"?

13

ON PERSEVERING PRAYER FOR OTHERS*

"And he said unto them, Which of you shall have a friend, and shall go unto him at midnight, and say unto him, Friend, lend me three loaves; For a friend of mine in his journey is come to me, and I have nothing to set before him? And he from within shall answer and say, Trouble me not: the door is now shut, and my children are with me in bed; I cannot rise and give thee. I say unto you, Though he will not rise and give him, because he is his friend, yet because of his importunity, he will rise and give him as many as he needeth" (Luke 11:5–8).

In speaking from this passage, I propose to observe:

- ► *There is a spontaneous impulse to pray for others.*
- ► *Why God has constituted us to feel we may and must pray for others.*
- ► *What this text teaches on the importance of perseverance.*
- ► *Why people do not pray more for others.*

There is a spontaneous impulse to pray for others.

The passage seems to have been designed to encourage us to pray for our friends and for others in general. The same is true of the Lord's Prayer, since many of its petitions obviously contemplate blessings upon others not less than upon ourselves. Indeed, the whole Bible is replete with instances and examples

---

The Oberlin Evangelist, January 17, 1855.

of prevailing prayer for others. I might begin with the case of Abraham interceding for Ishmael, for Abimelech, and yet again for Sodom. And then I might proceed to speak of Moses and of Samuel, of Jeremiah and other prophets, of the apostles, and of those who are continually in prayer for the Church. The Bible is full of this, and must make the impression on every attentive reader that intercession for others is a natural development of the Christian spirit.

It is equally a dictate of nature to pray for others as to pray for yourself. Who does not sometimes experience the spontaneous and irresistible impulse to cry out to God for others? It is utterly impossible for a parent to see a child in a house on fire, or sinking in deep waters, or in great peril, without crying to God for help. You who read the Bible must notice how God's people are continually in prayer for His Church and His cause on earth. You see there how parents pray for their children, how one prays for another under any circumstances of need. This is evident in every page of the whole Bible. No one who reads his Bible can fail to notice it.

From the mere light of nature, we expect God to hear our prayer for others. Consider this point and you will see it is so. Even the wickedest of men and of women pray for their children in distress, and indeed for others besides their own. They have an innate conviction that God should be sought in prayer, and that He will hear and help. Sometimes the impulse to pray for others is irresistible and insuppressible. You cry out spontaneously, "May God have mercy on their souls!" I doubt whether there is a person in the nation, however wicked, who could have stood by and have seen the train cars at Norwalk plunge off into the river without crying out, "May God save their souls!" This is quite as natural as to pray for ourselves, and shows fully the instinct of our minds. You may say what you please about there being no virtue in prayer, and you may try to believe what you will; yet nonetheless, this sort of prayer will come with the occasion that calls for it. The fact remains the same, in spite of all that people may strive to do by false philosophy to excuse themselves for praying so little.

I am aware that some people object, saying it is of no use to pray for others. But this objection is utterly shallow and groundless. It assumes that prayer never influences God, but ourselves only. They say the influence of prayer is wholly *subjective*; i.e., it mentally influences the person who prays; never *objective*; i.e., upon God, to move Him to act. It is strange that people should ever adopt a notion so absurd. This subjective influence never could be gained if people did not believe in the objective influence. How much good would it do your own heart to pray if it were the fact, and you absolutely knew it to be, that God *never* hears and answers prayer? Think how ridiculous for a person to go before God and pray to Him, "Lord, I don't expect my prayer to influence Thee in the least, for I know Thou canst not hear prayer at all; but I want to get a certain subjective effect on myself by this prayer; and therefore, I impose myself before Thy throne." How strange! Any man would be shocked at his own folly and absurdity.

Some of you, perhaps, do not fully understand when I say that prayer does not change God's nature and purposes. Some people say, "Prayer must change God's plans if He answers it." No, never. It has always been God's plan to hear and answer prayer. This has always entered into His purpose.

Again, God's immutability implies that He will answer prayer. It would be strange indeed if God should not change His course in answer to prayer if He is indeed immutable. If He were *not* to change for rightly offered prayer, it would prove He was not good; it would imply that He has ceased to be benevolent. Indeed, it would undeify Him at once. When you come to resolve this idea into its elements, you will see that it subverts the whole idea of God and of His attributes. It must imply that God's creatures might come into any position before Him, and He can never answer their prayers.

But many say, "I can see how prayer may benefit myself, but cannot see how it can benefit others." I reply that the latter can easily be seen. No one can read the Bible without seeing that this is the fact: prayer does benefit others. No one can study his own convictions without seeing evidence of it. If prayer never could benefit others, the fact would disappoint all our innate convictions.

I have said that to pray for others is a spontaneity of our nature. Even when our enemies are in sudden danger and trouble, we lift up our cry for them spontaneously. I doubt whether even an infidel could see a child struggling in pain and peril without crying out, "May God help!" Sometimes people in their sins have fallen into fearful circumstances, and have cried mightily to God, and God has intervened so remarkably as to astonish them. I have heard of many cases of this sort. I remember a case of a wicked man on the point of drowning who cried to God for help. It was remarkable that all his sins seemed to be concentrated into one present mass. He saw them, saw himself as that great sinner who had sinned so grievously; saw that he must turn from all his sins to God if he would ever hope for mercy. He did turn to God, saying, "I yield, and I will be thine forever." Immediately after this, he rose to the surface and floated to shore.

I have heard of another case of a man in his sins praying for a sick child. God heard, and it is wonderful to say, God answered, and the case made an impression on his mind which ended in his speedy conversion.

God hears the young ravens when they cry. He heard those heathen sailors who were in the ship with Jonah. He often hears sailors in distress as His Word most impressively declares. "For he commandeth and raiseth the stormy wind, which lifteth up the waves thereof. They mount up to the heaven, they go down again to the depths: their soul is melted because of trouble. They reel to and fro, and stagger like a drunken man, and are at their wit's end. Then they cry unto the Lord in their trouble, and he bringeth them out of their distresses. He maketh the storm a calm, so that the waves thereof are still. Then are they glad because they be quiet; so he bringeth them unto their desired haven" (Psalm 107:25–30). Many a sailor knows that God has heard him in his cry of distress. Some of them can gratefully testify, "God heard my cry and spared my life. Now, therefore, I will serve Him as long as I live." How often does God hear such prayer so obviously as to leave no doubt and no possibility of reasonable doubting!

Why God has constituted us to feel that we may and must pray for others.

They need our prayer. They may be mentally incapable of prayer. Or, their prayers for themselves may be utterly unavailing. Hence, they need the aid of someone who has power with God to pray for them. I can well remember that in my own case, one full year before I was married I had an irresistible conviction on my mind that I should lose my soul if I were to marry any other than a pious wife. I knew I could not pray for myself. An ungodly wife would not pray for me, but would only strengthen me in my sins. I therefore came fully to the conclusion that I should never marry any other than a pious woman. I had never heard my father or my mother pray, and had no reason to suppose they ever prayed for me. Hence, perhaps, I felt the more the need of a praying wife. But I have often heard other people say the same in regard to marrying pious wives. This may doubtless be abused. People may depend too much on others' prayers. Children often depend upon the prayers of their parents.

We need the exercise of praying for others. It will do us as well as them great good. This we may readily learn from our own experience.

Viewing God in His governmental relations and capacities, He needs this intercessory prayer for its influence on His creatures. He wants to interest His people in each other, and to cement their many hearts into one. It is His great desire to bring all His people to care for each other and to love each other.

Place before your mind the case of a great family. Suppose the father should not encourage his children to ask favors of him for each other. You say at once this would be very bad. Certainly a wise father would encourage that for the sake of strengthening the bands of mutual sympathy in his household. Some of the best families I have ever known have been remarkable for this. Each of the children were in the habit of asking favors not for himself but for his brothers or sisters. You can easily see the value of this in a family. Surely its value cannot be less in God's great family. It cannot be strange, therefore, that God should encourage His children to expect to be heard when they pray for their brothers and sisters. You can see how important it is that a father should encourage in his children the benevolent spirit of asking favors for each other, and should induce them to do so for the very purpose of cultivating benevolence in their hearts. It certainly is a most salutary arrangement in any family, or indeed in any government. Any good ruler loves to see his people interested in each other.

What do you think of a family, ten in number with which I was acquainted, who were accustomed when they met each evening around the family altar to detail briefly the state of their minds to each other. If anyone was in darkness or in sin, all would unite to pray for that one, or even, if the case seemed to call for it, would set apart an entire day of fasting and prayer in his behalf. Was not that a most admirable practice? Or what would you think of a church which prayed in this way for each other, and helped those especially who were in any affliction? And will not God encourage this spirit among His people? Most assuredly you know it must be so.

Prayer for each other draws us into a deeper consideration

of each other's needs. When you begin to pray for another, you are compelled to study his character, his temptations, his wants. This opens the way for a richer heart union.

Prayer for others draws us into sympathy with God's love and with His feelings toward His people. We may blame them more, or may pity them more; or it may be that we shall simply love them more. But however this may be, we shall be more likely to have the same mind toward them that God has.

It is intrinsically fit and proper that God should manifest His pleasure in every case of disinterested importunity for the souls of others. The case may be that of a stranger to you, yet your heart becomes deeply engaged and your very soul takes hold of the case. God sees this with delight. "What do you want, my child," says He. "I want for this soul to be converted," you reply. Is there not some propriety in God's being pleased with this prayer? God looks on this petitioner saying, "You come not to plead for yourself, not for life, not for any temporal good; but for your enemy. You come to pray for your enemy and you want me to convert his soul? I will do it." Indeed, I suppose that other things being equal, a sincere prayer offered for any enemy is more sure to be granted than any other prayer. But whether offered for an enemy, or for a friend, it is impossible that God should not be greatly influenced by self-sacrificing, really benevolent prayer. He must be if He loves real benevolence and seeks to promote it among His creatures.

Prayer for others needs this encouragement. If we were to pray earnestly for others and God did not regard it, we should lose confidence in prayer, not to say also in God himself.

This condescension on His part is of the utmost importance to the whole universe. People need to know that they can influence the Infinite Mind by prayer for fellow creatures, for this will encourage them to try to help each other by prayer, and will serve to knit the bonds of mutual affection and interest.

It is striking to notice how our dependent relations upon each other and upon God multiply the occasions of prayer for each other. It would seem that God loves to create these occasions and to multiply them continually. So He shuts us up by His providence, straitens us all round about, and thus compels us to feel the necessity of prayer. Oh, how He loves to multiply these occasions and bring up one subject of prayer after another, keeping our hearts ever warm with benevolent interest in our fellowman! All this time He is never weary of giving us audience and of inviting us into the secret chamber of His love.

Prayer for others supplies one important condition in the government of God upon which He can show mercy without detriment to any governmental interests. Everyone can readily see that a king might grant a favor to an offender for the sake of a mutual friend, which he could not grant for the offender's sake alone. Suppose a person in your city has committed a great crime. The governor cannot pardon him only on the strength of his own request. But if all the city were to unite their petitions, he might perhaps for their sakes grant the pardon. This principle has a wide and well known application.

Thus a parent might get a blessing for a child. The child may be guilty of high treason, but his father may have rendered so great service to the government that for the sake of these, and in answer to his prayers, the governor may honorably and safely pardon him. The governor would reply to the guilty son, "I cannot pardon you for your own sake, but for your father's sake I can." This principle has always been exercised in God's government.

For Abraham's sake God could bless Abimelech, Sarah, and almost the city of Sodom. Noah, Daniel, and Job are cited as examples of intercessors whom God would hear except under the extreme circumstances of guilt, when the nation had become extremely ripe for judgments.

God's language to Moses is striking and most significant. It was on the occasion of the golden calf that the Lord said to Moses, "I have seen this people, and, behold, it is a stiffnecked people: now therefore *let me alone,* that my wrath may wax hot against them, and that I may consume them: and I will make of thee a great nation" (Exodus 32:9, 10). God would not hear the people, but did hear Moses. Indeed, He speaks as if He could not go on in the course of just judgment against the people unless Moses would withdraw his intercession and let Him go on. How strong is the view thus given us of the power of prevailing prayer.

To pray for others, and to be heard and answered by God in our prayers, serves greatly to increase our love to God in the form of affection and our love to others in the form of benevolence. No one ever prayed for another, with real prayer, without feeling an increase of love toward that person no matter whether it is for a stranger or an acquaintance. So if a community or a church prays for some individual, the more they pray, the better they will love. Prayer creates a bond of union between our souls and the souls of those whom we love. Let one pray for others till he prevails. It results in a wonderful sympathy like that between a parent and a child. I have seen extraordinary cases of prayer for others in which a most mysterious connection seemed to be established between the party praying and the party prayed for, the latter seeming to know that blessings came through prayer, and almost adoring and idolizing the source through which they came.

We can often obtain for others what they cannot obtain for themselves. Abraham prayed for Abimelech and obtained for him blessings for which Abimelech's prayers might have been in vain. Job prayed successfully for his friends and God heard him when He would not hear them. Moses, in like manner, prayed for Aaron and Miriam, and God's hearing him, when He would not hear them, became a loud rebuke of their envy and pride. This illustrates a great principle in God's government, showing both that God means to encourage intercession for others, and that in order to pray acceptably, people must stand in favor before God—in a position which does not demand His rebuke, but which does at least justify manifestations of His favor. It is on this principle that God can and will hear the prayers of His humble, obedient, trusting children.

What this text teaches on the importance of perseverance.

I come next to the importance of *perseverance in prayer.* This text, like those of other sermons, is designed to teach this doctrine. You will notice how strong the case is made in our present text: "I say unto you, though he will not rise and give him because he is his friend, yet because of his importunity, he will rise and give him as many as he needeth." This, however, does not teach that God's friendship for His people fails to induce Him to give, but it is a strong case to show that Christians get for their importunity what they could not get without it.

There are cases where nothing short of importunity gains the desired blessing. The case of the Syrophoenician woman is to the same point. If she had given up after the first or the second rebuff, she would have surely failed to receive the great blessing. Daniel prayed on one occasion for twenty-one days and would not give up. At last deliverance came. Being obliged to press our suit so long compels us to study and to understand our case. It leads us into a deeper sympathy with God and with all His views and policy.

We can better appreciate the value of the blessing by how

much more it costs us and the longer we have to pray for it. The more intensely we feel in our prayer for a given case, the more fully we appreciate the blessing when it comes. It supplies a deeper want of our souls, and comes with a more refreshing consolation.

Such persevering prayer develops all the Christian graces— especially benevolence, the mother of all the rest. It brings this out in all its rich and varied phases.

It is often important that he who prays for another should have time and inducement to remove all obstacles out of the way. It is not, by any means, consistent with God's plans of moral government to hear your prayer for the conversion of a soul, so long as you yourself are laying a stumbling block in his way. By delaying the answer, God will surely give you time to search out and remove all such hindrances. Besides, providences must have time and scope to operate. Providential difficulties must be removed out of the way, and time may be requisite for this.

Often God delays that He may bring us lower in the dust before Him. He leads us into such humility that we will not be puffed up, so the blessing given will not injure us. To secure this object often delays the answer long. We are not low enough so that He can give us the blessing without mischief to ourselves. Study carefully the case of the Syrophoenician woman. Some said, "Send her away, for she crieth after us." Even Christ said He was not sent except to the lost sheep of the house of Israel. This was a dash of cold water upon her warm hopes, for it seemed as if Christ intended to discourage her. As if even this were not enough, He finally went so far as to say, "It is not suitable to take the children's bread and cast it to dogs." Did it not seem to her cruel that He should throw this foul Jewish prejudice into her teeth! But take note! What did she do? Did she resent it? Did she turn away discouraged? By no means. She seemed to say, "You don't mean to put me away. You cannot do that, I know the goodness of your heart too well." So she turned the very rebuke into an argument for her case. "Truth," she said, "but I do not ask for the children's bread. I only want the crumbs that fall from the table, and those it is surely proper to give to dogs." Now look at our blessed Lord. All overcome by such blended humility and importunity and faith, He yielded and cried out, "Oh, woman, great is thy faith; be it unto thee even as thou wilt." You see the great value of this importunity. All the world over wherever this story has been read, what rich lessons it has taught people on this subject!

The case of Jacob struggling with the angel of the covenant is another example here. It was only after he had safely passed the crisis and said, "I will not let thee go except thou bless me" that the Lord blessed him as he prayed.

Sometimes God delays for the sake apparently of drawing us into more and mightier prayer. We become straitened and agonized. Then God puts it into our hearts to do something yet more for the soul prayed for. Our experience in prayer reveals this. Then when we have done it, and are in every respect prepared, God sends an arrow and does the work.

Another reason for delay may be that you may become more deeply unified with the subject of your prayer. Sometimes you pray for a person till you become so unified with him that you say, "If that soul goes to hell, I must go with him." I have heard people say this as their own experience in prayer. So Christ himself seems to have prayed for His dying people. He grasped the masses, saying, "I must save them or sink to hell with them." Paul said, "I could wish myself accursed from Christ for my brethren, my kinsmen in the flesh." So, often God waits and delays His answer to prayer till the petitioner becomes so united that in sympathy they cannot be separated. Moses said, "Save this people, or blot out my name from this book."

I have seen precisely this in many cases. The Holy Spirit gives them such sympathy with the person they pray for, and such a hold of God's promise in prayer, they cry out, "I cannot live unless God hear and save! How can I live and see this people die!" Now, God loves this spirit and often waits till it comes up. In the case of parents, God frequently waits till they take hold of the case of their children in this very way. I well remember the striking case of a father who was so agonized in prayer for his children he told them he could not live unless he could see the salvation of the Lord among them.

Why people do not pray more for others.

People refuse to pray more for others mainly because they are not benevolent, but selfish only. They are selfish in the little prayer they do pray.

Or, sometimes, they are skeptical and unbelieving, and for this reason they do not lay out their strength in prayer. Or, they are presumptuous and assume that somebody else will pray enough to answer all purposes. Or, they are too carnal to have any spirit of prayer, and do not care for the souls of the perishing. Even their tender mercies are cruel. They see sinners going to hell, but are too carnal to pray for them. They offer no earnest, no agonizing prayer.

Brethren, what is your state of mind with regard to various objects of prayer around you? How do you feel for the young people gathered in your church? Do you sympathize earnestly in prayer for the elder members of the church? What is your state of mind toward the impenitent? Are you praying in earnest for those who have for a long time remained impenitent among us? Do you feel deeply for the strangers who are coming among us? Will you allow me to ask you in all faithfulness, "Have you the spirit of prayer for others?" As a preacher, I think I can tell when one prays by the light I experience in my mind when I study my sermons, and by the effect my words produce on the minds of my hearers. Do you not know that when some are agonizing in prayer some sinners are correspondingly struggling under conviction? Just in proportion to the amount and power of struggling prayer will be the struggles of those who are smitten with arrows of convicting truth.

Some of you who once prayed with earnestness and power, I fear have lost the spirit, or have let it sorely languish. Let me ask you all, "Have you as much of the spirit of prayer as you once had? Do you feel bowed down with grief because God's work revives no more? Some of you can answer in the affirmative. But some of you cannot. Some of you must say in truth, there has been a great falling off in prayer and of interest for souls.

On one occasion as I was preaching on this subject, a man who was represented to be one of the most pious men in the church rose and said, "I am the man, Mr. Finney! You need not say another word! I am the Achan in this camp of Israel! You need not look any further for the Achan—I am he!" What he said seemed to have more effect than everything else in the meeting and was the commencement of a glorious revival.

To students, let me say, Are you aware how much you can do by praying for each other? Are you in the habit of meeting in little circles for this purpose? Are some of your classmates in their sins, and can you let them live and die so? Are you not in fault for their impenitence? Have you set your hearts so intensely upon the conversion of these souls that you cannot live unless they are converted?

And will you not all pray for your teachers and make their

hearts strong by your concerns and your prayers in their behalf? Cry unto God for them that they may be made mighty through God for the converting and saving of precious souls. Oh, if all the church were filled with the spirit of prayer, what rush we should see toward the kingdom of heaven, even this very moment! What is your practice during meetings of inquiry? You do, I hope, have such meetings. Are you instant in prayer then? It always alarms me in a church to find that few or none inquire about the state of these meetings with anxious sinners. It shows that the hearts of the people are not there. Brethren, do you pray for those who have set their faces inquiringly toward Zion?

14

ON PRAYER FOR THE HOLY SPIRIT*

"If a son shall ask bread of any of you that is a father, will he give him a stone? or if he ask a fish, will he for a fish give him a serpent? or if he shall ask an egg, will he offer him a scorpion? If ye then, being evil, know how to give good gifts unto your children: how much more shall your heavenly Father give the Holy Spirit to them that ask him?" (Luke 11:11–13).

In discussing prayer for the Holy Spirit, I intend to show:

► *That this gift is easily obtained.*
► *How to account for the impression of the Holy Spirit being difficult to obtain.*
► *How conditions of prayer reconcile these verses with current experience.*

That this gift is easily obtained.

These verses form the concluding part of a very remarkable discourse of our Lord to His disciples on prayer. It was introduced by their request that He would teach them how to pray. In answer to this request, He gave them what we call the Lord's Prayer, followed by a forcible illustration of the value of importunity, which He still further applied and enforced by renewing the general promise, "Ask, and it shall be given you." Then to confirm their faith still more, He expands the idea that God is their Father and should be approached in prayer as if

---

*Charles G. Finney, *Sermons on the Way of Salvation* (Oberlin: Edward J. Goodrich, 1891), pp. 429–446. Also *The Oberlin Evangelist,* May 23, 1855.

He were an infinitely kind and loving parent. This constitutes the leading idea in the strong appeal made in our text. "If a *son* shall ask bread of any of you that is a *father*, will he give him a stone? or if he ask a fish, will he for a fish give him a serpent? or if he shall ask an egg, will he give him a scorpion? If ye then, being evil, know how to give good gifts unto your *children:* how much more shall your heavenly *Father* give the Holy Spirit to them that ask him?"

Remarking upon this text, I first observe that, when we rightly understand the matter, we shall see that the gift of the Holy Spirit comprehends all we need spiritually. It secures to us that union with God which is eternal life. It implies conversion, which consists in the will's being submitted to God's control. Sanctification is (1) this union of the will to God perfected and perpetuated; (2) the ascendancy of this state of the will over the entire sensibilities, so that the whole mind is drawn into union and sympathy with the mind and heart of God.

It is supremely easy to obtain this gift from God. In other words, it is easy to obtain from God all spiritual blessings that we truly need. If this is not so, what shall we think of these words of Christ? How can we by any means explain them consistently with fair, truthful interpretation? Surely, it is easy for children to get very good things from their father. Which of you, being a father, does not know it to be easy for your children to get good things from you? You know in your own experience that they obtain without difficulty, even from you, all the real good they need, provided it be in your power to give it. But you are sometimes "evil" and Christ implies that, since God is never evil but always infinitely good, it is much easier for one to get the Holy Spirit than even for your children to get bread from your hands. *"Much more!"* Every father knows there is nothing in the way of his children getting from him all the good things they really need and which he has to give. Every such parent values these good things for the sake of giving them to his children. For this, parents toil and plan for their children's sake. Can they then be reluctant or even slow to give these things to their children?

Yet God is much more ready to give His Spirit. My language, therefore, is not at all too strong. If God is much more ready and willing to give His children good things than you are to give to yours, then surely it must be easy, and not difficult, to get spiritual blessings, even to the utmost extent of our wants.

Let this argument come home to the hearts of those of you

who are parents. Surely, you must feel its force. Christ must be a false teacher if this is not so. It must be that this great gift, which in itself comprehends all spiritual gifts, is most easily obtained and in any amount which our souls need.

How very injurious and dishonorable to God are the practical views of almost all people on this subject! The dependence of people on the Holy Spirit has come to be the standing apology for moral and spiritual delinquency. People everywhere profess to want the Holy Spirit, and more or less to feel their need and to be praying for this gift; but continually and everywhere they complain that they do not get it. These complaints assume, both directly and indirectly, that it is very difficult to get this gift; that God keeps His children on a very low diet, and on the smallest possible amount even of that; that He deals out their spiritual bread and water in most stinted amount as if He purposed to keep His children only an inch above starvation.

Visit among the churches and hear what they say and how they pray. What would you think? How you would be shocked at the strange, may I not say, *blasphemous* assumptions which they make concerning God's policy in giving, or rather *not* giving, the Holy Spirit to those who ask Him! I can speak from experience and personal observation.

When I began to attend prayer meetings, this fact to which I have alluded struck me as very strange. I had never attended a prayer meeting till I had come to manhood, for my situation in this respect was very unlike some others. But after I came to manhood, and prayer meetings were held in the place where I lived, I used to attend them very steadily. It was a matter of great interest to me, more than I can explain or well express. I was filled with wonder to hear Christians pray, and all the more as I then began to read my Bible and to find in it such things as we have in our text. To read such promises and then hear Christians talk was surprising. What they did say, coupled with what they seemed to mean, would run thus: "I have a duty to perform at this meeting. I cannot go away without doing it. I want to testify that religion is a good thing, a very good thing, although I don't have much of it. I believe God is a hearer of prayer, and yet I don't think He hears mine—certainly not to much effect. I believe that prayer brings to us the Holy Spirit, and yet, though I have always been praying for this Spirit, I have scarcely ever received it."

Such seemed to be the strain of their talking and thinking, and I must say that it puzzled me greatly. I have reason to know that it has often puzzled others. Within a few years past, I have found this to be the standing objection of unconverted men. They say, "I could never make it if I should be converted. It is so difficult to get and to keep the Holy Spirit." They appeal to professing Christians and say, "Look at them. They are not engaged in religion; they are not doing their Master's work in good earnest, and they confess it. They have not the Spirit, and they readily admit and confess it. They bear a living testimony that these promises are of very little practical value."

Now, these are plain matters of fact and should be deeply pondered by all professing Christians. The Christian life of multitudes is nothing less than a flat denial of the great truths of the Bible.

Often, when I am urging Christians to be filled with the Holy Spirit, I am asked, Do you really think this gift is for me? Do you think all can have it who want it? If you tell them of instances, here and there, of persons who walk in the light and are filled with the Spirit they reply, Are not those very special cases? Are they not the favored few, enjoying a blessing that only a few can hope to enjoy?

Here you should carefully observe, the question is not whether few or many have this blessing; but, is it practically within reach of all? Is it indeed available to all? Is the gift actually tendered to all in the fullest and highest sense? Is it easy to possess it? These being the real questions, we must see that the teachings of the text cannot be mistaken on this subject. Either Christ testified falsely of this matter, or this gift is available to all and is easily obtained. For, of the meaning and scope of His language there can be no doubt. No language can be plainer. No illustrations could be more clear, and none could easily be found that are stronger.

How to account for the impression of the Holy Spirit being difficult to obtain.

There is an impression extensively pervading the Church that the Holy Spirit can rarely be obtained in ample, satisfying fullness, and then only with the greatest difficulty. This impression obviously grows out of the current experience of the Church. In fact, only a few seem to have this conscious communion with God through the Spirit; but few seem really to walk with God and be filled with His Spirit.

When I say *few*, I mean few relative to the whole number

of professing Christians. Taken absolutely, the number is great and always has been. Sometimes, some have thought the number to be small, but they were mistaken.

Elijah thought himself alone, but God told him there were many—a host, spoken of as seven thousand—who had never bowed the knee to Baal. Ordinarily, such a use of the sacred number seven is to be taken for a large, indefinite sum, much larger than if taken definitely. It may be so here. Even then, in that exceedingly dark age, there were yet many who stood unflinchingly for God!

It is a curious fact that people who have really the most piety are often supposed to have the least, so few there are who judge piety as God does. Those who preach the real gospel are often refreshed to find some in almost every congregation who manifestly embrace it. You can judge by their very looks. Their eyes shine and their faces are all aglow—almost like the face of Moses when he descended from the mount.

But theirs is not the common experience of professing Christians. The common one, which has served to create the general impression as to the difficulty of obtaining the Holy Spirit, is indeed utterly unlike this. The great body of nominal Christians has not the Spirit, within the meaning of Romans 8. They cannot say, "The law of the Spirit of life in Christ Jesus hath made me free from the law of sin and death." It is not true of them that they "walk not after the flesh, but after the Spirit." Comparatively few of all know in their own conscious experience that they live and abide in the Spirit.

Here is another fact. Many are praying, apparently, for the Spirit of God but do not get Him. If you go to a prayer meeting, you hear everybody pray for this gift. It is so, also, in the family, and probably also in the closet. Yet, strange to tell, they do not get Him. This experience of much prayer for this blessing and much failure to attain it is common everywhere. Churches have their prayer meetings, years and years in succession, praying for the Spirit, but they do not get Him. In view of this fact, we must conclude, either that the promise is not reliable or that the prayer does not meet the conditions of the promise. I shall take up this alternative later. Just now, my business is to account for the prevalent impression that the Spirit of God is hard to obtain and keep, even in answer to prayer—a fact which obviously is accounted for by the current experience of nominal Christians.

It should also be said that the churches have been taught

that God is a sovereign, in such a sense that His gift of the Spirit is only occasional, and is then given without any connection with apparent causes—not dependent, by any means, on the fulfilment of conditions on our part. The common idea of sovereignty excludes the idea that God holds this blessing free to all, on condition of real prayer for it. I say *real* prayer, for I must show you very shortly that much of the apparent praying of the church for the Spirit is not real prayer. It is this spurious, selfish praying that leads to much misconception as to the bestowment of the Holy Spirit.

Some of you may remember that I have related to you my experience at one time, when my mind was greatly exercised on this promise; how I told the Lord I could not believe it. It was contrary to my conscious experience, and I could not believe anything which contradicted my conscious experience. At that time the Lord kindly and in great mercy rebuked my unbelief and showed me that the fault was altogether mine, and in no part His.

Multitudes pray for the Spirit as I had done, and are in a like manner disappointed because they do not receive Him. They are not conscious of being hypocrites, but they do not thoroughly know their own spirits. They think they are ready to make any sacrifices to obtain this gift. They do not seem to know that the difficulty is all with them. They fail to realize how rich and full the promise is. It all seems to them quite unaccountable that their prayer should not be answered. Often they sweat with agony of mind in their efforts to solve this mystery. They cannot bear to say that God's Word is false, and yet, they cannot see that it is true. It is apparently contradicted by their experience. This fact creates the agonizing perplexity.

How conditions of prayer reconcile these verses with current experience.

How can we reconcile this experience with Christ's truthfulness? How can we explain this experience according to the facts in the case, and yet show that Christ's teachings are to be taken in their obvious sense, and are strictly true?

I answer, What is here taught as to prayer must be taken in connection with what is taught elsewhere. For example, what is here said of asking must be taken in connection with what is said of praying in faith—with what is said by James in asking and not receiving because men ask amiss that they may consume it upon their lusts. If any of you were to frame a will or a promissory note, binding yourself or your administrators to pay over certain moneys, on certain specified conditions, you would not think it necessary to state the conditions more than once. Having stated them distinctly once, you would go on to state in detail the promise; but you would not expect anybody to separate the promise from the condition, and then claim the promise without having fulfilled the condition, and even perhaps accuse you of falsehood because you did not fulfill the promise when the conditions had not been met.

Now, the fact is that we find, scattered throughout the Bible, various revealed conditions of prayer. Whoever would pray acceptably must surely fulfill not merely a part, but *all* of these conditions. Yet in practice, the Church, to a great extent, has overlooked, or at least has failed to meet these conditions. For example, people often pray for the Holy Spirit for selfish reasons. This is fearfully common. The real motives are selfish. Yet they come before God and urge their request often and long, perhaps with great importunity; but they are selfish in their very prayers, and God will not hear them. They are not in their inmost souls ready to do or to suffer all God's holy will. God calls some of His children through long seasons of extremest suffering, obviously as a means of purifying their hearts; yet many pray for pure hearts, for the Spirit to purify their hearts, who would rebel at once if God should answer their prayers by means of such a course of providence. Or God may see it necessary to crucify your love of reputation, and for this end may subject you to a course of trial which will blow your reputation to the winds of heaven. Are you ready to accept the blessings of a subdued, unselfish heart, even though it is given by means of such discipline?

Often, your motive in asking for the Spirit is merely personal comfort and consolation, as if you would live all your spiritual life on sweetmeats. Others ask for the gift really as a matter of self-glorification. They would like to have their names emblazoned in the papers. It would be so gratifying to be held up as a miracle of grace, as a most remarkable Christian. Alas, how many, in various forms of it, are only offering selfish prayers! Even a minister might pray for the Holy Spirit from only sinister motives. He might wish to have it said that he is very spiritual, or a man of great spiritual power in his preaching or his praying; or he might wish to avoid that hard study to which a man who has not the Spirit must submit, since the Spirit does not teach him nor give him unction. He might almost wish to be inspired, so easy would this gift make his preaching and his study. He might suppose that he really longed to be filled with the Spirit, while really he is only asking amiss, to consume it on some unhallowed desire. A student may pray for the Spirit to help him study, and yet only his ambition or his indolence may have inspired that prayer.

Let it never be forgotten, we must agree with God's reasons for our having the Spirit if we would hope to pray acceptably. There is nothing mysterious about this matter. The great end of all God's spiritual administrations toward us in providence or grace is to divest us of selfishness and to bring our hearts into harmony with His in the spirit of real love.

People often quench the Spirit even while they are praying to receive Him. One prays for the Spirit, yet that very moment fails to notice the Spirit's admonitions in his own heart, or refuses to do what the Spirit would lead and press him to do. Perhaps they even pray for the Spirit, that this gift may be a substitute for some self-denying duty to which the Spirit has long been urging them. This is no uncommon experience. Such people will likely think it very difficult to obtain the Spirit. A woman was once going to a women's prayer meeting and thought she wanted the Holy Spirit, making that her special errand at that meeting. Yet when there, the Spirit pressed her to pray audibly and she resisted and excused herself.

It is common for people to resist the Spirit in the very steps He chooses to take. They would make the Spirit yield to *them*; He would have them yield to *Him*. They think only of having their blessings come according to their own choosing; He is wiser and will do it in His own way or not at all. If they cannot accept His way, there can be no agreement. Often when people pray for the Spirit, they have in their minds certain things which they would dictate to Him as to the manner and circumstances. Such ought to know that if they would have the Spirit, they must accept Him in His own way. Let Him lead, and consider that your business is to follow. Thus it not infrequently happens that professing Christians maintain a perpetual resistance against the Holy Spirit, even while they are ostensibly praying for His presence and power. When He would eagerly draw them, they are thinking of dictating to Him, and refuse to be led by Him in His way. When they come really to understand what is implied in being filled with the Spirit, they draw back. It is more and different from what they had thought. *That* is not what they wanted.

REMARKS

The difficulty is always, and completely, in us, not in God. You may write this down as a universal truth, from which there can be no exceptions. The difficulty lies in our voluntary state of mind, not in anything which is involuntary and beyond our control. There is no difficulty in our obtaining the Holy Spirit if we are willing to have it; but this implies a willingness to surrender ourselves to His direction and discretion.

We often mistake other states of mind for a willingness to have the Spirit of God. Nothing is more common than this. People think they are willing to be filled with the Spirit and to have the Spirit do all His own work in their soul, but they are really under a great mistake. To be willing to be wholly crucified to the world and the world unto us is by no means common. Many think they have a sort of desire for this state, who would really shrink from it if they saw the reality near at hand. That people do make continual mistakes thinking themselves willing to be fully controlled by the Spirit, when they are not, is evident from their lives. The will governs the life, and therefore, the life must be an infallible index of the real state of the will. As is the life, so is the will; therefore, when you see the life alien from God, you must infer that the will is not wholly consecrated to His service, is not wholly in agreement with God's will.

When the will is really on God's altar, entirely yielded up to God's will in all respects, one will not wait long before he has the Spirit of God in the fullest measure. Indeed, this very consecration itself implies a large measure of the Spirit, yet not the *largest* measure. The mind may not be conscious of the deep union with God into which it may enter. The knowledge of God is a consciousness of God in the soul. You may certainly know that God's Spirit is within you, and that His light illumines your mind. His presence becomes a conscious reality.

The manner in which spiritual agencies other than human manifest themselves in the mind of man seems to some very mysterious. It is not necessary that we should know *how* those agencies get access to our minds; it suffices us to know, beyond all question, that they do. Christians sometimes know that the devil brings his own thoughts into the very chambers of their souls. Some of you have been painfully conscious of this. You have been certain that the devil has poured out his spirit upon you. Most horrid suggestions are thrust upon your mind—such as your inmost soul abhors, and such as could come from no other, and certainly from *no better* source than the devil.

Now, if the devil can thus make us conscious of his presence and power, and can throw upon our souls his own horrid suggestions, may not the Spirit of God reveal His? In fact, if your heart is in agreement with His suggestions and admonitions, may He not do much more? Surely none can doubt that He can make His presence and agency a matter of positive consciousness. That we can be conscious of nothing but the operations of our own minds is a very imperfect and even false view of the case. People are often conscious of Satan's thoughts, as present to their minds—a fact which Bunyan well illustrated where he supposes Christian to be alarmed by someone whispering in his ear behind him, pouring horrid blasphemies into his mind.

Cases often occur like the following: A man came to me in great distress, saying, "I am no Christian, I know of a certainty. My mind has been filled with awful thoughts of God." I replied, "But were those awful thoughts *your own* thoughts, and did you cherish them and give your assent to them?" "No, indeed," he said, "nothing could have agonized me more." "That is the work of the devil," I stated. "Well," he said, "perhaps it is, and yet I had not thought of it so before."

So God's Spirit within us may become no less an object of our distinct consciousness. And if you do truly and earnestly wait on God, you shall be most abundantly supplied of His fullness.

To be filled with the Holy Spirit, so that He takes full possession of our souls, is what I mean by sanctification. This glorious work is wrought by the Spirit of God; and that Spirit never can take full and entire possession of our hearts without accomplishing this blessed work.

It is no wonder some people deny the existence of any such state as sanctification. They do not know anything of being filled with the Holy Spirit. Ignoring His glorious way of working, we need not wonder that they have no knowledge of His work in the soul.

Often the great difficulty in the way of Christian progress is an utter lack of watchfulness. Some are so given to talking that they cannot hold communion with the Spirit of God. They have no leisure to listen to His "still small voice." Some are so fond of laughter, it seems impossible that their minds should ever be in a really serious frame. In such a mind, how can the Spirit of God dwell?

Often in our theological discussions, I am pained to see how difficult it is for people engaged in dispute and mutual discussion to avoid being chafed. Some of them are watchful and prayerful against this temptation, while others manifestly fall. If Christians do not shut down the gate against all abuse of the tongue, and, indeed, against every form of selfishness, there is no hope that they will resist the devil and the world as far as to be conquerors at last.

The Spirit of God troubles or comforts us, according as we resist or receive His great gift. The purpose of the gospel scheme was to accomplish this complete union and agreement between our souls and God, so that the soul could enjoy God's own peace and be in the utmost harmony with its Maker and Father. Hence, it is the great business of the Spirit to bring about this state. If we concur and if our will harmonizes with His efforts, He comforts us. If we resist, He troubles us; a struggle ensues. If, in this struggle, we come to understand God, and submit, then His blessings come freely and our peace is as a river; but so long as we resist, there can be no fruit of the Spirit's labor to us—only rebuke and trouble. To us He cannot then be the author of peace and comfort.

How abominable to God it must be for the Church to take a position in regard to the Spirit, which practically denies the truth of this great promise in our text! How dreadful that believers should hold and teach that it is a hard thing to be Christians! What abominable unbelief! How forcibly does the Church thus testify *against* God before the world! You might as well burn your Bible as deny that it is the easiest thing in the world to obtain the gift of the Holy Spirit. And yet, strange to tell, some hold that God is so sovereign, and is sovereign in such a sense, that few can obtain the Spirit at all—only those few to whom it may *happen,* and not by any means as the result of provision freely made and promise reliably revealed, on which any man's faith may take hold. Oh, how this notion of sovereignty contradicts the Bible! How long shall it be this way among professing Christians?

Do you, young people, really believe that your young hearts may be filled with the Spirit? Do you really believe, as our text says, that God is more willing to give His Spirit to those who ask Him than your own father or mother would be to give you good things? Many of you are in college far from your parents. But you know that even your widowed mother, much as she may need every cent of her means for herself, would gladly share the last one with you if you needed it. So would your earthly father. Do you really believe that God is as willing as they—as ready—as loving? Indeed, is He not *much more so,* as much more as He is better than your father and mother? And now, do you really need and desire this gift of the Spirit? If you do, will you ask for it in full confidence that you have a real *Father* in heaven?

Do you find practical difficulties? Do you realize how much you dishonor God if you refuse to believe His Word of promise? Some of you say, "I am so poor and so much in debt, I must go away and work somewhere and get money." But you have a father who has money enough. "Yes, but he will not help me. He loves his money more than he loves his son." Would not this be a great scandal to your father, a living disgrace to him? Surely it would. And you would be so keenly aware of this that you would not say it if it were not very true, then unless some very strong circumstances seemed to require of you the painful testimony. If your mother, being amply able, yet would not help you in your education or in your sickness, you would hardly tell of it—so greatly would it discredit her character.

And now will you have the face to say, "God doesn't love me. He doesn't want to educate me for heaven. He utterly refuses to give me the Holy Spirit, although I often ask Him and beseech Him to do so?" Will you even *think* this? And can you go even further and act it out before all the world? Oh, why should you thus dishonor your own God and Father!

15

ON PRAYING ALWAYS*

"He spake a parable unto them to this end, that men ought always to pray, and not to faint" (Luke 18:1).

In discussing the subject of prayer, presented in our text, I propose to inquire:

▶ *Why people should pray at all.*
▶ *Why people should pray always and not faint.*
▶ *Why people do not pray always.*

Why people should pray at all.

Our dependence on God is universal, extending to all things. This fact is known and acknowledged. None but atheists presume to call it in question.

Prayer is the dictate of our nature. By the voice of nature this duty is revealed as plainly as possible. We feel the pressure of our needs, and our instincts cry out to a higher power for relief in their supply. You may see this in the case of the most wicked people, as well as in the case of good people. The wicked, when in distress, cry out to God for help. Indeed, mankind has given evidence of this in all ages and in every nation, showing both the universal necessity of prayer and that it is a dictate of our nature to look up to a God above.

It is a primitive conviction of our minds that God does hear and answer prayer. If people did not assume this to be the case,

---

*Charles G. Finney, *Sermons on the Way of Salvation* (Oberlin: Edward J. Goodrich, 1891), pp. 413–428. Also *The Oberlin Evangelist*, January 3, 1855.

they wouldn't pray. The fact that people do spontaneously pray shows they really expect God to hear prayer. It is contrary to all our original belief to assume that events occur under some law of perpetual continuity, as a chain too rigid for the Almighty to break, and which He never attempts to adjust according to His will. People do not naturally believe any such thing as this.

The objection to prayer that God is unchangeable, and therefore cannot turn aside to hear prayer, is altogether a fallacy and the result of ignorance. Consider what is true about God's unchangeableness. Surely, it is not that His course of conduct never changes to meet circumstances; but it is this—that His *character* never changes; that His nature and the principles which control His voluntary action remain eternally the same. All His natural and moral attributes remain forever unchanged. This is all that can rationally be implied in God's immutability.

How, His hearing and answering prayer imply no change of character, no change in His principles of action. Indeed, if you ask why He ever answers prayer at all, the answer must be, *because He is unchangeable.* Prayer brings the petitioner into a new relationship to God's kingdom; and to meet this new relationship, God's unchangeable principles require Him to change the course of His administration. He answers prayer because He is unchangeably benevolent. It is not because His benevolence changes, but because it does *not* change that He answers prayer.

Who can suppose that God's answering prayer implies any change in His moral character? For example, if a person in prayer repents, God forgives. If He does not repent of present sin, God does not forgive. And who does not see that God's immutability must require this course at His hands? Suppose God did not change His conduct when men change their character and their attitude toward Him. This would imply fickleness, an utter absence of fixed principles. His unchangeable goodness must therefore imply that when His creatures change morally, He changes His course and conforms to their new position. Any other view of the case is simply absurd, and only the result of ignorance. Strange that people should hold it to be inconsistent for God to change, and to give rain in answer to prayer, or give any needed spiritual blessings to those who ask them!

Communication with God is a necessity of moral beings, a necessity of their natures. No doubt this is true in heaven itself, and the fact that this need of their natures is so gloriously supplied there makes it heaven. The Bible represents spirits in heaven as praying. We hear them crying out, "How long, O Lord, holy and true, dost thou not judge and avenge our blood on them that dwell on the earth?" (Revelation 6:10). True, their subjects of prayer are not in all respects the same as ours. We have things to pray for which they have no occasion to ask for themselves. They are neither sick nor sinful, but can you suppose they never pray "Thy kingdom come"? Have they lost all sympathy with those interests in Zion? Far from it! Knowing more of the value of those interests, they no doubt feel more deeply their importance and pray more earnestly for their promotion.

From the nature of the case, God's treatment of the inhabitants of heaven must be conditioned on their voluntary course with regard to Him and His kingdom. It must be governed and determined by their knowledge, their progress in knowledge, and their improvement of the means and powers at their command. Obviously, their voluntary worship, gratitude, thanksgiving, and service of every sort, must vary their relationships to God; and consequently, His course toward them. He will do many things to them and for them which He could not do if they did not pray, and praise, and love, and study, and labor.

This must be true, even in heaven, of apostles and prophets, and of all glorified saints. God makes to them successive revelations of himself, each successively higher than the preceding, and all dependent on their voluntary devotion to Him and to His glory. They are forever advancing in His service, full of worship, praise, adoration, and this only prepares them the more to be sent on missions of love and service, and to be employed as the interests of God's kingdom require. Hence, we see that God's conduct toward saints in heaven depends on their own voluntary course and bearing toward Him.

This is a necessity of any and every moral system. If saints in heaven are moral agents, and God's government over them is also moral, all these results must follow. In this world, sin exists; and in this fact we see an obvious necessity for this law of moral administration. But the holy in heaven are no less moral and responsible than the sinning on earth. The great object of God's administration is to assimilate moral beings to himself; hence, He must make His treatment of them depend on their moral course toward Him.

With regard to saints on earth, how can God do them any

good unless He can draw them to himself in prayer and praise? This is one of the most evident necessities that can be named. People irresistibly feel the propriety of confession and supplication in order to have forgiveness. This feeling lies among the primitive affirmations of the mind. People know that if they would be healed of sin, they must seek and find God.

Why people should pray always and not faint.

The case presented in the context is very strong. Whether it is history or parable does not affect the merits of the case to illustrate importunity in prayer. The poor widow persevered. She kept coming and would not be discouraged. By perseverence simply, she succeeded. The judge who cared not for God or man did care somewhat for his own comfort and quiet, and therefore thought it wise to listen to her story and grant her request. Upon this case our Lord seized to enforce and encourage importunity in prayer. Hear His argument. "Shall not God"—who is by no means unjust, but whose compassions are great and deep—"shall not such a God avenge his own elect, who cry day and night unto him, though he seem to bear long" in delaying to answer their prayers? "I tell you he will avenge them speedily."

People ought to pray always because they always need the influence of prayer. Consider what is implied in prayer and what prayer does for you. Prayer bathes the soul in an atmosphere of the divine presence. Prayer communes with God and brings the whole mind under the hallowed influence of such communion. Prayer goes to God to seek pardon and find mercy and grace to help. How obvious, then, that we always need its influence on our hearts and lives! Truly, we need not wonder that God should enjoin it upon us to pray always.

God needs prayer from us as a condition of His doing for us all that He would. He loves us, and sees a thousand blessings that we need, that He would delight to bestow. Yet, he cannot bestow them except on condition that we ask for them in Jesus' name. His treatment of us and His bestowment of blessings upon us must depend upon our views and conduct: whether we feel our dependence on Him, whether we confess and forsake all sin, whether we trust Him and thoroughly honor Him in all things. His action toward us must depend upon our attitude toward Him.

It is essential in the management of a moral system that

we should pray and trust in order that He may freely and abundantly give, and especially that He may give in a way safe to us and honorable to himself. Nothing can be substituted for our own praying, either in its relation to God or to ourselves. We cannot get along without the personal benefit of prayer, confession, trust, and praise. You cannot substitute instruction, ever so much or so good. For these things must enter into the soul's *experience*. You must feel them before God and carry out the life and power of these truths in your very heart before the Lord; else they are worse than unknown to you. You are not likely to understand many of these things without prayer. And even if you were to understand them, and yet not pray, the knowledge would only be a curse to you.

What can be so useful to us, sinners, as direct communion with God: the searching of the heart which it induces, the humility, the confessions, the supplications? Other things have their use. Instruction is good. Reading God's Word may be a blessing. Communion with the saints is pleasant. But what are they all compared with personal communication with God? Nothing else can make the soul so sick of sin and so dead to the world. Nothing else breathes such spiritual life into the soul as real prayer.

Prayer also prepares us the better to receive all blessings from God, and hence should be constant.

Prayer pleases God as Governor of the universe, because it puts us in a position in which He can bless us and gratify His own benevolence.

Search the history of the world, and you will find that where there has been most true prayer, and the soul has been most deeply imbued with the divine presence, there God has most abundantly and richly blessed the soul. Who does not know that holy men of old were eminent for usefulness and power according as they were faithful and mighty in prayer?

The more we pray, the more we shall be enlightened; for surely they are most enlightened who pray most. If we go no further in divine things than human reason can carry us, we get little indeed from God.

The more we pray, the more we will love prayer, and the more we will enjoy God. On the other hand, the more we pray—in real prayer—the more God will delight in us. Observe what I say—*delight*; the more God will truly delight in us. This is not merely the love of benevolence, for God is benevolent to all; but He delights in His praying children in the sense of having deep satisfaction or complacency in their character. The Bible often speaks of the great interest which God takes in those who live near Him in much prayer. This is naturally and necessarily the case. Why should not God delight in those who delight in Him?

The more we pray, the more God loves to manifest to others that He delights in us and hears our prayers. If His children live lives of much prayer, God delights to honor them as an encouragement to others to pray. They come into a position in which He can bless them and can make His blessings on them result in good to others—thus doubly gratifying the benevolence of His heart.

We can never reach a position in which we shall not need prayer. Who believes that saints in heaven will have no need for prayer? True, they will have perfect faith, but this, so far from precluding prayer, only the more ensures it. People have strangely assumed that if there were only perfect faith, prayer would cease. Nothing can be more false and groundless. Certainly, then, we can never get beyond prayer.

If I had time I should like to show how the manner of prayer varies as Christians advance in holiness. They pray not less, but more, and they know better *how* to pray. When the natural life is mingled largely with the spiritual, there is an outward effervescing which passes away as the soul comes nearer to God. You would suppose there is less excitement, and there *is* less of animal excitement; but the deep fountains of the soul flow in unbroken sympathy with God.

We can never get beyond the point where prayer is greatly useful to us. The more the heart breathes after God, and rises toward Him in heavenly aspirations, the more useful do such exercises become. The aged Christian finds himself more and more benefited in prayer as he draws more and more near to God. The more he prays, the more he sees the wisdom and necessity of prayer for his own spiritual good.

The very fact that prayer is so great a privilege to sinners makes it more honorable to God to hear prayer. Some think it disgraceful to God. What a sentiment! It assumes that God's real greatness consists in His being so high above us as to have no regard for us whatever. Not so with God. He regards both the flight of an archangel and the fall of a sparrow. Before His eye no possible event is too minute for His attention—no insect too small for His notice and His love. His infinite glory is manifest in this very fact, that nothing is too lofty or too low for His regard. None are too insignificant to miss sympathy—none too low to share His kindness.

Many talk of prayer as only a duty, not a privilege; but with this view of it, they cannot pray acceptably. When your children, full of wants, come running to you in prayer, do they come because it is a duty? They come because it is their privilege. They regard it as their privilege. Other children do not feel this way toward you. And it is a wonderful privilege! Who does not know it and feel it to be so? Shall we then ever fail to avail ourselves of it?

Finally, we are sure to prevail if we thoroughly persevere, and pray always, and do not faint. Let this suffice to induce perseverance in prayer. Do you need blessings? And are they delayed? Pray always and never faint, so you shall obtain all you need.

Why people do not pray always.

In the case of some, the enmity of their hearts toward God is such that they are shy and dread prayer. They have so strong a dislike for God, they cannot make up their minds to come near to Him in prayer.

Some are self-righteous and self-ignorant, and therefore have no heart to pray. Their self-righteousness makes them feel strong enough without prayer, and self-ignorance prevents their feeling their own real needs.

Unbelief keeps others from constant prayer. They don't have enough confidence in God, that He is ready to answer prayer. Of course, with such unbelief in their hearts, they will not pray always.

Inconsistent reasoning and sophistry prevent others. I have alluded to some of its forms. They say, God, being immutable, never changes His course; or they urge that there is no need of prayer, inasmuch as God will surely do just right even if nobody prays. There are acclaimed *little* sophistries, the kind ignorant minds dream up and stumble over. It is amazing that any minds can be so ignorant and so unthinking as to be influenced by these untrue ideas.

Many years ago, these objections to prayer came up before my mind, but were instantly answered and set aside, because they seemed so absurd. For instance, that God had framed the universe so wisely that there is no *need* of prayer, and indeed, no *room* for it. My answer was ready. What was God's object in making and arranging His universe? Was it to show himself to be a good *mechanic*, so skillful that He can make a universe to run itself without His constant agency? Was *this* His object? No! His object was to plant in this universe intelligent minds and then reveal himself to them, drawing them to love and trust their own infinite Father. This object is every way noble and worthy of a God. But the other notion is horrible! It takes from God every endearing attribute, and leaves Him only a *good mechanic*.

The idea that God is personally involved continually in human affairs prevails everywhere among all minds in all ages. Everywhere they have seen God revealing himself. They expect such revelations of God. They have believed in them, and have seen how essential this fact is to that confidence and love which belong to a moral government.

On one occasion when the weather had been very wet and became suddenly very dry, the question arose, How can you defend the providence of God? At first the question stung me; I stopped, considered it a few moments and then asked, What can His object be in giving us weather at all? Why does He send and not send rain? If His object is to raise as many potatoes as possible, then our weather has not been the wisest course. But if His object is to make us feel our dependence, this is the wisest course possible. What if God were to raise harvests enough in one year to supply us for the next ten? We might all become atheists. We should be very likely to think we could live without God. But now, every day and every year, He shuts us up to depend on Him. Who does not see that a moral government ordered on any other system would work ruin?

Another reason for not praying much is, people have no real sense of sin or of any spiritual lack; no consciousness of guilt. While in this state of mind, it need not be expected that they will pray.

In the other extreme, after becoming deeply convicted of sin, they fall into despair and think it does no good to pray.

Another reason for not praying much is found in self-righteous conceptions of what is requisite to success in prayer. One says, I am too degraded and not good enough to pray. This objection is founded altogether in self-righteous notions, assuming that your own goodness must be the ground or reason for God's hearing your prayer.

A reason why many pray so little is their worldly-mindedness. Their minds are so filled with thoughts of a worldly nature that they cannot get into the spirit of prayer.

Again, in the case of some, their own experience discourages them. They have often prayed, yet with little success. This brings them into a skeptical attitude in regard to prayer. Very likely the real reason of their failure has been the lack of perseverance. They have not obeyed the precept that urges men to pray always and never faint.

REMARKS

It is no loss of time to pray. Many think it chiefly or wholly lost time. They are so full of business, they say, and assume that prayer will spoil their business. I tell you, that your business, if it is the sort that ought to be done at all, will go all the better because of much prayer. Rise from your bed a little earlier and pray. Get time somehow—by almost any imaginable sacrifice, sooner than forego prayer. Are you studying? It is no loss of time to pray, as I know very well by my own experience. If I am to preach, with only two hours for preparation, I give one hour to prayer. If I were to study anything—let it be Virgil or geometry—I would by all means pray first. Prayer enlarges and illumines the mind. It is like coming into the presence of a master. You know how sometimes this electrifies the mind, and fires it with boundless enthusiasm. So, and much the more, does real access to God.

Let a physician pray a great deal; he needs counsel from God. Let the mechanic and the merchant pray much; they will testify, after trial of it, that God gives them counsel, and that, consequently, they lose nothing and gain much by constant prayer.

None but an eminently praying man is a safe religious teacher. However scientific and literary, if he is not a praying man, he *cannot* be trusted.

A spirit of prayer is of much greater value than human learning without it. If I were to choose, I would prefer conversation with God in prayer before the intellect of Gabriel. I do not say this to disparage the value of learning and knowledge, for when great talents and learning are sanctified with much prayer, the result is a mind of mighty power.

Those who do not pray cannot understand the facts in regard to answers to prayer. What can they know? Those things seem to them utterly incredible. They have no such experience. In fact, all their experiences go in the opposite direction. State a case to them; they look incredulous. Perhaps they will say, "You seem to think you can prophesy and foreknow events!" Let them be answered that "the secret of the Lord is with them that fear him."

Those who keep up a living conversation with God know many things they do not tell, and had better not tell. When I was a young convert, I knew an aged lady whose piety and prayer seemed to me quite extraordinary. You did not feel like talking much in her presence; there was something in it that struck you as remarkable. The subject of sanctification came into discussion, and meeting me on one occasion, she said, "Charles, take care what you do! Don't do things to be sorry for afterward." A son of hers became a Christian and was astonished at the manifestations of his mother's piety. She had prayer for him long and most earnestly. When, at length, his eyes were opened, she began to say, "I did not tell anybody my experiences, but, in fact, I have known nothing about condemnation for thirty years past. In all this time I am not aware that I have committed a known sin. My soul has enjoyed uninterrupted communion with God, and constant access to His mercy seat in prayer."

Prayer is the great secret of ministerial success. Some think this secret lies in talent or in tact; but it is not so. A man may know all human knowledge, but without prayer, what can he do? He cannot move and control men's hearts. He can do nothing to purpose unless he lives in agreement and open-faced communion with God. Only so can he be mighty through God to win souls to Christ. Here let me not be understood to depreciate learning and the knowledge of God. By no means. But prayer and its power are much greater and more effective. Herein lies the great mistake of theological seminaries and of gospel ministers. They lay excessive stress on learning, and genius, and talents; they fail to appreciate duly the paramount importance of much prayer. How much better for them to lay the principal stress on bathing the soul in God's presence! Let them rely, first of all, on God, who worketh mightily in His praying servants through His Spirit given them; and, as to resources, let them estimate above all other means, prayer— prayer that is abundant, devout, earnest, and full of living faith. Such a course would be an effectual correction of one of the most prevalent and perilous mistakes of the age.

16

THE USE AND PREVALENCE OF CHRIST'S NAME*

"Hitherto have ye asked nothing in my name: ask, and ye shall receive, that your joy may be full" (John 16:24).

In covering the "Conditions of Prevailing Prayer," I briefly mentioned that prayer should be made in the name of Jesus Christ. In speaking further on this subject, I shall endeavor to show:

► *What is implied in an acceptable offering of prayer in the name of Christ.*
► *The state of mind that can acceptably use Christ's name in prayer is indispensable to prevailing with God.*
► *The reasons for which we are required to pray in Christ's name.*

What is implied in an acceptable offering of prayer in the name of Christ.

There is some good reason, doubtless, for our being required to pray in Christ's name. In this case, our Lord was addressing His disciples. While He lived, it was natural that they should not clearly understand their exact position with regard to God, in such a sense as to fully comprehend the reason for using Christ's name in prayer. We must endeavor to ascertain our

*The Penny Pulpit, No. 1,562, May 24, 1850, delivered at the Tabernacle, Moorfields. Last in the series of three lectures on the "Conditions of Prevailing Prayer": chapters 10, 11, and 16 in this book.

209

real relationship to the government of God. We are outlaws, criminals, under condemnation. True Christians are not outlaws and criminals in such a sense as to be under condemnation; still, they never come into such a relationship with God as to be accepted in their *own* name. In their acceptance with God, they must remember always their relationship to God through Christ and their position in His government.

When people are under sentence for any capital offense, they are regarded as outlaws. The government, as such, does not even recognize their existence while they occupy such a position in relation to it. Being outlawed, they are civilly dead; that is, the government regards them as dead and so far as it is concerned, to all intents and purposes, they are not legally in existence. The government has no communication with them, knows nothing of them; they are treated as if they were not.

This is the true governmental position, and precisely under God's government the position in which the sinner stands when viewed as a sinner and separate from Christ. They are criminals, and He as head of the universe knows nothing of them, only as being cast out and condemned to die, outlawed.

But, even when people come to be Christians, they do not come into such a relationship to God as to have no more need of coming to Him through Jesus. An unconverted person stands condemned. He is under sentence of eternal death. Suppose a person is convinced of sin, convicted by his own conscience as well as by the law of God; the sentence is gone out against him. How is such an individual to appear in God's presence? Why, he cannot have even access to God! How can an individual, who has been sent to prison under sentence for a capital crime, have any connection with the government of his country? He is governmentally dead. And it behooves the government to treat him as such. While in such a position, he can have no relationship to government but as a dead man.

Yet the head of the government may have no ill will or wrong feeling toward him. He might even be disposed to treat him with great affection and regard him as a living man. This he might do in his individual capacity, but as the head of a government, he has necessarily a public as well as a private character to sustain, and this he must not overlook. He must not act as a mere private individual; public reasons forbid him to do so; and whatever his private relationships and feelings may be, he must remember his public relationships and character for the sake of the public good.

Now, let us look at such an individual as he stands before God and is subject to His laws and government. Such is the sacredness of the governmental character and relationships of the sovereign, that when the law has pronounced sentence against him, there are laws which place the ruler and the ruled in certain relationships to each other. The ruler cannot justly overlook these relationships. Now, when the law has once pronounced sentence against an individual, it has committed the public character of the lawgiver against him. And for the government by any public act to go against this is to depart from its principles and to take up arms against the law.

This is so in human governments, and if so in human governments, are not the reasons infinitely stronger in God's government for maintaining His public character? God must be careful that He gives no opportunity for any individual to draw a false inference as to His position. Once convicted, the sinner comes before God. What can he do? He is governmentally dead. The whole human race stands in that position before God, condemned criminals, outlaws, under the sentence of death. God's public character and relationships are such that He cannot so much as have the least communication, nor let them so much as to take His name on their lips without offense; He can regard them only as criminals. If He acts contrary to this, He forfeits the confidence of the universe. It is His public character and relationship that render it necessary, that if sinners are to approach Him, *there must be a mediator.*

Sinners must not come in their own names, for if they do He will not know, hear, or look at them. They must be so united to Christ that Christ may be virtually the petitioner, that from a governmental point of view it is Christ who approaches God. Unless you come to Him through Christ, and virtually as Christ, in Christ's very Spirit, unless you can do this, God will not so much as look at you or allow you to approach His presence.

The sinner, when he comes to God, must approach Him in this way. He must put on Christ, appropriating to himself all that Christ has done, taking to himself the very work of Christ. He must come in the person and name of Christ, with Christ's Spirit; then the request he makes will virtually be Christ's own Spirit making intercession. The sinner is in Christ, and governmentally united with Him. The greatest sinner in the world, as well as the least, may come in this way. Only let them do this, and they will be accepted as really as Christ is accepted, *because* Christ is accepted. He lives in Christ and is governmentally regarded as being found in Christ. If he comes repenting, believing, putting on the Lord Jesus Christ, he is as really, freely, and fully accepted as Christ himself; for now he is come into a state of mind in which he really comes in Christ's name. He now comes to be found in Christ, and governmentally he is known only as a part of Christ, one of Christ's family, a member of Christ's own body, a part of Christ himself. In this capacity he is known in the government of God.

May Christ now be laid aside? By no means. Unless you abide in the same state of mind, in the possession of the same proportion of Christ, you are cast out. The Bible everywhere teaches us this. Nor will it ever be otherwise to all eternity, since he will be found in Christ and accepted only on His account. This governmental relationship will always exist; and the relationship of His saints to Christ will be the sole and only reason they are received into heaven. What Christ has done will not save anyone who is *out of* Him. There is no dropping Christ's name, His interposition, and our relationship to Him when we approach God.

This leads me, in the next place, to remark that the use of Christ's name implies that we recognize our relationship to God as sinners, truly abhorring ourselves and repenting. We must truly and fully concede to God the entire justice and propriety of His treating us as rebels and refusing so much as to look at us unless we come to Him through Christ.

The use of His name acceptably also implies a state of mind which can and does receive these truths into the inmost hearts. For unless we really renounce and abhor our own righteousness, and wholly give up all expectations of approaching God and prevailing in our own name, and come to God in Christ's name alone, we can never prevail with Him.

Some say, "Why come in Christ's name more than in the name of Paul or of Moses?" What idea can a Unitarian have of Christ's name, when he denies His divinity and sacrifice? The Unitarian cannot understand this. He professes great love to God, and to worship "his heavenly Father," and so forth. I have heard much of this, but what shall I call such slang except slang? I have heard them say they are "fond of God, and God is fond of them," but they have nothing beyond a type of sentimentalism, very far from a recognition of their relationship to the Creator. This governmental relationship must be ever kept in view. It must be an ever-present consideration, and in such a degree as always to influence us in our approach to God.

There are thoughts which take possession of the mind, and are always there and have their influence, though we may not at all times be conscious of it. For example, people who have children: this fact always acts upon them; hours may glide away and their children remain unthought of. Yet, the fact that they *have* children is an influence always acting upon them. When people approach God, they must have not only an idea that they sustain certain relationships to Christ; but in order to approach Him acceptably, there should be a vivid recollection of this. When the name of Christ is used, they should know well why they use it. The idea of their governmental relationship and character without Christ must have its due weight with them. Do not, for a moment, once think of coming without Christ.

But again, to use this name acceptably implies a *realizing sense of our character and relationships, and of His character and relationships;* God's character and governmental position and our character and governmental position. Now, unless the mind realizes what it ought to mean in using Christ's name, it does not do so acceptably. We are to understand why we use Christ's name. Praying in His name implies the most implicit confidence in His influence at His Father's court, an entire confidence that in coming to God in His name we shall really obtain what we ask in His name.

When people really and truly use the name of Christ, there is a very important sense in which they *pray for Christ.* I do not mean by praying for Him that Christ *needs* to be prayed for as a sinner, as one who needs forgiveness, or any favor from God *for himself.* I mean that the Church is Christ's, God having given the world to Him in such a sense that every favor bestowed on them is regarded, governmentally, as bestowed on Him. The saints are Christ's servants. This is Christ's world in such a sense that when the government of God grants anything to the inhabitants thereof, it yields it to Christ. Prayer has been made for Him, it is said, continually.

The state of mind that can acceptably use Christ's name in prayer is indispensable to prevailing with God.

To pray in His name, we must ask the thing not for ourselves, because we are not our own. We do not own ourselves; and of course therefore, we can own nothing else. The fact is we are Christ's, and when we seek anything in Christ's name, we seek it for Him. We are Christ's servants; and as children, we belong to Christ. If we want anything for ourselves, separate from Christ, to glorify ourselves, we cannot have it. But if we want it for His sake, because we belong to Him, and ask it as something to be given to us only *because* we belong to Him, then we can have it.

Suppose, for example, we pray for anything whatever, and ask it merely for ourselves alone, we ask it selfishly "that we may consume it upon our lusts." We have no right to come and plead Christ's name to obtain things for ourselves as not belonging to Him. We are not authorized to use His name in any such sense as that. We are not authorized to make use of His name to get things merely to please ourselves as distinct from pleasing Him. Many regard the Gospel and Christ's name in such a light as if they might use Christ's name as a mere speculation for their own selfish purposes. But Christ has never given permission for any such use of it. The fact is, we must ask for things, recognizing that they are His and that whatever we ask for, even our daily bread, is to be used for Him. The very air we breathe is to be inhaled for Him. The clothing we wear is to be worn for Him; and unless we recognize this practically, unless we really come to regard ourselves as asking for things for Christ's sake, we cannot expect an answer to prayer.

What is meant by the phrase *"for Christ's sake"*? Do you mean for *your* sake, in Christ's name? Do you not know that, as I have said, you belong to Christ and have no right to approach God except in Christ's name? If, however, you overlook this fact, or think it only a speculation, no wonder you don't prevail. You have no right, as I have said, to pray at all unless you pray as for Christ, recognizing that all you are and have are His. If you want the Spirit of God that you may use the grace received for Him, you may have it. But you must have a single eye to His glory. If you do not so regard it, if you ask for yourselves, as distinct from Him, you cannot have it.

We must remember, too, that for God to give anything to the inhabitants of this world, as such, without Christ, would be inconsistent with His position. God promises things to Christ, who distributes them to His children. All the promises are in Christ to the glory of God, and we must recognize this if we would use Christ's name rightly and expect the fulfillment of the promises made through Him. These promises are all yea and amen in Christ Jesus. God is infinitely sincere in giving them to Christ, who receives them and gives them to people. They are given in the utmost good faith, so that coming in His name it is, "Yes, yes, as often as you please; if you really come in Christ's name, you may approach Me with the utmost confidence and boldness—not *impudence*, but boldness." We are infinitely welcome. There need be no hesitation. You are thoroughly welcome to as much as you want, only be sure you come meaning what you ought to in the use of Christ's name.

We should also recognize the fact in the use of Christ's name that *there is so good a reason for this use of it that for God to promise us anything in any other way, or encourage us to approach Him in any other way, would be to forfeit His governmental position.* The true idea of faith in Christ is a heart-recognition of the fact that, apart from and out of Christ, God is to us necessarily "a consuming fire." But in Christ, we are as safe and as welcome as Christ himself. We may come to His house, to His mercy seat, yes, to His very feet with every possible freedom. It is impossible that the angels themselves should be more welcome. We may rise, as it were, above the angels, and approach even nearer to God, perhaps, than they are allowed to do. If we only clothe ourselves with Christ as with a garment, renouncing and abhorring self, there is no language that can express the fullness and the freedom with which we can approach Him, and receive as largely as we can ask or think—in fact, exceeding abundantly above all that we can ask or think.

To use Christ's name acceptably also implies that you do it *in faith*. By faith you must rely implicitly on Christ, trusting in Him as your wisdom, sanctification, and redemption, expecting that He will accept you as freely and as fully as He has promised. The truth is that really to accept Christ implies a great deal more than is often supposed. I have been struck with the extent to which Christ is lost sight of in many of His relationships, and has come to be viewed simply as a Savior for whose sake our sins are forgiven—losing sight of sanctification and justification.* "What!" said a doctor of divinity to me a few years ago; "What! Christ, the second person in the Trinity, our sanctification? I never heard of such a thing!" Well now, I cannot tell you how shocked I felt. Never heard the apostle say, "Who,

---

*See especially, Charles G. Finney, *Principles of Union With Christ* (Minneapolis: Bethany House Publishers, 1985), *Principles of Holiness* (Minneapolis: Bethany House Publishers, 1984), and *Principles of Sanctification* (Minneapolis: Bethany House Publishers, 1986).

of God, is made unto us wisdom, and righteousness, and sanctification, and redemption"? It was as much one as the other. No one understands what it is to put on Christ thoroughly, properly, until he has learned something more than that he maintains to Him merely one relationship.

Lastly, it implies *really and universally depending upon Him*. People are dependent upon Him, but there is a difference between being really dependent and depending. Every sinner in the world is really dependent upon Him, but every sinner does not really depend upon Him in the sense of depending upon His name. We must come to depend not upon our prayers, states of mind, feelings—not upon anything we have done, or ever expect to do at all—but we must depend on Him really understanding that such is our relationship to God that we can never expect to be accepted unless we are found in Him, that we must put on Christ even to approach God.

The reasons for which we are required to pray in Christ's name.

Our relationships to God's government, when viewed out of relationship with Christ, are really those of sinners under sentence for a capital crime, "condemned already," governmentally regarded as dead. There are two senses in which sinners are represented in the Bible: "dead in trespasses and sins," that is, unconverted persons; and secondly, they are civilly dead—viewed governmentally, they are outlaws under sentence of death. These are acts which no one can dispute. If a man is a sinner, the law of God has condemned him, and the sentence of death is already out against him. A man can no more deny this than he can deny his own existence. There is not a moral agent in the world who does not know that, as far as God's law is concerned, he is regarded as an outlaw and a rebel; he can no more doubt or deny it than he can doubt or deny his own existence. These facts are not only revealed in the Bible, but are most clearly manifest to our own consciousness; our very conscience testifies to their truthfulness.

Now, if we don't believe what God says on this subject, we make Him a liar; and if we don't believe our own nature, we make Him a liar again; for we must not overlook the fact that God is as really the Author of our own nature as of the Bible itself. Does your conscience accuse you of sin? It is as truly a revelation from God as anything can be. It is God's own testimony in this sense—God has given us a power by which we irresistibly condemn ourselves. He has implanted within us a law which, when we sin, irresistibly compels us to condemn ourselves. This is God's own voice and revelation; and he who disbelieves it is guilty of making God a liar. If, then, we approach Him in our own name, we virtually deny the truth of these things, and pour contempt upon His governmental relationships and the sacredness of His character. The truth is that His character and governmental relationships are such that no one can be accepted of God who violates or overlooks these relationships.

Again, *it is an absolute insult to the majesty of God,* as Governor of the universe, to overlook these solemn facts so plainly revealed to us both in His Word and in our hearts. And he who would approach God in this manner is a deluded wretch, rushing rudely into the face of his Maker.

Again, *it is pouring contempt upon God's authority,* and virtually denying the wisdom and necessity of His method of accepting us. Bear in mind that a merciful disposition on the part of God is no reason why He should accept people holding certain relationships. Suppose the Queen of England felt compassion for a certain rebel, so much so indeed that in her private apartments she really wept. And suppose this rebel, hearing of this, should attempt to force himself upon her regardless of the sacredness of the place because she has compassion on him. May he force himself into her presence? No, indeed! The fact is the same with God. These relationships must not be lost sight of. The good of society, as well as individual interest, demand they should not be overlooked, but well pondered. And every act of both parties should have reference to these relations. It is precisely this way under God's government. And if it is necessary in human governments to recognize these relationships, is it not infinitely more so under God's government?

These truths appear everywhere within, without, upon the page of inspiration, and in our minds. It is clear that out of Christ and apart from Him, God can have no conversation with sinners. Apart from Christ, sinners are under sentence, condemned outlaws, rebels whom God is pledged to destroy unless they can find a Mediator. To come to God without Christ is a virtual denial of the necessity of a Mediator. To come without Christ is to appear at the feast in our own filthy garments instead of throwing over us His righteousness. Under the Old Testament dispensation, many truths were taught in an impressive manner. There were the holy vestments in which the high priests were obliged to appear before God, and without which they were not allowed to approach God. So must we, as it were, throw Christ over us as a robe. This is the lesson the ceremony was designed to teach.

But let me say again that not to use Christ's name in approaching God in prayer is *to scorn the advocacy of Christ.* In other words, God has made Him our advocate, and not to pray in Christ's name is to thrust Him aside and become our own advocates. It is to have low and blasphemous conceptions of God's relationship to us as Creator. The real saints under the Old Testament dispensation understood this method of approach to God. Daniel prayed for the Lord's sake. He and all the real saints doubtless understood the way of approach as shadowed forth in the typical dispensation. We can well enough account for the fact that there is now so little prevailing in prayer, because comparatively so few use Christ's name rightly. They have no definite idea of the reasons for using it. In their hearts they are really in a state in which they do not make proper use of His name. I have often feared that multitudes of people *pray for themselves*, and in such a sense as really to be selfish. In their supplications they do not recognize themselves as belonging to Christ and as deserving answers to their prayers for Christ's sake.

When people do this, they make use of Christ's name just as a man would make use of his master's name to get money to speculate with himself. A clerk or agent takes a check, goes to the bank and draws money, but it is for his employer. He is certainly going to use it himself; but, take note, he does it in the name and for the sake of his employer—not to further his own private interests but the interests of his master. Now, if we would come to Christ in a proper manner, we must regard ourselves as His servants in this sense— wanting what we want and obtaining what we obtain for the purpose of serving Him and glorifying His name. While we separate ourselves from Him and seek things for ourselves, no wonder our religion profits us so little—no wonder Christ's name on our lips is of no avail! To refuse to come in Christ's name is as effectual a hindrance to our prayers being answered as if there were no Christ at all. Who does not believe that if a man neglects or refuses to use Christ's name in the sense in which He requires us to use it, it is just as effectual a bar to His acceptance as if there had been no Christ? The same reason requiring Christ's interposition for us requires that we should recognize these reasons and *always* on our approach to God have respect to them.

I have often feared that *many use His name without hardly knowing why* they do so. It is done by them as a mere matter of form. Perhaps they have never so much as inquired what state of mind was requisite to the proper use of Christ's name. I fear some people simply suppose that to append the phrase "for Christ's sake" to their prayers is enough. But this is a grievous error. If we come in Christ's name, we may claim as our due whatever God has promised to Christ. Now, Christ has rendered great service to the government of God, and of this we as His children are to have the full benefit. We are not to suppose that what Christ has done has merely rendered it *possible* that God may forgive us. He has rendered the most important service to the government of God that can be conceived. He has placed God's character, government, and relationships, and the entire question of revelation in such an aspect as to give the whole universe a great deal of new light on the subject. He has arrested the progress of rebellion and established the authority of God over all being. Angels sinned, and God exercised the law upon them. Man sinned, and who knows where it might have ended had it not been for Christ's intervention. He has done that which amply entitles Him to receive gifts for men, to bestow them upon those for whom He died. The government of God can well afford to let Him do so, seeing how wonderfully He rebuked sin and revealed the divine character. So great a thing has He done in His death that the government of God can well afford to dispense favors to all who belong to Him; and they are bestowed as freely as they can flow forth from a heart of infinite love.

In himself, God is disposed to do all He can in behalf of His creatures. And *our greatest governmental obstacle Christ has completely removed.* He has, moreover, so wonderfully magnified the law and made it honorable that, instead of there being an obstacle in the way, there is a direct invitation from God to come to Him that He may come out and show the infinite largeness of His heart by giving Christ's people all the riches of His glorious kingdom. So that, as I have said, the Head of the very government which stood in the way now invites us to come to Him that the deep tides of His love and salvation may burst forth—that His grace may infinitely abound, like a sea with neither shore nor bottom, whose waves flow on with boundless universality. The door is open wide to every sinner.

We are never constricted in God, but in our own hearts, on account of our stinted faith and limited confidence. Christ, as our representative, became poor that we might become rich. The divine government can now well afford to come forth, because, as I have said, of Christ's unspeakable services, and the glorious Head of that government can let His compassions flow to sinners. He may use language toward us it would not be fitting for Him to use, if it were not for what Christ has done. Christ now offers you His righteousness and mediation that guilty and condemned as you are, deserving as you are to be thrust out, notwithstanding all this, He has set the door wide open. Now, therefore, instead of standing on the Court of the Gentiles, in the Court of the Hebrews, or even in the Court of the Priests, the veil is rent, and access is free to the mercy seat itself, where the cherubim stand with the Shechinah amid a flood of glory.

Put on Christ, then, and come confessing your sins, renouncing your own righteousness, recognizing God's governmental relationships. Oh, come! Come quite up to the mercy seat! God invites you to come, if you will do so in the way I have described. No one is a Christian until he believes, until in fact he does the very thing I am now exhorting you to do. Believe in Christ— that is be a Christian. Do you say, "Has Christ died for me?" Yes, He died for you as really as if there were no other sinner in the universe. Do you say, "May I have access to Him in my own behalf, clad in the filthy rags with which I have been trying to cover myself?" Yes! Do as blind Bartimeus did. The poor blind man sat by the wayside. Great multitudes were thronging along, some before, some behind, crowding around the person of the Savior. Bartimeus naturally inquired the cause of this unusual gathering, and was told it was Jesus passing. He had heard of Him and exclaimed aloud, "Jesus, thou Son of David, have mercy upon me!" They told him to be still, as if there were something improper in his actions. But he would not be silenced. He believed Jesus would restore his sight, and he lifted up his voice above all the noise: "Jesus," he cried out, "thou Son of David, have mercy on me!" Christ stopped, "What is that?" Why, a blind man. "Bring him here." "What wilt thou have me to do?" "Lord, that I might receive my sight." He would not be kept away. He threw himself upon Christ in faith and instantly received the object of his wishes.

Now, sinner! Why don't you follow the example set here? I wish I had more time to the subject. Oh, that Christians would but understand what they may have by prayer if they really use Christ's name rightly! You are either infidels or you believe that you will receive what you pray for in Christ's name. Now, do you *get* what you ask? Do you use Christ's name effectually? Do your families know that God hears and answers your prayers? Can you honestly say, "I believe God hears me"? If you can, I am glad. But if you can't, remember you are not using Christ's name rightly. He will not hear you till you do so.

17

THE PRIMITIVE PRAYER MEETING*

"These all continued with one accord in prayer and supplication" (Acts 1:14).

In the context we have an account of Christ's last interview with His disciples. They had assembled at His request. He met them, "spoke to them of the things pertaining to the kingdom of God"; commanded them not to depart from Jerusalem, but to wait for the promise of the Father, assuring them that they "should be baptized with the Holy Ghost not many days hence." And then He was taken up from their sight. They returned to Jerusalem, went into an upper room, and there "all continued with one accord in prayer and supplication." These, in brief, are the circumstances of this wonderful prayer meeting.

I propose to notice:

► *The object of this prayer meeting.*
► *Its characteristics.*
► *Its results.*

The object of this prayer meeting.

The special object of this meeting was to pray for the outpouring of the Spirit upon themselves and the world. It had been promised, even from Abraham, down the long line of holy prophets, that in connection with the advent of Christ, the Spirit should be given. Christ reminded His disciples of this

*The Oberlin Evangelist, November 22, 1854.

great promise and bade them tarry in Jerusalem and wait for its fulfillment. He had given them their great commission, to go forth into all the world and preach the Gospel to every creature. But He would have them plainly understand that they could do nothing without His Spirit, and therefore they must by all means wait in Jerusalem till they had received this anointing of the Father. That they might the better understand this baptism, He referred to John's mission and work, saying, "John truly baptized with water; but ye shall be baptized with the Holy Ghost, not many days hence." That baptism was only a type; this was to be the very thing symbolized.

This meeting to pray for the descent of the Spirit continued not less than ten days. From the Passover at which Christ suffered, He met with them on various occasions during forty days; then ascended to heaven. The feast of Pentecost was, as its name signifies, just fifty days after the Passover. The interval from the ascension to Pentecost, ten days, was the duration of this remarkable prayer meeting. For we are told that when the day of Pentecost was fully come, they are still "all with one accord in one place."

Its Characteristics.

Of the *characteristics* of this meeting, the first to be noticed is that the brothers and sisters *were all present*. This is a prominent peculiarity and deserves distinct and special notice. The sacred historian is careful to call attention to the fact. "Peter stood up among them; the number of names together were about one hundred and twenty." All the eleven were there, "with the women and Mary the mother of Jesus and with his brethren." No one could be spared. What do you suppose Christ would have thought if only two or three had come and the rest had been too indifferent or too much engrossed in other business to be there? They did not allow any other business to detain them. They honored God enough to meet on His special call and to stay till the object of the meeting was accomplished.

They were all interested in the object. This is obvious by the fact that they all came and all remained together so long— indeed until the object was attained. Not only were they all there, but all held on through those long sessions. This shows they were really in earnest.

They *expected* the promised blessing. They knew Christ had promised it, and they believed His promise. Of course their faith became a strong and definite expectation.

Yet again they were *united*. Over and over again, we are told they were all with one accord in one place. United in the one desire to obtain this great blessing, and of one heart in regard to the motives which led them to pray, there was the most entire unanimity, as if the whole company had but one heart, and that was strong and true in its impulse and purposes.

They were united in *fraternal confidence*. There is no hint of any loss or lack of confidence in each other. Hence they could edify each other. The communion of soul was deep and precious.

They *persevered*. "These all *continued* with one accord in prayer and supplication." They could not think of giving up and abandoning their effort before the blessing came. They said as Jacob in his wrestlings, "I will not let thee go, except thou bless me." What could they do without the Spirit! Besides, Christ had distinctly told them not to go until the blessing came.

I said that both the brothers and sisters were there. This was contrary to the doctrine and practice of the Jews then, and indeed is so to this day. They do not admit women to sit with them in their holy places, in their seasons of worship. Women are allowed to occupy only the galleries, from which they may look down as spectators, not being expected to join as associate worshipers. In public acts of devotion they might have no part. Not so under the Gospel. In Christ there must be no distinction between bond and free, male and female. All were to be one in Him. All their old Jewish prejudices were discarded. This was a most important fact in the constitution of the Christian Church. Until Christ came, no such meeting of brothers and sisters on the same level had been known. The particularity with which this circumstance is recorded shows that a new era had opened. No partition wall is henceforth to thrust the female sex into the court of the women, or into the distant galleries; all sexes are counted alike as brethren in Christ Jesus.

Observe also that there is no sectarian or party spirit or party strife among them. No party prejudice was there; all were true Christian brethren. The division of the Christian Church into parties and sects, now so great an evil, was then unknown. Men were not then sticklers for little things, were not building up new denominations on a basis so unworthy as a mere difference in forms or even in the forms of a form. The controversies of later days about ordinances had not yet begun to distract and rend the body of Christ. Nor was there then any strife for leadership. Diotrephes and his sect had not yet appeared in the Christian Church.

You may think me censorious in having intimated that the ambition of leadership makes sects. I wish there was no truth in this intimation. But who does not know it to be but sadly true!

Moreover, there was no carping against the truth, or against judiciously proposed measures. Suspicion had no room in their kindred bosoms. They had no disposition to resist each other's prayers; there were none to whisper—I am not edified with this brother's prayer or by the prayer of that sister. *All with one accord*, as well as all in one place. This must have been a charming season, a meeting in which loving hearts blended in holy sympathy.

Finally it was a *deeply earnest meeting*. No apathetic souls were there, lagging and hanging as dead weights on the general heart of the assembly. All seemed to take an equally deep and warm interest in the great supplications they were convened to pour out before their ascended Lord for the great blessing of the Christian dispensation.

Its results.

In brief, these are soon told. Three thousand were converted under one short sermon. The Holy Spirit fell on the disciples with great power, and from them the blessing diffused itself on every hand to the thousands who believed. The little band found themselves launched forth upon the greatest enterprise ever undertaken by mortals; and by that enterprise, drawn into such relationships of faith and sustaining strength toward God and their ascended Savior as had never been realized on earth before. The conversion of the world to Jesus had fairly begun and the mission of the Spirit was opened.

REMARKS

This is doubtless to be taken as a model prayer meeting. It was substantially, in its spirit and leading circumstances, what a prayer meeting ought to be. Why not? There is nothing here that should not be in all prayer meetings for objects of similar importance.

Yet who can fail to notice that most prayer meetings are nearly the reverse of this in all their characteristic features? What do you see now in prayer meetings appointed to pray for the conversion of sinners? Only a little handful of Christians present; the rest of the church pouring contempt on the very call for a meeting! It is easy to see that this must be regarded by Christ as a real insult. A meeting is called, yet few have interest enough to attend! What would you think if a notice were given out for a meeting at your church to invite some distinguished personage to come and visit—say the President of the United States or the King and Queen of England, or someone to whom the nation were under the very greatest obligations; the call for a meeting is given out; it appears in the daily papers; but when the hour arrives, only a very few are present? The people do not come! Suppose this distinguished stranger is informed how small this meeting is; will he come? Will he not deem the very call an insult? So when meetings are appointed to invite the Lord Jesus and almost none attend, why should He come? There is no unanimity in the invitation. The understanding is they are not unanimous in inviting Him to come.

You will say, perhaps, that you did not intend your absence to mean just that. You did not mean to say that you did not want the Savior to come. You had your special reasons for being absent. You had an excuse; but do you think such excuses would avail in the case of any distinguished personage? Suppose the meeting had been called to invite and honor a great general; but very few attend it; yet they sent him their excuses for non-attendance. They told him they were all very busy: some had sickness in their family; some were taking care of various home concerns; they really felt the highest respect for him, etc. Would their apologies avail! Would it not be regarded as a downright insult to ask so great a man to come among you, and yet in a meeting called to invite him, have only a mere handful present?

Now, does not this apply in the case of prayer to God? Indeed it does. The prayer meeting is especially called for the purpose of inviting Him to come among us. It is important to know *who* wants Him to come, *how many* there are, and *how much* they desire His coming. The call of a meeting is the proper way to test and determine all these points. If the result shows that but very few care enough about it to even appear at the meeting, what can be expected but a failure in the great object of inducing Him to make us a visit, and bring revival?

Suppose the meeting at the day of Pentecost and during those previous days had been very thin, would the blessing have descended? Who can suppose it would?

We may have a prayer meeting and urge the very strongest

reasons for the descent of God's Spirit; but what good does it do if we are only a small minority of those who are in the church?

How much worse still is the case in our modern prayer meetings if even those who do attend are manifestly not by any means earnest in prayer! How often we see this to be undoubtedly the case. They do not press their plea for a visitation of mercy from on high. They do not struggle long and earnestly as those praying souls did in the first great primitive prayer meeting. These pleas and prayers are as different from those as can well be imagined. Let no one wonder that these movements are so unavailing!

People think they cannot take time for continuous prayer. To keep up a prayer meeting a whole week is quite too much to think of! They have by no means brought their views up to the point of praying till the blessing comes. They do not feel earnest enough, nor are they sufficiently pressed with a sense of *need* to make this seem a small thing compared with the greatness of the blessing sought. They think they do well if they pray a little at one meeting per week, keep up one weekly meeting, and spend even that mostly in something else than prayer. What can be expected from such efforts?

Perhaps there is not unanimity enough, nor brotherly love enough to sustain even one weekly prayer meeting. This is the case in many churches and in many neighborhoods. Is it so in your church?

Even where general prayer meetings can be kept up, and are so, yet neighborhood prayer meetings fall through. Alienations of feeling arise among brothers and sisters; bickerings, bad blood and bad words are there; they lose confidence in each other, and cannot pray together! How awful! How different from the spirit of the day of Pentecost! There, all the assembled brothers and sisters were of one heart and one soul! The tears were scarcely dry on the cheek of the penitent Peter; Thomas had not recovered from the deep mortification, shame and grief of his unbelief, yet even these feelings did not stand in the way of the most entire union of heart and soul in prayer for the great promised blessing.

Yet in how many churches you are astonished to find the prayer meeting abandoned; the hearts of brethren soured and alienated; confidence almost gone, and worse than all the rest, few left to mourn over this deplorable state of Zion. You may find, here and there, a brother or a sister mournfully asking, "What shall we do for a prayer meeting in our neighborhood?

There is not brotherly love and confidence enough here to sustain one." You would be astonished to know how often this is the case.

Sometimes a family prayer meeting drops to pieces in the same way. Alienation in some form arises; they lose confidence in each other's prayers, and interest in each other's welfare; and, of course, they cease to pray with and for each other. Under such influences, Christians are not interested in each other's prayers, and are not led onward and edified by mutual prayer. When alienation exists, and mutual sympathy is lacking, there can be no union of heart in prayer and no spiritual edification.

You have often noticed in a prayer meeting that the brothers and sisters will be greatly quickened and edified by one brother's prayer and not at all by another's. When one prays, it is most obvious that the hearts of all are moved; there is a sighing, an uplifting of heart, a general response; but when another leads, you see no such tokens of general agreement. You can tell who can lead the hearts of the brethren in real prayer. You will always notice that no one can do this unless the people have confidence in him, and unless they feel the deep pulsations of his heart moving upon their own. Sometimes this is seen in the family. The head of the family prays, but all have lost confidence in him and are doing anything and everything else but uniting in his words of prayer. Is it amazing that such prayer avails nothing? Indeed, the very expressions which such a man may use in prayer will be interpreted as only so much hypocrisy! Alas, the spirit of prayer cannot be there! The spirit of dissent, and not the spirit of union, is there. They do not and cannot pray together. They are not united in prayer. A spirit of alienation exists, unexpressed, but deep; perhaps their will is upset about something. Even husband and wife do not pray together; they are chafed in their feelings toward each other, and are indulging a state of mind which forbids a spirit of mutual prayer. Often our prayer meetings die out by reason of little bickerings and heart burnings.

Brothers and sisters, will you not look to this?

Often when people stay away from meetings for prayer, they assign other than the true and real reason. They do not say frankly, I stay away because I cannot hear this or that brother pray. They profess to be too busy—too much and too urgently occupied; but really they do not assign even themselves the true reason, the very thing which has kept them back from the meeting.

At the Pentecostal meeting, they neglected all other business. They were poor in this world's goods, and had, no doubt, business enough to do. Their women, also, had enough to do; yet they were all there. But suppose it had been the case that they felt their business to be too important to be dropped. Suppose they had said, "Oh, it cannot be necessary for us all to go; we are so full of business, and so pressed every way, and so fatigued by all this." Do you believe that, making such excuses for neglect of prayer, they could have had the blessing? If they could not fulfill the condition, could they hope to receive the promise? If they would not meet the demand made by the condition, obviously the way would not be open for Christ to fulfill His promise. He could not grant them the blessing without virtually giving a bounty to remissness and unfaithfulness.

The fact is, brothers, our modern prayer meetings are too cold and too constrained. Christians are not earnest in prayer. Their souls cannot become deeply burdened and earnestly agonized in supplication; they do not thirst enough for spiritual blessings, and have not the deep communion with God which is requisite for prevailing prayer. You know what a burden is felt in the prayer meeting when the heart is thoroughly broken; when pride is abased, the soul humbled, and the entire energies are drawn out in earnest supplication. But there are few such meetings for prayer now. There is a lack of sustaining unanimity.

It is a law of mind that union of heart sustains the interest and power of prayer. Did you never observe how you can sustain another in prayer if you enter deeply into his sympathies? You uphold his faith and his fervor. I have often thought that the practice common among the Methodists is useful, if not abused. The responses that truly come from the heart serve to quicken and sustain genuine prayer. The responses introduced in the service of the Church of England are excellent, provided only that the heart be in them. I love to hear these sustaining responses and to know that I have the sympathizing heart of those who profess to be praying with me.

Often our prayer meetings are cold and profitless because there is no liberty and no free utterance. The spirit of prayer is straitened because the natural expressions of deep feeling are repressed. Said an English Congregationalist, "I do wish our people could learn from the Methodists how to have a prayer meeting." He felt the need of an unconstrained utterance and of a free expression of feeling. Now I would not sanction heartless noise and vociferation; that is not prayer and cannot help real prayer. There is a wide difference between that and a meeting in which the heart has free scope, and the Spirit of God is not straitened, but ranges with free scope and melting power. I have seen prayer meetings in which obviously the whole congregation went forth before God in mighty prayer. Some of you have seen such prayer. The hearts of the people were moved as the trees of the forest before a mighty rushing wind. Words seem as if freighted with irrepressible emotion. You can see that God is there. Everyone feels it. An awe of the Holy Presence pervades each heart. And yet they are not afraid, but are drawn into sweet confidence and most earnest pleading. Literally they seem to pour out their hearts before him. This is true prayer, and meets the idea of social praying. It is a union of hearts before God's mercy seat, the Spirit coming down to make intercession with their spirit with groanings that cannot be uttered. Every prayer meeting should bear this character, modified only according to the type of those circumstances that call for prayer.

18

REPENTANCE BEFORE PRAYER FOR FORGIVENESS*

"Repent therefore of this thy wickedness, and pray God, if perhaps the thought of thine heart may be forgiven thee. For I perceive that thou art in the gall of bitterness, and in the bond of iniquity" (Acts 8:22, 23).

These words were addressed to Simon Magus. A revival of religion was in progress in Samaria under the labors of Peter and Philip. Many were converted to God, and among them Simon Magus also professed conversion. He had been a great man in that place and had deceived many by his magic arts. Seeing the greater wonders wrought by these Christian apostles, he was struck with surprise, and his ambitious spirit caught at the idea of augmenting his own power over men by obtaining this new secret. Hence he offers the apostles *money* to buy this new power. Peter saw his heart at once and nobly replied, "Thy money perish with thee; thou hast neither part nor lot in this matter, for thy heart is not right in the sight of God." He then gave him directions as in our text, "Repent therefore of this thy wickedness, and pray God, if perhaps the thought of thine heart may be forgiven thee."

Following the order of thought as in the text, I shall show:

- ▶ *The principle developed here in the light of which Peter saw this man as yet in his sins.*
- ▶ *What repentance is.*

---

*The Oberlin Evangelist, November 19, 1851.

▶ *What is implied in repentance.*
▶ *Why sinners are exhorted first to repent and then to pray for pardon.*
▶ *The importance of following this example in all our dealings with men.*

The principle developed here in the light of which Peter saw this man as yet in his sins.

Peter did not profess to learn Simon Magus' character by inspiration. He had no such omniscience. Inspiration he doubtless had, but inspiration taught general truth, not individual character. Peter saw his heart to be selfish, and not at all in harmony with the gospel spirit. Simon still had his old spirit, and wanted power to give the Holy Spirit to whom he pleased for the same reason that he had before sought and valued his magic powers. Hence he offered money, as if the apostles were as greedy as himself. Peter saw that he was selfish and therefore blind, far indeed from understanding the subject of Christianity. Hence Peter exhorted him to *repent.*

What is repentance?

Repentance should always be distinguished from conviction for sin. The latter is an involuntary state of mind, and of course has no virtue in it. There may be as much of it as there is in hell itself, and yet no virtue. There is awful conviction in hell; but no genuine repentance.

Neither does repentance consist merely in sorrow. Indeed, this is properly and strictly no part of it, for sorrow does not belong to the thinking department of the mind; much less does it pertain to the will and to the department of voluntary action.

Again, repentance is not the same thing as *remorse.* Remorse, though it amount to the keenest and most galling self-condemnation, does not necessarily imply repentance. There may be in it no *change of mind* whatever.

Repentance is simply and precisely a *change of mind.* The original term denotes, a thinking again—a turning of the mind—as when one finds himself going wrong and turns about to pursue the opposite course. The term, when applied to evangelical repentance, means not merely a turning of the mind, but a change of the entire purposes of action, change in the entire attitude of the will. Repentance, therefore, is not remorse, is not sorrow, nor anything of this kind, but is the mind turning away from selfish attitudes to benevolent attitudes, from being selfish to being genuinely benevolent.

What is implied in repentance.

Conviction of sin as a wrong committed against God is implied in repentance. Without this there can be no rational repentance.

The sinner must become truly honest with God. He must honestly admit the truths affirmed by his reason and pressed on his soul by his conscience. Especially must he recognize God's rights: that he himself is God's property and belongs truly to God.

He must become just and equitable toward men, truly an honest man. Selfishness is the greatest dishonesty in the world. No one is radically honest who is selfish, unless a person can be honest in essentially denying everybody's rights but his own. No; selfishness is the perfection of dishonesty. It is absurd for a wicked person to pretend to be honest. He has not a particle of genuine honesty, no more than Satan has! What is honesty? Respecting other's rights and especially God's rights, according to their true value. But the sinner sets himself up for an honest person, while he utterly denies God's rights. How false their pretensions! They respect their neighbor's rights only for their own interests, only because in some way they expect to reap good to themselves from the respect they hypocritically show to their neighbor's interests. The fact is people are totally deceived if they think themselves honest toward other people while they are not really honest toward God. The heart of honesty is not in them. If they do not love their neighbor as themselves, they are not honest. No one has a right to say practically that his rights and interests are greater than his neighbor's. The practical assumption of this is both false and dishonest.

No one is penitent who is not honest in the sense that he renders to God what is God's and to man what is man's. He must begin with restoring to God his stolen self. God has created him, has kept him alive, and has redeemed him: this threefold claim God has on him; and yet he sets himself up in opposition against God and has no sympathy with God whatever. No person is honest until he repents toward God. The first step is to give himself back to God; and with himself whatever remains of his time, his talents, his property and his influence.

It is always implied in true repentance that you make full restoration of everything.

Repentance implies confession of sin to God and to all those whom you have injured. Let no one think himself truly penitent until he has made confession in all things where it is due. Some sins are known only to God, and some are committed only against God. These should be confessed to God. In some excepted cases, God holds people to the duty of confessing secret sins. This, however, is the exception and not the rule.

I cannot enter now into those various applications possible which should be made on this subject. But obviously where restitution cannot be made without confession, as for example, where character is injured, there you persist in the wrong unless you confess. You have deceived many in respect to your neighbor, to his hurt, and this wrong which you have done him, you must *undo,* or you cannot suppose yourself to be really penitent.

But besides confession, *restitution* is always implied in repentance. Each person should make it to the extent of his power. This is always implied, because the penitent man is also benevolent. He loves his neighbor as himself, and therefore like Zaccheus he hastens to restore, and thinks it no hardship even to restore *fourfold.*

Repentance implies the entire abandonment of all courses of life and of business which are inconsistent with Christian character. Do you think that a man, really benevolent in spirit, could pursue a business adapted to ruin instead of save men? No indeed! Shall a man who loves the well-being of others as he does his own devote himself to traffic in or destroy human flesh? No sooner than he would sell his own flesh and blood, his own person into bondage, or the bodies and souls of his own wife and children.

Repentance also implies not only an abandonment of all selfish branches of business, but of all selfish modes of transacting business. Selfish men often pursue a good business in a bad way—on most selfish principles and policy. This also repentance precludes, because repentance is a change of the heart and life from selfishness to real benevolence. It implies an abandonment of all selfishness.

Repentance implies a *universal reformation* of life, a reformation extending to all forms of sin. Penitent men turn from all sin *as sin,* because they regard it as sin, and therefore can have no sympathy with it. All *known sin* therefore they at once abandon. And since to *them* nothing can be sin except what is known to be such, the forsaking of all known sin is really a forsaking of all sin. No one is truly penitent who allows himself to continue in some chosen sin, and who picks and chooses his indulgences. This is not repentance at all.

When I speak of *abandoning* sin, I do not imply that the penitent man never for even a moment relapses into it; but I imply that he sets himself against it in real honest earnestness.

Finally, true repentance implies confidence in God and in Jesus Christ. If a man truly repents of sin, he will of course believe on Jesus Christ.

Why sinners are exhorted first to repent and then to pray for pardon.

He assumed that Simon Magus was totally depraved, totally alienated from God, and hence unwilling to give up his sins. Hence he could not exhort him to pray for pardon while yet in his sins. Peter knew full well that Simon would spring at the idea of being forgiven before he repented; but he meant to caution him in the strongest way against such a delusion. He knew that his sin consisted of cleaving to his selfishness, and therefore told him first to give up his sins and then to ask forgiveness. Peter assumed that his unwillingness to give up his selfishness was his great sin first of all to be repented of and put away.

Peter assumed that God could not forgive him until he should put away his sin. Peter knew Simon's great difficulty. He knew that he held on to his course as an ambitious and selfish man; and therefore Peter assured him that mercy could come to him only after full repentance.

Peter did not regard Simon as having any right to ask or wish for pardon until he had repented. You will observe that Peter saw Simon impenitent and selfish. Hence, he assumed that he had no right to ask or expect forgiveness while in this state of mind. He did not tell him to pray for repentance, because he knew he was unwilling to repent, and therefore such a prayer would only be mocking God.

Yet many direct the sinner to pray for repentance! Ah, do you want the sinner to mock God? Peter did not direct Simon to pray for repentance, for he knew that this would be only mocking God until he should himself be willing to repent; and he could not invite him to insult Jehovah.

Peter also assumed that he was abundantly *able* to repent.

People sometimes teach sinners to pray that God would make them *able* to repent, and many even imply that the sinner is trying as hard as he can to repent, and therefore needs only cry unto God to help him repent, the only difficulty in his case being that God does not give him enough strength!

"Trying to repent" always implies two things: a willingness to repent and a lack of power to do it. *Trying* is making an effort to accomplish that on which the mind is set, and, if unsuccessful, implies that the failure results from lack of power.

Now Peter understood this whole subject. Peter knew that this man had enough free will and ability to repent if he would. Therefore he directs him first to repent and then ask pardon. Asking forgiveness before repenting would only blaspheme God, and Peter could not advise him to do that.

Peter implies that he had conviction enough, and therefore need not wait for more. Hence he did not tell him to wait for it, but at once to *repent.* This of course assumed that he had conviction enough. Many set sinners to praying for conviction just as if they needed more and desired to have it, neither of which are usually true.

Peter assumed that the sinner is without excuse for either his sin or his remaining impenitence. He insisted on repentance as the present duty of that man, which of course implies that in God's judgment, it is the duty of every sinner to repent. Now it must be of the very first importance for us to *know how God judges* in this matter. It is a remarkable fact that both Peter and all other inspired teachers concur in representing God as requiring sinners at once to repent.

The importance of following this example in all our dealings with men.

The direction to repent before asking forgiveness, and this only, is consistent with the facts in the case.

For what are the facts? Simply these. The sinner is a free-acting, voluntary agent. In this capacity he sets himself selfishly against the demands of God's law of love. Now, what shall God require him to do? *Change* his course to be sure—in other words, *repent.* Nothing can be plainer than that a voluntary agent who is voluntarily doing wrong should turn about and voluntarily do right. This, and this only, is consistent with the facts and with the right of the case.

But suppose you undertake to give direction to a sinner who

is still selfish, that is, devoted to self-pleasing. First of all you set him to praying. Praying for what? That God would give him the desire of his heart? Of course, if he prays without first changing the purpose of his heart, he will pray for what he desires; that is, he will pray that God would grant him the selfish desires of his heart. His prayer would be, "O Lord, let me have heaven without holiness. Lord, pardon my sins, and yet let me live on in sinning, for I have no heart to repent!"

Now, can such mocking of God be of any use? Would you suppose it probable that the Bible would give such directions to awakened sinners?

If men are really *willing* to repent and forsake all sin, God asks no more of them, for the willing is essentially the doing; but there can be no greater mistake in this world than to assume that sinners are willing to repent and want to repent before they actually do it.

The usual order in which inquirers after salvation are set at work is the reverse of that enjoined in the Bible, as if the sinner was ready and God not ready, and therefore the sinner supposedly needs to use means to make God ready and to urge God forward to do His duty.

To set the sinner to praying for repentance is to assume that he is willing to repent but *cannot*, and therefore he needs God's power to help him.

The truth is no man can will to renounce sin without doing so; for to *will it* is to *do* it.

To direct sinners otherwise than God does in the Bible is to deceive them. Thousands have been deceived thus to the ruin of their souls forever. If you set them to pray for pardon before they repent, you leave them under the delusion that they are doing something they ought to do—are doing their duty; whereas they are not doing their duty until they repent! What a horrible doctrine this is! Teach an impenitent sinner, still holding on to his sins, to pray for pardon! This would ruin a world of sinners. It would leave them all deceived and deluded in their sins and under God's wrath forever!

To tell the sinner to pray for the Holy Spirit is only the same thing in a slightly different form. Nothing can be more deceptive than to tell the sinner to pray for the Holy Spirit while you know he is only resisting the Holy Spirit, and while you allow him to go on, still resisting. "Ye do always resist the Holy Spirit," says the Word of God through one of its most faithful and truthful preachers. What does the Holy Spirit do? He takes truth and reveals it to the sinner in impressive aspects. This is His office work respecting the sinner. As soon as the sinner yields to the truth as presented and enforced by the Holy Spirit, he is converted. Until he repents he only resists the Spirit.

What good does it do then, to direct him to pray for the Spirit, so long as he is resisting the Spirit? What can his prayer be while pursuing this course except mocking God? The thing he should do is not to pray for the Holy Spirit, but to yield to His influence as already exerted on his mind. The first thing and the only right thing for the awakened sinner to do in reference to the Spirit is yield his heart to the demands of God's revealed truth. Let him do this and he will be converted in a moment. He should be told that he does not feel his need of the Spirit, and therefore cannot pray intelligently for its greater influence on his mind. He should also be told that the only honest thing he can do in the first place is to cease to resist the Spirit.

Peter did not say to Simon, "Pray for the Holy Spirit to strive with you, or to repent for you, or to make you repent, or even to help you repent": but simply, " 'Repent yourself', repent first of all, and then ask forgiveness."

To direct a sinner yet in his sins to pray instead of repenting is to leave him under the impression that after he has prayed he has done his duty. You tell him to pray. He prays and then says, "Now I have done my duty and why am I not converted?" But if you tell him as Peter did, first to repent and then to pray, and if he follows your direction, he is converted. Then his prayer can be acceptable to God.

The opposite course; that is, the reverse order which puts prayer before repentance virtually casts the blame of continued unrepentance upon God. If you direct the sinner to pray first instead of repenting first, you virtually imply that the difficulty in the sinner's way is one that God must remove—that the reason why he has not repented lies in God and not in himself. If the sinner prays before he repents, then having prayed he says, "Why am I not converted and saved? I have prayed; God does not convert me; the blame be on God and not on me!" How horrible must the influence of this course be on the sinner's mind!

No inspired writer warrants any other course than this of the text. Search the Scriptures from beginning to end, and you will find no directions to sinners different from this. You might well wonder in amazement if you should; for to tell the sinner to go and pray first before repenting overlooks the very nature of repentance and of a sinning state of mind.

Every doctrine of Scripture is consistent with the course of directions given in the text and with no other course. Every doctrine of Scripture shuts the sinner up to doing his present duty. The whole Bible urges him to do present duty and if he is in unrepented sin, it tells him that his first duty is to *repent*. People have designed a strange way when they have directed sinners to do something else than repent, because the Bible holds steadfastly to the only consistent course: urging evermore on every sinner that first of all he should REPENT.

John came crying in the wilderness of Judea, "Repent". Jesus Christ followed him and preached the same thing. "Repent," said He, "for the kingdom of heaven is at hand." So every prophet, and every apostle, each in his place, cried aloud: *Repent, Repent,* as if there was nothing else they dared to say till this first duty was done.

This is the only biblical and rational course—the only course which is based upon Scripture, upon reason, and upon the true science of mind. Every sinner knows that he is a sinner. You no more need the Holy Spirit to make you see yourself a sinner than to make you see that you exist. This shows why the Bible always faces the sinner with the assumption: "You are a sinner, and the facts need no proof." Every sinner knows it.

Sinners are often very willing to pray, but not to repent. Only let him get away from the heart work of repenting, and he will gladly do many other things. A young man once said to me, "I would travel to any part of the world if I might thereby be saved." "Yes," said I, "but one thing you will not do; you will not give up your self righteousness, and be saved on Christ alone, without doing anything meritorious yourself."

So with every sinner. Tell him to pray for conviction. Oh yes, he will pray for conviction, but he will *resist* conviction until he repents. Tell him to pray for the Holy Spirit. Oh yes, he will pray for the Holy Spirit, but still he will perhaps resist the Holy Spirit continually. He is ready to do the outside work, but not the heart work. He will readily cleanse the outside of the cup and platter, but the turning of his own heart from his sins and selfishness, that is the hard thing, the thing which of all others he is reluctant to do.

Sinners are prone to assume in self-vindication that it is impossible for them to control their own hearts. They admit they can control their muscles. If Jesus were on earth, they could come to Him and bow their knees before Him; but then inconsistently they say they cannot come with their hearts and bow their hearts to Him. But what is the heart that you cannot control it? You are controlling your own hearts all the time, and the very thing God complains of is that you control it too stubbornly, so that His truth and His Spirit cannot move you. You control it *wrongly* and with so much obstinacy as to baffle all His efforts to save you. Therefore He cries, "Turn ye, turn ye, for why will ye die?"

REMARKS

But you ask, "Should not a sinner pray?" The answer depends on what the question means and implies. If it means, "Shall a sinner mock God?" The answer is "NO." If you mean, "Shall he truly pray in sincerity and honesty?" "YES." "Shall he lie to the Holy Spirit?" "NO." "Shall he turn to God?" "YES."

But the sum of all that need be said on this point is that the sinner should be told to *repent* and pray, not *pray* and then *repent*. Let him observe the scriptural order—an order founded in reason and in the nature of the case.

This order of duties is *eminently reasonable*. Suppose a sinner had stolen money. He knows that God is greatly displeased with him for this, and he is also afraid of being detected and disgraced. Now he says, "What shall I do? Shall I repent and then pray God to forgive me, or shall I pray first?" Greatly disliking to confess, repent, and restore, he says, "I will do the other thing; I will pray. I will go alone and pray about it, and then perhaps I will repent." See him. He takes out his stolen money. He passes it from one hand to the other; I am greatly distressed, he says, "What shall I do? Shall I put it in my pocket and go and pray?" No, sinner, *no*. Carry it back: repent first, and then go and pray. Don't go and pray for the Holy Spirit first. There is no need of that. The Holy Spirit is already convicting you of your great sin. Don't insult Him by refusing to yield to His persuasions and by pretending to pray for His guidance and help.

Stealing money is only one form of sin; but let it represent all forms of sin. You, sinner, are fully committed to living for yourself. You have robbed God by wresting yourself away from His service. God says, "*Restore!* Give yourself back to Me and to My service." But you reply, "What shall I do? Shall I not go and pray?" God says, "Restore first; give back the stolen goods first; then you may pray." What should you pray for until you have restored what you have stolen? You surely will insult God by praying for pardon before you have restored what you have stolen. You need not pray for the Holy Spirit unless you restore, for to pray and not restore is only resisting and mocking the Spirit of God.

But the sinner says, "You talk as if I could repent." Yes, and so does God. God in His Word always speaks as if you could repent, and as if you ought to know that you can. What if Simon Magus had said, "But you don't expect me to repent, do you?" You will observe he *did not* say any such thing. His own conscience neither suggested nor allowed such a defense, nor did the preaching of the apostles encourage it.

But you say, "Does the Bible always assume that I can repent?" Yes, everywhere, in all its commands, by every prophet, every apostle, by the lips of every forerunner of Christ, by the lips of Christ himself. Every inspired command, every inspired direction holds the same language and makes the same implication. You can repent and you *ought to do it immediately*!

When the sinner says, "I can't repent," he virtually charges God with being a tyrant. For what is tyranny but charging God with requiring you to do impossibilities?

But some say, "Does not the Bible teach that God gives men repentance?" Yes, and in the same sense as He gives you daily bread; which, however, you must yourself provide and yourself eat. God does not give you your daily bread as long as you persist in starving yourself. So God gives you repentance by persuading you to repent, by drawing you, by impressing truth on your heart and conscience. Indeed there is no other possible way in which He can give you repentance. It is only by bringing truth before your mind, impressing it by a thousand ways upon your heart and conscience. For repentance is a rational, voluntary act—an act done by the sinner because he sees that truth and reason demand it.

Every sinner should see and feel that immediate repentance is what God requires. He should see that he is shut up to this precisely and to nothing else.

Nor is there anything strange or absurd in this. Suppose a man had committed murder, and you should tell him to repent of this great sin. Is there anything mysterious in this? Or if you see a man engaged in any particular form of wickedness and you exhort him to desist and repent, is there in this course anything strange or unreasonable? How then can there be anything unreasonable in requiring a sinner to repent of *all his sins* or of that which embraces the sum of all wickedness?

Some of you are so afraid you will repent, that even under the most solemn preaching, you try to keep from thinking of your own sins; and then when you do, you pretend that you cannot repent, and eagerly imply that you would repent if you could! Is not this horribly inconsistent?

Many professing Christians are greatly backslidden from God; they pray in form, but don't repent. Many talk about praying as if they make up in prayer what they lack in pleasing God by sinning. Once I asked a young lady, "Do you pray?" "Yes, Sir," she replied. "When?" I pressed. "On retiring to rest at night." "What for?" "That God would take me to heaven if I should die before morning." "Do you expect God would do so?" "No." "You expect then to go on in sin. Now be so honest as to tell God the truth. Say to Him, 'Lord, forgive my sins, give me strength by sleep and food that I may sin a little more; I have sinned all the day past. I don't intend to repent; I only want to be taken to heaven if I die, for I cannot bear to sink down to hell. Lord, help me to sin on against thee as long as I live, and then take me up to heaven!!' "

You are shocked; but what shocks you? Your practice, or my language?

Observe the sinner. He gets on his knees to tell God that he wants repentance, but he lies in saying so every moment until he does in fact repent. And you, backslidden professor, lie to God in every word of your pretended prayer. Do you say, "I will not repent. I don't intend to repent"? If you say anything else than this you lie to God, for nothing else is true *until you do in fact repent*. The truth is, so long as you continue in your selfish, impenitent state, *you don't mean to repent*. Therefore, let him pray as he will, his true meaning is, "I have no intention of repenting of my sins." This is always true until he does repent.

But can this be praying when sinners in their sins do not mean to repent? Hear him, "O Lord, I beseech thee to search my heart." No, you don't mean any such thing; you are covering up your own heart all the time. "O God, come near to me." But you are pushing away from God every moment and as you strive to get away, you only look back over your shoulder and cry to God to reveal His face and draw near to your soul. Hark, hear what the Bible says. "He that turneth away his ear from hearing the law, even his prayer shall be an abomination." And what is your course but this?

Let me tell you, God is infinitely ready to meet and bless you. He comes with pardons in His hands, pardons all sealed with blood. You need only renounce your sins and come to Him; then all will be well. The very first moment you come before God with a penitent heart, He will meet you with smiles of lovingkindness.

His parable of the prodigal son both illustrates and proves this. See, the wandering son comes to himself. Instead of staying away and trying to live on husks, he turns his face toward home, and comes with a confession on his lips and tears of penitence on his cheeks. He is coming; and now see the aged father. He spies him in the distance; he recognizes his long-lost son. See how he leaps from his door and rushes to embrace this returning son. Oh, how *ready*! Oh, how much more than merely *ready*!! Oh, how ready God is in your case to meet you with the fullest pardon, and wipe all your tears away and soothe your aching heart!

Now, don't go away and say I told you not to pray. If I should tell you not to go into your closet, get on your knees and swear and blaspheme God, could you honestly say that I told you not to pray? So I do not teach you not to *pray*; but I do teach you to be *honest*. I warn you, when you pray *do not mock God*. I entreat you, when you pray give your heart to God and repent of all your sin. When I first repented, I did it on my knees and in the act of prayer. I knelt down an unrepentant sinner, and rose up a repentant. In the very act of speaking to God, my heart broke; I yielded myself to God. This is the way. And do you ask, "Can I believe God?" "Yes." "Can I pray in faith?" "Yes." "Can I give my heart to God in penitence?" "Yes." Why not you as well as Paul, as well as Peter, as well as others who have done this very thing and have found mercy?

19

PRINCIPLES OF COMMUNION WITH GOD*

"Ye ask, and receive not, because ye ask amiss, that ye may consume it upon your lusts" (James 4:3).

In a former discourse I mentioned, among other conditions of prevailing prayer, that confession should be made to those whom our sins have injured, and also to God. It is most plain that all sins should be confessed to God that we may obtain forgiveness and be reconciled to Him; else how can we have communion of soul with Him? And who can for a moment doubt that our confessions should not omit those of our fellow beings whom we have injured?

Following this thought, I want to show:

▶ *That restitution should be made to God and to man.*
▶ *That in infinite goodness God welcomes back penitent sinners.*
▶ *That we must be reconciled to our brother.*
▶ *That we must have an honest and good reason for our prayer.*

That restitution should be made to God and to man.

To man, we should make restitution in the sense of undoing as far as possible the wrong we have done, and repairing and

---

*The Oberlin Evangelist, July 21, 1847. The third in a series of three sermons formerly titled, "Conditions of Prevailing Prayer." The first two sermons in the series were combined in sermon number 7 in this book.

making good all the evil. If we have impeached character wrongfully, we must recall and undo it. If we have injured another even by mistake, we are bound, if the mistake comes to our knowledge, to set it right; else we are criminal in allowing it to remain uncorrected. If the injury done by us to our neighbor affects his property, we must make restitution.

But I wish to call your attention more especially to the restitution which we are to make to God. And in respect to this, I do not mean to imply that we can make good our wrongs against God in the sense of really restoring that which we have withheld or taken away; but we can render to Him whatever yet remains. The time still given us we can devote to Him, although the past has gone beyond recall. Our talents and influence and wealth, yet to be used, we may freely and fully use for God. Obviously God and reason require this of us, and it would be vain for us to hope to be accepted in prayer unless we seriously intend to render all the future to God.

Let us look more closely into this subject. How many of you have been robbing God, robbing for a long time and on a large scale? Let us see.

We all belong to God. We are His property in the highest possible sense. He brought us into being, gave us all we have, and made us all we are; so that He is our rightful owner in a far higher sense than that in which any man can own anything whatever.

All we have and are, therefore, is due to God. If we withhold it, we are guilty of robbing God precisely as much as we have withheld. And all this robbery from God, we are unquestionably bound, as far as possible, to make up.

Do any of you still question whether men ever do truly rob God? Examine this point thoroughly. If any of you were to slip into a merchant's store and filch money from his drawer, you cannot deny that the act is theft. You take criminally from your fellowman what belongs to him.

Now can it be denied that, whenever you withhold from God what is due Him, you as actually rob God as anyone who steals from a merchant's drawer? God owns all men and all their services in a far higher sense than that in which any merchant owns the money in his drawer. God rightfully claims the use of all your talents, wealth, and time for himself, for His own glory and the good of His creatures. Just so far, therefore, as you use yourselves *for yourselves*, you actually rob God as if you appropriated to yourself anything that belongs to your neighbor.

Stealing differs from robbery chiefly in this: the former is done secretly; the latter, by violence, in spite of resistance, or, as the case may be, of protest. If you go secretly, without the knowledge of the owner, and take what is his, you steal. If you take anything of his openly—by force—against his known will, you rob. These two crimes differ not essentially in spirit: either is considered a serious trespass upon the rights of a fellowman. Usually, robbery has this aggravation: it puts the owner in fear. However, the owner may do all he wisely can to prevent being robbed, yet you may rob him without exciting alarm and causing him the additional evil of fear. Even in this case, there might still be the essential ingredient of robbery: forcibly taking from another what is his and not yours.

Now, how is it that we sin against God? The true answer is, we tear ourselves away from His service. We wrest our hearts by a sort of moral violence away from the claims He lays upon us. He says, "Ye shall serve me, and no other God but me." This is His first and great command; none can be greater. No claim can be stronger than God's upon us.

Still, it always leaves our will free to rebel and wrest ourselves away from the service of God if we will do so. And what is this but real robbery?

Suppose it were possible for me to own a man. I know we all deny the possibility of this, our relationships to each other as men being what they are. But for illustration, let's suppose I have created a man and hence own him in as full a sense as God owns us all. Still he remains a free agent, yet solemnly bound to serve me continually. But despite my claims on him and all I can wisely do to retain him in my service, he runs away, tears himself from my service. Is not this real robbery? Robbery too of a most absolute kind? He owed me everything; he leaves me nothing.

So the sinner robs God. Availing himself of his free agency, he tears himself away from God in spite of all his rightful owner can do to enlist his affections, enforce his own claims, and retain his willing allegiance. This is robbery. It is not done secretly, like stealing, but openly and violently, too, as in the case of common robbery. It is done in spite of all God can wisely do to prevent it.

Hence, all sin is robbery. It can never be anything less than wresting from God what is rightfully His. It is therefore by no figure of speech that God calls this act robbery. Will a man rob God? "Yet ye have robbed me, even this whole nation." Sin is never anything less than this: a moral agent owned by the highest possible title, yet tearing himself away from his rightful owner, despite all persuasions and all claims.

Hence, if any man would prevail with God, he must bring back himself and all that remains not yet squandered and destroyed. Yes, let him come back, saying, "Here I am, Lord; I have played the fool and have erred exceedingly. I am ashamed that I have used up so much of thy time—have consumed in sin so much of that strength of mind and body which is thine— ashamed that I have employed these hands and this tongue and all these members of my body in serving myself and Satan and have wrested them away from thy service. Lord, I have done most wickedly and meanly; thou seest that I am ashamed of myself and I feel that I have wronged thee beyond expression."

So you should come before God. See that thief coming back to confess and make restitution. Does he not feel a deep sense of shame and guilt? Now unless you are willing to come back and humbly confess and freely restore to God the full use of all that yet remains, how can you hope to be accepted?

You may well be thankful that God does not require of you that you restore all you have wrested from Him and guiltily squandered—all your wasted time and health and influence. If He were to demand this, it would at once render your acceptance before Him, and your salvation, too, impossible. It would be forever impossible, on such a condition, that you should prevail in prayer.

Blessed be God, He does not demand this. He is willing to forgive all the past, but remember, only on the condition that you bring back all the rest, all that yet remains to be used of yourself and of the powers God has given or may yet give you.

All of this God must require as a condition; and why should He not? Suppose you have robbed a man of all you can possibly get away from him and you know that the facts are all known to him. Yet you come before him without a confession or a blush and ask him to receive you to his confidence and friendship. He turns upon you, "Are not you the man who robbed me? Where is that money which you took from me? You come to me as if you had never wronged me and as if you had done nothing to forfeit my confidence and favor. Do you come and ask my friendship again? Monstrous!"

Now, would it be strange if God were, in a similar case, to repel an unhumbled sinner in the same way? Can the sinner who comes back to God with no heart to make any restitution or any consecration of himself to God expect to be accepted? Nothing can be more unreasonable.

That in infinite goodness God welcomes back penitent sinners.

It is indeed nothing less than infinite goodness that God can forgive trespasses so great, so enormous as ours have been: "Oh, what a spectacle of lovingkindness is this!" Suppose a man had stolen ten thousand dollars from you and, having squandered it all, should be thrown in his rags and beggary at your door. There you see him wasted and wane, hungry and filthy, penniless and wretched; and your heart is touched with compassion. You freely forgive all. You take him up, you weep over his miseries, you wash him, clothe him, and make him welcome to your house and to all the comforts you can bestow upon him. How all the world would admire your conduct as generous and nobel in the very highest degree!

But Oh, the lovingkindness of God in welcoming to His bosom the penitent, returning sinner! How it must look in the eyes of angels! They see the prodigal returning, and hear him welcomed openly to the bosom of God's family. They see him coming weak, haggard, guilty, ashamed, in tattered and filthy robes, and downcast in manner—nothing attractive in his appearance. He does not look as if he ever was a son, so terribly has sin defaced the characteristics of sonship; but he comes and they witness the scene that follows. The Father spies him from afar, and rushes forth to meet him. He owns him as a son; falls upon his neck, pours out tears of gladness at his return, orders the best robe and the fatted calf, and fills his mansion with all the testimonies of rejoicing.

Angels see this, and oh, with what emotions of wonder and delight! What a spectacle this must be to the whole universe— to see God coming forth thus to meet the returning penitent! To see that He not only comes forth to take notice of him, but to answer his requests and enter into such communion with him and such relationships that this once apostate sinner may now ask what he will and it will be done for him.

I have sometimes thought that if I had been present when Joseph made himself known to his brethren, I would have been utterly overwhelmed. I can never read the account of that scene without weeping.

I might say the same of the story of the prodigal son. Who

can read it without tears of sympathy? Oh, to have seen it with one's own eyes, to have been there, to have seen the son approaching, pale and trembling, and the father rushing forth to meet him with such irrepressible tenderness and compassion. Such a spectacle would be too much to endure!

And now let me ask, "What if the intelligent beings of the universe might see the great God receiving to His bosom a returning, repentant sinner?" Oh, what an interest must such a scene create throughout all heaven! But just such scenes are transpiring in heaven continually. We are definitely told that there is joy in the presence of the angels of God over one sinner that repents. Surely all heaven must be one perpetual glow of excitement—such manifestations are ever going forward there in infinite compassion toward sinners returning from their evil ways.

Yet we must remember, no sinner can find a welcome before the face of God unless he returns most deeply penitent. Ah! you do not know God at all if you suppose He can receive you without the most thorough penitence and the most ample restitution. You must bring back all that remains unwasted and unsquandered. You must look it all over most carefully and honestly and say, "Here, Lord, is the pitiful remnant, the small amount left; all the rest I have basely and most unprofitably wasted and used up in my course of sin and rebellion. Thou seest how much I have squandered and how very little is left to be devoted now to thy service. Oh, what an unprofitable servant I have been—and how miserably unprofitable have I made myself for all the rest of my life!"

It would be well for every hearer to go minutely into this subject. Estimate and see how many years of your life have gone, never to be recalled. Young people have more years remaining, according to the common laws of life, than we who are farther advanced in years. Yet even you have sad occasion to say, "Alas, how many of the best years of my life are thrown away, yes, worse than thrown into the sea, for in fact they have been given to the service of the devil. How many suits of clothing worn out in the ways of sin and the work of Satan. How many tons of provisions—food for man, provided under the bounty of a gracious Providence—have I used up in my career of rebellion against my Maker and Father! Oh, if it were all now to rise up before me and enter with me into judgment, if each day's daily bread used up in sin were to appear in testimony against me, what a scene would the solemn reckoning be!"

Let each sinner search his heart and think of the position he must occupy before an abused, yet most gracious God, and then say, "How can I expect to prevail with God if I do not bring back with a most penitent and devoted heart all that remains yet to me of years and of strength for God?"

How much more, if more be possible, is this true of those who are advanced in years. How fearfully have we wasted our substance and our days in vain! How then shall we hope to conciliate the favor of God and prevail with Him in prayer unless we bring back all that remains to us and consecrate it a whole offering to the Lord our God.

That we must be reconciled to our brother.

On this subject you will at once recollect the explicit instructions of our Lord: "If thou bring thy gift to the altar, and there rememberest that thy brother hath aught against thee; leave there thy gift before the altar, and go thy way; first be reconciled to thy brother, and then come and offer thy gift."

This passage states very distinctly one important condition of acceptable prayer, and shows that all men are not at all times in a fit state to pray. They may be in a state in which they have no right to pray at all. If they were to come before the Lord's altar in this state, He would bid them suspend their offering of prayer, go back at once, and be reconciled to their brother.

It is important for people to understand that they should approach God in prayer only when they have a right to pray. Others seem entirely to misconceive the relationships of prayer to God and to themselves and think that their prayers are a great favor to God. They seem to suppose that they lay the Lord under great obligations to themselves by their prayers, and if they have made many prayers, and long, they think it quite hard if the Lord does not acknowledge His obligation to them and grant them a speedy answer. Indeed, they seem almost ready to fall into a quarrel with God if He does not answer their prayers.

I knew one man who on one occasion prayed all night. Morning came, but there was no answer from God. It made him so angry with God that he was tempted to cut his own throat. Indeed, so excited were his feelings and so sharp was this temptation that he threw away his knife the better to resist it. This shows how absurdly people feel and think on this subject.

Suppose you owed a man a thousand dollars and decided to

discharge the debt by begging him to release and forgive it. You renew your prayer every time you see him, and if he is at any distance, you send him a begging letter by every mail. Now, inasmuch as you have done your part as you suppose, you fall into a passion if he won't do his and freely relinquish your debt. Would not this be on your part sufficiently absurd, sufficiently ridiculous, and wrong?

So it is with the sinner and God. Many seem to suppose that God ought to forgive. They think He is under obligation to them to pardon and put away from His sight all their sins the moment they choose to say.

Now, God has indeed promised on certain conditions to forgive, and the conditions being fulfilled, He certainly will fulfill His promise, yet never because it is claimed as a matter of justice or right. His promises all pertain to an economy of mercy, not of strict justice.

When people pray rightly, God will hear and answer, but if they pray as a mere duty or pray to make it a demand on the score of justice, they fundamentally mistake the very idea of prayer.

But I must return to the point under consideration.

Sometimes we have no right to pray. When "thou bringest thy gift to the altar, and there rememberest that thy brother hath aught against thee; leave there thy gift before the altar, and go; first be reconciled to thy brother, and then come and offer thy gift." The meaning of this precept seems to be plain. If you are conscious of having wronged your brother, go at once and undo that wrong. If you know that he has any good reason for having anything against you, go and remove the reason as far as it lies in your power to do so. Otherwise, how can you come before God to ask favors of Him?

Here it is important to understand certain cases, which, though they may seem to, do not actually come under the spirit of this rule. Another man may suppose himself to have been injured by me, yet I may be entirely conscientious in feeling that I have done nothing but right toward him. Still, I may be utterly unable to remove from his mind the impression that I have wronged him. In this case, I am not cut off from the privilege of prayer.

Thus it often happens when I preach against backsliders. They feel exceedingly hurt and think I have wronged them unpardonably; whereas, I may have been only honest and faithful to my Master and to their own souls. In such a case I am not to be debarred the privileges of prayer because of their feelings toward me. It would indeed be most absurd that this should shut me away from the mercy seat. If I am conscious of having done no wrong, the Lord will draw me near to himself. In such a case as this, I can make no confession of wrongdoing.

But the case contemplated by our Lord is one which I know I have done wrong to my neighbor. Knowing this, I have no right to come before God to pray until I have made restitution and satisfaction.

Sometimes professing Christians have come to me and asked, "Why are we not heard and answered? We pray a great deal, yet the Lord does not answer our prayers."

Indeed, I have asked them, "Do you not recollect many times when in the act of prayer you have been reminded of having injured a brother, and yet you did not go to him and make restitution, or even confession?" "Yes," many have said, "I can recollect such cases, but I passed them over and did not trouble myself with them. I do not know that I thought much about the necessity of making confession and restitution. At all events, I know I soon forgot those thoughts of having wronged my neighbor."

You did, indeed; but God did not forget. He remembered your dishonesty and your neglect, or perhaps contempt of one of His plainly taught conditions of acceptable prayer, and He could not hear you. Until you have gone and become reconciled to your brother, what have you to do with praying? Your God says to you, "Why do you come here before Me to lie to My very face, pretending to be honest and upright toward your fellow beings, when you know you have wronged them and have never made confessions and restitution?"

In my labors as an evangelist I have sometimes entered a community in which the majority of the residents were in this horrible state. Perhaps they had sent for me to come among them, saying that they were ready and ripe for a revival and thus constrained me to come. On coming among them, I have found the very opposite to be the fact. I would preach to the impenitent, and many would be convicted; an awful solemnity would prevail, but no there would be no conversions. Then I would turn to the church and beg them to pray. Soon the fact would come out that they had no fellowship with each other and no mutual confidence. Almost every brother and sister had hard feelings toward one another. Many knew they had wronged their brethren and had never made confession or restitution; some had not even spoken kindly to one another for months; in short, it was a state of real war. How could the Dove of Peace abide there and how could a righteous God hear their prayers? He could do no such thing till they repented in dust and ashes and put away these abominable iniquities from before His face.

It often happens that professing Christians are exceedingly careless in respect to the conditions of prevailing prayer. What! Christian men and women in such a state that they will not speak to each other! In such relationships to each other that they are ready to injure one another in the worst way—ready to mangle and rend each other's characters! Away with it! It is an offense to God! It is an utter abomination in His sight! He loathes the prayers and the professed worship of such people, as He loathes idolatry itself.

Let it be known that God is infinitely honest, and so long as He is so, He will not hold communion and fellowship with one who is dishonest. He expects us to be honest and truthful, willing ever to obey Him, and ever anxious to meet all the conditions of acceptable prayer. Until this is the case with us, He cannot and will not hear us however much and long we pray. Why should He? "Thou requirest truth in the inward parts," said the Psalmist of his God, as if fully aware that entire sincerity of heart, and of course uprightness of life toward others, is an unalterable condition of acceptance before God. It is amazing to see how much insincerity there often is among professing Christians, both in their mutual relationships to each other and to God.

That we must have an honest and good reason for our prayer.

We ought always to have an honest and good reason for praying and for asking for the specific things we pray for. Remember that God is infinitely reasonable, and therefore does nothing without a reason. Therefore in all prayer you should always have a reason or reasons that will commend themselves to God as a valid ground for His hearing and answering our prayers.

You can have a rational confidence that God will hear you only when you know what your reasons are for praying and have good grounds to suppose they are such as will commend themselves to the infinitely wise and righteous God.

Beloved, are you in the habit of giving your attention sufficiently to this point? When you pray, do you ask for your own reasons? Do you inquire, now have I such reasons for this prayer that God can sympathize with; such reasons that I can suppose will have weight with His mind?

Surely this is an all-important inquiry. God will not hear us unless our reasons satisfy His own infinite intelligence, such that He can wisely act in view of them, such that He will not be ashamed to have the universe know that on such grounds He answered our prayers. They must be such that He will not be ashamed of them himself. For we should always consider that all God's doings are one day to be perfectly known. It will yet be known why He answered every acceptable prayer and why He refused to answer each one that was not acceptable.

Hence, if we are to offer prayer, or do anything else in which we expect God to sympathize with us, we ought to have good and sufficient reasons for what we ask or do.

You cannot help seeing this at your first glance at the subject. Your prayer must not be selfish, but benevolent. Otherwise, how can God hear it? Will He lend himself to patronize and befriend your selfishness?

Suppose a person asks for the Holy Spirit to guide him in any work. Or suppose he asks for that Spirit to sanctify him and his friends. Let him always be able to give a good reason for what he asks. Is his ultimate reason a selfish one? For example, does he pray for the Holy Spirit so he may become more distinguished in the world, or may achieve some favorite scheme for himself and his own glory or his own selfish good? Let him know that the Lord has no sympathy with such reasons for prayer.

Thus a child comes before his parent and says, "Do give me a favor." "Your reason, my child," says the parent; "give me your reason. What do you want it for?"

Now, God says to us, His children, "Your reason, My child; what is your reason?" You say, it may be for an education. Why do you want an education? You say, "Lord, furnish me the means to pay my tuition bills and my board bills and my clothing bills, for I want to get an education." "Your reason, my child," the Lord will answer; "your reason; for what purpose do you want to get an education?" You must be able to give good reasons for your requests. If you want these things only that you may consume them upon your lusts; if your object is to climb up to some higher post among men, or to get your living with less toil, or with more respectability, you have small ground to expect the Lord to sympathize with any such reasons. But if your reasons are good; if they are such that God will not be ashamed to recognize them as His own reasons for acting, then you will find Him infinitely ready to hear and to answer. Oh, He will bow His ear with infinite grace and compassion.

Your hope of success in prayer, therefore, should not lie in the *amount of prayer*, but in the quality of your prayers. If you have been in the habit of praying without regard to the reasons why you ask, you have probably been in the habit of mocking God. Unless you have a reason when you come before the Lord, it is mocking to come and ask for anything. There should always be something which you need. Now, therefore, ask yourself, "Why do I want this thing which I ask of God? Do I need it? For what end do I need it?"

A woman of my acquaintance was praying for the conversion of an impenitent husband. She said, "It would be so much more pleasant for me to have him go to church with me, and to have him think and feel as I do." When she was asked, "Is your heart broken because your husband abuses God, because he dishonors Jesus Christ," she replied that she had never thought of that. Never! Her husband had troubled and grieved her, she knew; but she had not once thought of his having abused and provoked the great and holy God.

How infinitely different must that woman's state of mind become before the Lord can hear and answer her prayer! Can she expect an answer as long as she takes only a selfish view of the case? No, never until she can say, "O my God, my heart is full of bleeding and grief because my husband dishonors thee. My soul is in agony because he scorns the dying blood and the perfect sacrifice of Jesus Christ."

So when parents urge their requests for the salvation of their children, let them know that if they sympathize with God He will sympathize with them. If they are chiefly distressed because their children do not love and serve their own God and Savior, the Lord will most assuredly enter into the deep sympathies of their hearts and will delight to answer their requests. So of the wife when she prays for her husband, so universally when friend prays for friend. The great God seems to say, "If you sympathize with me, I will sympathize with you." He is a being of infinite sympathies, and never can fail to reciprocate the holy feelings of His creatures. Let the humblest subject in His universe feel sincere regard for the honor and glory of God and the well-being of His kingdom. Then how suddenly it is reciprocated by the Infinite Father of all! Let one of the myriads of His creatures in earth or heaven be zealous for God, then assuredly will God be zealous for him and will find means to fulfill His promise: "Those that honor me I will honor." But if you will not feel for Him and will not take His part, it is vain for you to ask or expect that He will feel for you and take your part.

It is indeed a blessed consideration that when our own interests merge in the interests of God and of His kingdom, then He gathers himself all around about us, throws His banner of love over us, and draws our hearts into inexpressible nearness of communion with himself. Then the Eternal God becomes our own God, and underneath us are His almighty arms. Then whoever would touch us, would touch the apple of His eye. There can be no love more watchful, more strong, more tender than that borne by the God of infinite love toward His affectionate, trustful children. He would move heaven and earth if need be to hear prayer offered in such a spirit.

Oh, to immerse and bathe ourselves, as it were, in the sympathies of God: to yield up our whole hearts to Him until our deepest and most perfect emotions should gush and flow out only in perfect harmony with His will, and we are swallowed up in God, knowing no will but His and no feelings but in sympathy with His. Then wave after wave of blessings would roll over us, and God would delight to let the universe see how intensely He is pleased with such a spirit in His creatures. Then you would need only put yourself in an attitude to be blessed and you could not fail to receive all you could that would be actually good to your soul and to God's kingdom. Almost before you should call, He would answer and while you were yet speaking He would hear. Opening wide your soul in large expectation and strong faith before God, you might take a large blessing, even "until there should not be room enough to receive it."

20

MUTUAL CONFESSION OF FAULTS, AND MUTUAL PRAYER*

"Confess your faults one to another, and pray one for another, that ye may be healed" (James 5:16).

In the present discourse, the following points demand our attention:

- ► *What is intended by the injunction, "Confess your faults one to another."*
- ► *What is implied in obeying this injunction.*
- ► *The reasons for this injunction.*
- ► *What is meant by praying one for another.*
- ► *What is implied in obeying this injunction.*

What is intended by the injunction, "Confess your faults one to another."

There is no reason for supposing that this text gives any validity to the Roman Catholic doctrine of confession to priests. Please understand, the doctrine so long prevalent in that institution is under the name of "Auricular Confession," because it was made in the private ear of the priest. This doctrine holds that all are bound to make auricular confession of every act and of every thought upon which their conscience is at all troubled. Consequently the system makes the priest the repository of all the sins of the church—of all the most private sins of all its members, male or female, to be confessed on pain of damnation.

The Oberlin Evangelist, January 17, 1849.

Everyone who is acquainted with the results of this system knows that they have been naturally pernicious to the purity and morals of both priest and people. It is most manifest that the apostle did not contemplate and could never sanction such a system. Confessing faults one to another is not the same as confessing *all* faults to the *priest only.*

Although there is nothing in the text which especially defines the sins contemplated, yet we are doubtless to understand the apostle here to refer primarily to faults committed against others, and to enjoin the confession of faults to those whom we have injured. The doctrine of confession in this form is abundantly taught and implied in the Scriptures, and is therefore, we may suppose, the particular thing intended here.

The principle involved in this may, however, extend somewhat further; to the confession or disclosure of our besetting sins and of our peculiar temptations and weaknesses. It is plain that by making our confidential Christian friends acquainted with these temptations and besetments of ours, we may enlist their concern and prayers in our behalf, and thus secure valuable aid in resisting and overcoming these temptations.

The principle of the text may also include these sins which though not properly committed against particular individuals are yet naturally committed in the presence of others, and therefore become a scandal to religion and a stumbling block to our associates. For example, *irritability*, which so often stumbles others and becomes a besetting sin. *Censoriousness*, the practice of speaking harshly of others, and which is often a sore grievance not merely to those against whom we speak evil, but against every benevolent mind that hears us. It is plain that these and other sins of this class should be confessed.

In saying this you will observe I do not mean that people must reveal everything they know, even such as are known only to themselves and God. It does not appear that the Bible makes the duty of confession to men this universal.

What is implied in obeying this injunction.

That we are thoroughly convinced of our sin; that we not only admit the fact, but also its wickedness, as a sin against God and our neighbor. It is one thing for a man to confess his fault as a real *fault* and a *sin*, and quite another to acknowledge the fault without recognizing its heinous guilt. Hence, our text must imply that we really understand and sincerely confess the actual guilt of our sin; that we repent and renounce our sin. Confession is no better than an insult to God and man if unaccompanied by repentance and renunciation of confessed sin.

Humility is also implied. By this is meant that disposition which loves to take its own place, though it be a very low place—which does not seek to excuse, but really unmasks oneself and naturally seeks the very place which seems to belong to us.

The most common difficulty found in confessing is that people are too proud. They do not love to place themselves as low in the estimation of others as they ought to be. Now, humility is the opposite of pride and implies a willingness to come down to its own low place.

A forced and extorted confession is not the thing enjoined in the text. When a man confesses under the sting of a scorpion conscience, or because convicted by public disclosures and confronted by appalling revelations, he cannot do otherwise and yet maintain any show of Christianity. Such confessions, though they may cost a proud man a prodigious struggle, are yet in real value exceedingly cheap.

Genuine confession implies readiness to make restitution for the wrong we have done. Indeed, confession is in one sense an element of restitution—as far as you can. This is really implied in the spirit of this injunction. No one in his right mind could suppose that if he had stolen, his confession would be worth a straw without ample restitution. And the same principle should certainly apply in all cases where restitution is possible.

It is implied that the confession be full and free, not scanty and constrained. Let it be made with a free, full, and honest heart, in such a spirit and manner as will satisfy the reasonable views of the injured party. How can we suppose that God will be satisfied with anything less?

Suppose you have wronged a man and he knows and feels it. You come to him and after a sort you confess; but instead of making a full and satisfactory confession, you merely hint at your wrong deeds. He knows that you are not an honest man, and that you have not even answered the demands of your own conscience. Such a confession can do neither yourself nor your neighbor any good. Confession, therefore, should be poured out free as water, full and thorough.

Legitimate confession implies and involves throwing yourself upon mercy. When people thoroughly confess their sins to

God, they cease to justify themselves before Him and throw themselves entirely upon His mercy. They rest upon His clemency alone and leave themselves wholly in the hands of God. In a similar way, when you confess to man, you throw yourself upon his clemency; you confess your wrong and forego all pleas of justification.

Where people confess their besetting sins, the act implies a sincere desire to be holy and an honest determination to give up sin and be rid of it forever.

I have often been struck with the different manner in which individuals hear the announcement of the doctrine of sanctification. Proclaim to a body of professing Christians the fact that through grace they may in this life be delivered from all sin, and the reception of it will often speak volumes in revealing their real character. It serves to show their precise attitude toward sin. For example, I once preached in Rochester on this subject, and no sooner had the congregation dispersed than one man came to me, saying with great earnestness, "Mr. Finney, that is too good news to be true." There was a minister in that audience, however, who did not regard it as good news at all. He did not seem to treat the doctrine as if he had any desire to wish it were true.

Who has not observed this very difference? Preach the doctrine of a present salvation from sin to a man really panting to be delivered from sin, and he will hail it with intense interest, if not at once with openhearted welcome. He will receive it most readily if he thinks it may be true. He will long to have it prove true, and his heart will throw no obstacles in the way of his candidly investigating its evidence and cordially embracing all that evidence can be found to sustain.

But if he does not want it to prove true, he will criticize it bitterly; that is, criticize it while evading the issue—will repel its evidence stubbornly, and of course will be likely to reveal himself unconsciously as the enemy of all righteousness. He will show that he takes no interest in being made free from sin *at present*—no real interest in ever being free from sin.

These developments of character are vastly better testimony to one's real state of mind than can otherwise be given. No one ever yet railed against this doctrine who in heart longed to become holy. Even if he does not believe the doctrine true, and hence feels constrained to oppose it, there will be no spirit of rancor. When you see men object to any doctrine without good reason, you may know they do not want it to be true. It is not congenial to their hearts.

Who does not know that the doctrine of entire sanctification has received a great deal of opposition under a pretense of zeal for the truth and opposition to error. But this opposition, after all, has been nothing more nor less than a manifestation of a spirit of criticism and obvious opposition to truth and disinclination to have that doctrine proved true? It has been mournful and appalling to notice the exhibition of real opposition to holiness which has manifested itself in many quarters within the last few years. I am sure I do not say this censoriously. It is what everybody knows to be true who has kept his eye open to the real manifestations which have been made through the pulpit and the press, through ecclesiastical organizations and in many other ways against the doctrine of holiness in this life.

But to return to our thoughts on confession. When Christians reveal their deep sin to their brethren, it is always implied that they are really panting after holiness—that they abhor these sins which they confess, and are ready to do anything, however humiliating, to mortify these horrible sins they so much detest.

The reasons for this injunction.

With respect to personal injuries inflicted upon others, the injunction is founded in justice. Confession is a necessary element of restitution. We cannot be just toward our injured brother without it.

Confession is indispensable to peace with God. It is naturally impossible that we can have peace with God without confession of known offenses against our neighbor. Who needs to be told that God can have no fellowship with injustice, and of course none with those who act unjustly! Does not His eye notice all iniquity? Your injured neighbor might go before the Lord and say, "Lord, he has wronged me, Thou knowest, and now wilt Thou hold fellowship with him?"

Confession is just as indispensable to peace of mind as it is to peace with God. Suppose, if it were possible, all the world were at peace with us, suppose God were too; yet we could not persuade ourselves that we were right. Conscience will forever upbraid us until we confess and do all we possibly can under the circumstances to make restitution for our wrong deeds.

Confession is indispensable to peace with those whom we have injured. Although the injured man may have no ill will toward us—no spirit inconsistent with the Gospel, no disposition to retaliate—yet it is impossible for him to have the spirit of Christian sympathy and harmony with us as long as he knows we are impenitent and unwilling to confess known wrongs. This is a difficulty, a barrier, between us, which cannot be removed until he is satisfied that I am honest; and this satisfaction he cannot have till I confess my fault.

Confession is indispensable to peace and sympathy with all the just and good. While it is true that neither God nor the injured party can be at peace with the wrongdoer till he confess, the same is equally true of all holy beings. Their minds cannot be in a peaceful and harmonious state toward me while they know that I am guilty of wrongdoing and will not confess. So long as they know me to be in this state, they must regard me as as a transgressor, and this must create an everlasting barrier between me and them. They may have no disposition to retaliate or injure me; on the contrary, they may be most earnest in prayer for me that God would humble me and break down my pride. Their position toward me may be no other than that of true benevolence; yet till I confess, they cannot be in Christian sympathy and friendship with me. The thing is naturally impossible.

The same is true even of the wicked. They cannot be at peace with me until I confess my wrongs. It is remarkable that a wicked man as truly condemns wrongdoing as a good man does, although he may do the very same thing himself. His moral decisions upon the right and the wrong may be just and truthful notwithstanding his own bad character. Let him have a case in which his own selfishness does not bribe his conscience and blind his intelligence, and he will decide that wrong is wrong, and ought to be confessed and put away. You cannot therefore have the respect even of wicked men unless you will confess your known wrongs. Even the wickedest of men or devils in hell cannot be satisfied with your course as right until you confess. They might not love you if you were to become holy, but certainly they never can esteem you until you do—never till you confess and abandon all your known wrongdoings. They can never justify and approve your sins.

Confession of wrong is indispensable to self-respect. It is naturally impossible to respect yourself while you withhold proper confession of your sins. By the very laws of your moral nature, this can never be. Who does not know that? If you do not know this, you certainly ought to, and by a very little careful attention to the admonitions of your own conscience, you certainly may know it. Surely you can get no good by resisting the claims of an enlightened conscience, for if all the universe should let you alone in your sin, your conscience would not and could not. Still its voice would ring in your ear, and you could not silence its upbraidings.

Have you not sometimes been ashamed of yourself because you were too proud to confess? This very shame of making confession has filled your soul with bitter agony and the keenest self-reproach, making you sometimes feel that it is a greater shame and a deeper guilt than the original wrong itself. Suppose you were to meet the very man whom you have wronged. The best opportunity is afforded to make the confession which you know to be due—but shame and pride seal your lips. Not a word of confession is lisped. You go away full of remorse and a sense of guilty shame, for you can scarcely help feeling that the last sin is worse than the first. A physician under these circumstances once cried out, *"Oh, how full of hell I am!"* So you perhaps are sometimes constrained to say. You know if you experience in your soul an earnest of hell, for you are sure you deserve the deepest, darkest place in the dwellings of the damned.

Nobody else can have confidence in you or respect for you as long as it is understood that you will not confess known wrongs. You may labor to restore yourself in their confidence, but you are doomed to labor in vain. You may think to live it down, and wash out by good deeds the foul stain attached to you because of unconfessed bad deeds, but you will certainly toil to no purpose. Who can think you an honest man? The truth is, they know better; for you have given them the best possible evidence of your being supremely proud and selfish. Put on the air of the saint as much as you will, you cannot make them confide in you as an honest Christian until you confess your sins wherever confession is necessary and demanded.

Consider, further, that you can never regain the confidence of discerning people until you are willing to go further in confession than you are absolutely compelled to go. It often happens that people will go as far as they must, but no further. They show clearly that they agree to confession only because they are so pushed they cannot help it. Step by step, one step at a time, just as fast as they must, but no faster, they move along.

I have often looked on with astonishment to see this unique process. The guilty man finds that one thing is out too far to be denied any longer; so he confesses that, but nothing more. "No," he says, "that's all." Soon another feature of the same transaction comes out, blacker than the first. "Sir, you are guilty of this too!" "No, I am not. You cannot prove it." "Yes, my friend, it is proved beyond all question." "Oh, well then, I confess that. I am very sorry, but that's all." There is nothing more. Well, by the next day some new point is brought up, and the same road is traveled over again. Denial, conviction, confession, and then to save all the rest of his character, he will beg you to accept his solemn word that there is nothing more of the sort to be revealed.

Now, such a person often uses up his character faster than he is aware. He little thinks how cheap his forced confessions become, and how little confidence is reposed in his most solemn protests of having made clean work in confession. It is vastly better to go to the bottom in the outset. Yes, go to the bottom, pour it all out, *all*, so thoroughly that neither man nor God can find anything more belonging to that subject. Do this, and there is hope for you. People will say to you, "Now we know he is honest-hearted, and though he has done wrong, yet he lays his heart all open and we can trust him again." It is not in human nature to resist the appeal which earnest, honest-hearted confession makes to the human heart.

Confession of personal wrongs is exceedingly useful to both parties concerned. It greatly relieves the guilty man, rolling off a mountain-sized weight from his soul, and restoring sweet peace and joy again. On the other side it often seems to be necessary to the party wronged.

You may recollect the case which I just cited of Dr. Hopkins, whose deep and full-hearted confessions were the means of converting his wicked brother-in-law. Confessions will often do what nothing else can. It often serves to show wicked men that Christians are in spirit utterly unlike themselves. The wicked are conscious that they do not confess their faults—that they know nothing about such brokenness of spirit. Hence, the confessions of a humble Christian reach their conscience as nothing else can.

Often I have known people to scatter conviction like fire through a congregation by a simple confession of their own sins. I recall the case of a minister who by a confession to his people set on foot a glorious revival. He had been to Rome during the great revival there, and became deeply convicted of his great guilt in having cared so little for the salvation of his people. He returned home, prepared a sermon for his people, but when he entered the pulpit the next Sabbath, he could not preach it. His heart was full, ready to burst, and he told the people that he could not preach a word. "Oh," said he, "I have been among you so many years, and alas how little have I cared for your souls! I have tried to please *you* and have discharged my regular duties in a way too heartless; but, ah, my guilt in having so overlooked the salvation of your dying souls!"

Well, he had scarcely begun to confess in this fashion before the deacon wanted to confess, and then other members of the church, and that house became another Bochim. The Lord was there, and His work moved on with power. You can readily see the bearing of that minister's confession. Everyone said, "If our minister has sins to confess, so have we! If he has reason to confess with such contrition and bitter weeping, how much more reason have we!" Thus, his confessions effected what no sermon of his ever did.

Again, sincere confessions are highly honorable to the party who makes them. There is perhaps no other way in which people evidence more strongly their earnest and sincere approval of the *right*. It is surely no small testimony to the integrity of a person's character if he shows that he approves the right so fully and strongly that he does not shrink a moment from condemning himself for any known deviation. His love of right prevails over his pride of character. His confessions are a nobel testimony to his deep sincerity of heart.

How strange it is that people should be ashamed to confess their sins! They could not make this great mistake if they did not "put darkness for light and light for darkness." *Is* it not most honorable for a person who has done wrong to make restitution—for a person who has sinned to make a full and free confession? How strange that people should be afraid to confess! They might as well be ashamed to expose their honesty, ashamed to let the world see that they approve the right more than they value an undeserved reputation, a reputation for being what they are not.

Confessions serve to unburden the mind of the injured person and lead him to exercise forgiveness. Injuries inflicted especially by professing Christians often become great snares and temptations. Many are overcome by them, and fall into a bad state of mind in which divine truth and grace seem to have no good influence on their hearts. They know, perhaps, that it is wrong for them to indulge such feelings, but they have been sorely abused by a professing Christian, and they do not find it easy to divest their minds of the impression thus made. Now in such cases, an honest confession by the offending party is the natural remedy. It usually does more to remove that dreadful stumbling block than anything or everything else.

Christian, is any sinner stumbled thus by any sin of yours? Take care that you do not ensnare his soul to his ruin. Take care that the blood of his soul is not found on your hands!

I have sometimes known a person to provoke another till he has made him angry, and then reproach him for this very anger instead of reproaching himself for having caused it. This is cruelly wicked. The person who has thus provoked another to anger ought to humble himself to most thorough confession and say, "I have most meanly tempted you to sin and then reproached you for yielding to my temptation, when I ought to have most reproached myself. I am sorry. I deplore and condemn my own wickedness."

You may perhaps recall a case in which it is said that a man who was opposing Wesley's views of sanctification and who wanted to prove that a certain believer in those views was not perfectly sanctified took a washbowl of filthy water and threw it in his face. Now, we will suppose that the injured man took offense and got angry, and seeing this, the offending party exults and says, "Fine sanctification this—to get angry on so slight a provocation!" But note how ineffably mean and wicked is the course of this tempter to sin. Let him break down and confess his own sin with shame. Let him say, "I have been the guilty wretch in this matter!" Let him do this and repentance would flow freely from both their hearts.

Again, confession tends strongly to secure the prayers of those against whom you have sinned and to whom you confess. Nothing tends more strongly to beget instantly the spirit of prayer in your behalf. How naturally they cry out, "O Lord, forgive the man, for he confesses his wrong; forgive all his sins and show him the light of thy face." The confession of our besetting sins otherwise than to an injured party, and for the purpose of getting aid to overcome them, is exceedingly useful. It usually interests our Christian brethren very much in our behalf. Who does not know how powerfully the heart is drawn out to pray for those who in this manner confess their besetting sins? Have you not had some experience in this?

What is meant by praying one for another.

The text implies that we interest ourselves deeply in the spiritual welfare of those who confess their faults and use our influence with God to secure their pardon. It is as if we were to sign a petition for their acquittal from the sentence of a broken law.

Suppose your neighbor has broken the laws of the state and, being convicted, is sent to the state prison for life; but he repents most deeply and gives evidence that he is a changed man. Now a petition for his pardon is laid before you to sign. Will you join in the prayer? You will say, "Does he confess his sin? If he does, I can pray for his pardon."

So when people confess their sins to God and to men you should pray God to forgive them. God requires you to do it.

What is implied in obeying this injunction.

Obedience to this requirement implies a real spirit of forgiveness—a desire that God should forgive and an expression of this desire in real prayer to God. This is too obvious to need illustration.

In the case where besetting sins are confessed, it is implied that we interest ourselves in their sanctification and pray earnestly to God for this great result.

REMARKS

Wrongs committed against the public should be confessed publicly. Of this no one can have any doubt. If confession should be made at all, it should be made to those against whom the sin is committed.

Wrongs against individuals may be committed either publicly or privately, and in either case the confession should correspond to the manner and publicity of the offense. If any man injures another in the public estimation by writing or preaching a libel against him, the sin is public, and confession of it should obviously be coextensive with the extent of the offense. You are bound to make the retraction as broad as the wrong done if you can.

You may see why many people never overcome their besetting sins. They are never humble and open enough to confess them. Instead, they pour out their hearts before their brethren so as to secure their sympathy and prayers in their own behalf. They never take advantage of the great moral lever which confession puts under a man's giant sins to dig them up and roll them out and away forever.

You may see the error of supposing that it is enough to confess to God, and that confession to man is useless and not required. The Catholic doctrine of confession has driven many Protestants to the opposite extreme, so that many churches are opposed to having any confessions at all made before men. But it does not follow at all that because Catholics have abused the doctrine of confession, therefore it should be all cast away. It does not follow that we are not under obligation to confess to those whom we have injured. By no means. If this principle were a just one, we should soon lose all our Bibles.

I have often known people to labor a long time under a load of sins unknown to others, sins which might not need confessing to men, except for their great pride. But God saw that their pride must be humbled, and He could not give peace to their souls until it was. Now let such a man go to those whose good opinion he most values and confess his sins; let him really take up his cross in this thing and spare not his proud heart at all. He will find it a most excellent antidote to pride. I have often seen this done. A man goes to some person whom he esteems very highly and says, "I am ensnared by my pride; it is dragging me away from God, down to hell, and I am determined it shall be subdued." So he pours out his confessions of sin.

Now this is seizing the great club to crush the serpent's head—the head of cursed pride—and it is commonly successful.

People in this situation will often find confession quite indispensable.

When in a case of personal fault both parties are to blame, one should never wait for the other to begin the confessions. Let each hasten to be most hearty and full of his own confession, and then a right spirit will obtain, and each will provoke the other to good. It often happens that one holds back lest the other should make bad use of his confessions. No matter if he does. I mean comparatively speaking it is no matter, worth only a moment's regard. It is infinitely more important that you should do what is right before God, the world, and the man you have injured, than that you should withhold confession to prevent him from abusing it. Besides this, there is little danger of his doing it. If he does, the responsibility is his alone.

In a case of this sort I once knew a man who said, "I will confess my wrong, and if my neighbor does not choose to confess his, or pleases to make a bad use of what I confess, he must bear the responsibility alone." He poured out his confessions like water, found sweet relief and peace of soul, and soon after died. That neighbor and every enemy he had mourned over his ashes in bitterness, and confessed that there had lived at least one good man.

I have known the case of a church involved in great difficulty, pitted against each other with strong prejudices and party feelings; but ultimately the spirit of confession began to prevail. Each one felt himself more to blame than his neighbor, and now the only strife was to see which should confess first and most. The controversy now was not that each should prove his neighbor at fault, but that he himself had been the chief sinner and had been the great cause both of his own sins and of his neighbor's. Every man was ready to take his hand off his neighbor and lay it on himself. This was good. If you could have seen those humbled, confessing Christians, you would have said, "It is good to *come down* and get the spirit of confession."

Under such circumstances mutual confession seems to be the only thing that can save Christian character and the church. When people have done wrong, they must humble themselves and confess their faults one to another. To see two brethren meet in the spirit of mutual confession, forgiveness, and prayer is a blessed sight. God rejoices in it, and every holy angel strikes a fresh note of joy and praise in heaven. It is one of the loveliest scenes ever known on earth.

Prayer offered in such circumstances is especially prevalent. Suppose you had been wronged. The wrongdoer is prosecuted, convicted, and sentenced; but in process of time he repents; you are ready to forgive him and you send your petition to the governor for his pardon. Now who does not know that your name will have tenfold more weight because of your peculiar relation to that crime?

So it was in the case of Job and his three friends. They had spoken unkindly of him, and there was good reason for their asking his forgiveness. God's wrath was kindled against them. What did God say? "Go," said He, "to my servant Job. . .my servant Job shall pray for you: for him will I accept." They had accused Job of being a hypocrite. Now let them make up the matter with Job and obtain his intercessions with the Lord in their behalf and they can be forgiven. He of all others is the man to pray for them. God can hear him.

Have you wronged a brother? Go, make your confession to him, and beg his prayers in your behalf. He is the man to pray for you. God can hear him. Humble yourself at his feet till he can feel a spirit of faith to pray for you; then you may hope for prayer that will avail before the Lord.

"Oh," said a dying slaveholder, "how can I die here on my bed and have no prayer offered up for my guilty soul?" His sympathizing wife asked, "What shall I do? Shall I send for the minister?" "No, no," said the dying man; "send for my slave, Tom. I have heard him pray in my barn many a time—send for him." Tom came softly in, dropped his hat under his arm and walked toward the bed: "What does Massa want?" The slaveholder replied, "I want you, Tom, to pray for your dying master, I have wronged you and robbed you of your liberty these many years; I am sorry. Oh, if I could live to reward you, but if you can pray for a poor lost sinner, do pray!" And who would not rather have the prayers of the man he had enslaved and wronged than the prayers of all other men on earth. Such a prayer is worth a world of other prayers! But how can you have it *without confession?*

21

AN APPROVING HEART—CONFIDENCE IN PRAYER*

"Beloved, if our heart condemn us not, then have we confidence toward God. And whatsoever we ask, we receive of him, because we keep his commandments, and do those things that are pleasing in his sight" (1 John 3:21, 22).

In discussing this subject, I shall show:

▶ *If our heart does not condemn us, we have confidence toward God that He accepts us.*

▶ *If we have confidence that our heart does not condemn us, we may also have confidence that God will grant us what we ask.*

▶ *Why this is so, and why we know it to be so.*

If our heart does not condemn us, we have confidence toward God that He accepts us.

If our heart really does not condemn us, it is because we are conscious of being conformed to all the light we have, and of doing the whole will of God.

While in this state it is impossible that, with right views of God's character, we should conceive of Him as condemning us. Our intelligence instantly rejects the supposition that He does or can condemn us for our *present state.* We may be most deeply conscious that we have done wrong heretofore. We may feel

*Charles G. Finney, *Sermons on the Way of Salvation* (Oberlin: Edward J. Goodrich, 1891), pp. 391–412. Also *The Oberlin Evangelist*, March 3, 1847.

ourselves to be most guilty for this, being sure that God disapproves of those past sins of ours and would condemn us for them even now if the pardoning blood of Christ had not intervened. But where pardon for past sins has been sought and found through redeeming blood, "there is therefore no more condemnation" for the past. And in reference to the present, the obvious truth is that if our conscience fully approves of our state, and we are conscious of having acted according to the best light we have, it contradicts all our just ideas of God to suppose that He condemns us. He is a father, and He cannot but smile on His obedient and trusting children.

Indeed, ourselves being in this state of mind, it is impossible for us *not* to suppose that God is well pleased with our present state. We cannot conceive of Him as being otherwise than pleased; for, if He were displeased with a state of sincere and full obedience, He would act contrary to His own character. He would cease to be benevolent, holy, and just. We cannot, therefore, conceive of Him as refusing to accept us when we are conscious of obeying His will so far as we know it. Suppose the case of a soul appearing before God, fully conscious of seeking with all the heart to please God. In this case the soul must see that this is a state that must please God.

Let us turn this subject over till we get it fully before our minds. For what is it that our conscience rightly condemns us? Plainly for not obeying God according to the best light we have. Suppose now we turn about and fully obey the dictates of conscience. Then its voice approves and ceases to condemn. Now all just views of the Deity require us to consider the voice of conscience in both cases as only the echo of His own. The God who condemns all disobedience must of necessity approve of obedience; and to conceive of Him as disapproving our present state would be, in the conviction of our minds, to condemn Him.

It is therefore by no means presumption in us to assume that God accepts those who are conscious of really seeking supremely to please and obey Him.

Again, let it be noted that in this state with an approving conscience, we should have no self-righteousness. A man in this state would at this very moment ascribe all his obedience to the grace of God. From his inmost soul he would say, "By the grace of God, I am what I am"; and nothing could be further from his heart than to take praise or glory to himself for anything good. Yet I have sometimes been exceedingly astonished to hear some, and even ministers of the Gospel, speak with surprise and incredulity of such a state as our text presupposes, a state in which a person's conscience universally approves of his moral status. But why be incredulous about such a condition? Or why deem it a self-righteous and sinful state for person in this state to be as far as can be from ascribing glory to himself? No state can be further from self-righteousness. So far is this from being self-righteous, that the fact is, every other state but this is self-righteous, and this alone is exempt from that sin. Mark how the man in this condition ascribes all to the grace of God. The Apostle Paul when living in conscious uprightness most heartily ascribes all to grace. "I labored," says he, "more abundantly than they all, *yet not I, but the grace of God that is in me.*"

But, observe, that while the apostle was in that state, it was impossible that he should conceive of God as displeased with him. Paul might greatly and justly condemn himself for his past life, and might feel assured that God disapproved and had condemned Saul, the proud persecutor, though He had since pardoned Saul, the praying penitent. But the moral state of Paul the believer, of Paul the untiring laborer for Christ, of Paul, whose whole heart and life divine grace has now molded into His own image—this moral state Paul's conscience approves, and his views of God compel him to believe that God approves.

So of the Apostle John. Hear what he says: "Whatsoever we ask, we receive of him, *because we keep his commandments, and do those things that are pleasing in his sight.*"

But here rises up a man to rebuke the apostle. "What!" he says, "did you not know that your heart is corrupt, that you never can know all its latent wickedness, that you ought never to be so presumptuous as to suppose that you 'do those things that please God'? Did you not know that no mere man does ever, even by any grace received in this life, really 'keep the commandments of God so as to do those things that are pleasing in his sight'?" "No," says John. "I did not know that." "What!" rejoins his reprover. "Not know that sin is mixed with all you do, and that the least sin is displeasing to God?" "Indeed," replies John, "I knew I was sincerely trying to please God, and verily supposed I did please Him and did keep His commandments, and that it was entirely proper to say so—all to the praise of upholding, sanctifying grace."

Again, when a person prays disinterestedly, and with a heart in full and deep sympathy with God, he may and should have confidence that God hears him. When he can say in all honesty before the Lord, "Now, Lord, thou knowest that through the grace of thy Spirit my soul is set on doing good to men for thy glory. I am grieved for the dishonor done to thee, so that 'rivers of water run down my eyes, because men keep not thy law,' " then he cannot but know that his prayers are acceptable to God.

Indeed, no one having right views of God's character can come to Him in prayer in an unselfish state of mind and feel otherwise than that God accepts such a state of mind. Now since our heart cannot condemn us when we are in a disinterested state of mind, but must condemn any other state, it follows that if our heart does not condemn us, we shall have, and cannot but have, confidence that God hears our prayers and accepts our state as pleasing in His sight.

Again, when we are conscious of agreeing with God himself, we may know that God will answer our prayers. There never was a prayer made in this state of sympathy with God which He failed to answer. God cannot fail to answer such a prayer without denying himself. The soul, being in sympathy with God, feels as God feels; so that for God to deny its prayers is to deny His own feelings and refuse to do the very thing He himself desires. Since God cannot do this, He cannot fail to hear the prayer that is in full agreement with His own heart.

In the state we are now considering, the Christian is conscious of this fact. Do not some of you know this? You who thus live and walk with God, do you not know that the Spirit of God helps your infirmities and makes intercession for you according to the will of God? Are you not very conscious of these intercessions made for you, and in your very soul, as it were, with groanings that cannot be uttered? Your heart within pants and cries out after God, and is lifted up continually before Him as spontaneously as it is when your heart sings, pouring out its deep outgushings of praise. You know how sometimes your heart sings, though your lips move not and you utter no sound; yet, your heart is full of music, making melody to the Lord. Even so, your soul is sometimes in the mood of spontaneous prayer, and pours out its deep-felt supplications into the ears of the Lord of Hosts just as naturally as you breathe. The silent and ceaseless echoing of your heart is, "Thy kingdom come, thy kingdom come." And although you may not utter these words, and perhaps not any words at all, yet these words are a fair expression of the overflowing desires of your heart.

And this deep praying of the heart goes on while the Christian is still pursuing the common vocations of life. The carpenter, perhaps, is in his workshop driving his plane, but his heart is communing or interceding with God. You may see a farmer behind his plow, but his heart is deeply engrossed with his Maker. He follows on, and only now and then starts up from the intense working of his mind and finds that his land is almost finished. The student has his book open to his lesson; but his deep musings upon God, or the irrepressible longings of his soul in prayer consume his mental energies, and his eye floats unconsciously over the unnoticed page. God fills his thoughts. He is more conscious of this deep communion with God than he is of the external world. The team he is driving or the book he professes to study is by no means so actually and so vividly a matter of conscious recognition to him as is his communion of soul with his God.

In this state the soul is fully conscious of being perfectly submissive to God. Whether he uses these words or not, his heart would always say, "Not my will, O Lord, but thine be done." Hence, he knows God will grant the blessing he asks if He can do so without a greater evil to His kingdom than the resulting good of bestowing it. We cannot but know that the Lord delights to answer the prayers of a submissive child of his own.

Again, when the conscience sweetly and humbly approves, it seems impossible that we should feel so ashamed and confounded before God as to think that He cannot hear our prayer. The fact is, it is only those whose heart condemns them who come before God ashamed and confounded, and who cannot expect God to answer their prayers. These people cannot expect to feel otherwise than confounded until the sting of conscious guilt is taken away by repentance and faith in the Redeemer's blood.

Yet, again, the soul in this state is not afraid to come with humble boldness to the throne, as God invites him to do; for he recognizes God as a real and most gracious Father, and sees in Jesus a most compassionate and condescending High Priest. Of course he can look upon God only as being always ready to receive and welcome him to His presence.

Nor is this a self-righteous state of mind. Oh, how often have I been amazed and agonized to hear it so represented! But how strange is this! Because you are conscious of being entirely honest before God, therefore it is maintained that you are self-righteous! You ascribe every good thing in yourself most heartily to divine grace, but yet you are (so some say) very self-righteous notwithstanding! How long will it take some people to learn what real self righteousness is? Surely it does not consist in being full of the love and Spirit of God; nor does humility consist in being actually so full of sin and self-condemnation that you cannot feel otherwise than ashamed and confounded before both God and man.

If we have confidence that our heart does not condemn us, we may also have confidence that God will grant us what we ask.

This must be so, because it is His Spirit working in us that excites these prayers. God himself prepares the heart to pray; the Spirit of Christ leads this Christian to the throne of grace, and keeps him there; then presents the objects of prayer, kindles desire, draws the soul into deep sympathy with God; and now, all this being wrought by the grace and Spirit of God, will He not answer these prayers? Indeed He will! How can He ever fail to answer them?

It is a remarkable fact that all real prayer seems to be summed up in the Lord's Prayer, and especially in those two most comprehensive petitions: "Thy kingdom come; thy will be done on earth as it is in heaven." The mind in a praying frame runs right into these two petitions, and seems to center here continually. Many other and various things may be specified; but they are all only parts and branches of this one great blessing: "Let God's kingdom come, and bear sway on earth as it does in heaven." This is the sum of all true prayer.

Now let it be observed that God desires this result infinitely more than we do. When, therefore, we desire it, too, we are in harmony with the heart of God, and He cannot deny us. The blessing we crave is the very thing which, of all others, He most delights to bestow.

Yet let it be noted here that God may not answer every prayer according to its letter; but He surely will according to its spirit. The real spirit is always this, "Thy kingdom come, thy will be done"; and this God will assuredly answer, because He has so abundantly promised to do this very thing in answer to prayer.

Why this is so, and why we know it to be so.

The text affirms that "whatsoever we ask, we receive of him, because we keep his commandments and do those things that are pleasing in his sight." Now we might perhaps understand this to assign our obedience as the *reason* of God's giving the blessing sought in prayer. But if we should, we should greatly err. The fundamental reason always of God's bestowing blessings is His goodness and love. Let this never be forgotten. All good flows down from the great fountain of infinite goodness. Our obedience is only the *condition* of God's bestowing it, never the fundamental reason or ground of its bestowment. It is very common for us, in rather loose and popular language, to speak of a condition as being a *cause* or fundamental reason. But on a point like the present, we ought to use language with more precision. The true meaning on this point undoubtedly is that obedience is the condition. This being fulfilled on our part, the Lord can let His infinite benevolence flow out upon us without restraint. Obedience takes away the obstacle; then the mighty gushings of divine love break forth. Obedience removes the obstacles; never merits or draws down the blessing.

If God were to give blessings upon any other condition, it would deceive multitudes, either respecting ourselves or God himself. If He were to answer our prayers, we being in a wrong state of mind, it would deceive others very probably. For if they did not know us well, they would presume that we were in a right state, and might be led to consider those things in us to be right, which are in fact wrong.

Or, if they knew that we were wrong, and yet knew that God answered our prayers, what must they think of God? They could not avoid the conclusion that He patronizes wrongdoing, and lifts up the smiles of His love upon iniquity: and how grievous must be the influence of such conclusions!

It should be borne in mind that God has a character to maintain. He must maintain His reputation as an indispensable means of sustaining His moral government over other creatures. It could not be benevolent for Him to take a course which would peril His own reputation as a holy God and as a patron and friend of holiness and not of sin.

God is well pleased when we remove the obstacles out of the way of His benevolence. He is infinitely good, and lives to do good, and for no other purpose, for no other end whatever than to pour forth blessings upon His creatures wherever He can without peril to the well-being of other creatures under His care and love. He exists forever in a state of entire consecration to this end. Such benevolence as this is infinitely right in God, and nothing less than this could be right for Him.

Now, if it is His delight and His life to do good, how greatly must He rejoice when we remove all obstacles out of the way! How His heart exults when another, and yet another, opportunity is afforded Him of pouring out blessings in large and rich measure! Think of it, sinner, for it applies to you! Marvelous as you may think it, and most strange as it may seem, judged of by human rules and human examples, yet of God it cannot fail of being always true that He delights supremely in doing you good, and only waits till you remove the obstacles; then would His vast love break forth and pour its ocean tides of mercy and of grace all around about you. Go and bow before your injured Sovereign in deep submission and real penitence with faith also in Jesus for pardon, and thus put this matter to trial! See if you do not find that His mercies are high above the heavens! See if anything is too great for His love to do for you!

And let each Christian make a similar proof of this amazing love. Place yourself where mercy can reach you without violating the glorious principles of God's moral government; and then wait and see if you do not experience the most overwhelming demonstration of His love! How greatly does your Father above delight to pour out His mighty tides of blessings! Oh, He is never so well pleased as when He finds the channel open and free for these great currents of blessings to flow forth upon His dear people!

A day or two ago, I received a letter from the man in whose behalf I requested your prayers at a recent church prayer meeting. This letter was full of precious interest. The writer has long been a stranger to the blessedness of the Gospel; but now he writes me, "I am sure you are praying for me, for within a week I have experienced a peace of mind that is new to me."

I mention this now as another proof of the wonderful readiness of our Father in heaven to hear and answer prayer. Oh, what love this is! To what shall I compare it! How shall I give you any adequate view of its amazing fullness and strength? Think of a vast body of water, pent up and suspended high above our heads, pressing and pressing at every crevice to find an outlet where it may gush forth. Suppose the bottom of the vast Pacific Ocean should heave and pour its ocean tides over all the continents of the earth. This might illustrate the vast overflowings of the love of God. How grace and love are mounting up far and infinitely above all the mountains of your sins! Yes, let the deep, broad Pacific be elevated on high and there pent up, and then conceive of its pressure. How it would force its way and pour out its gushing floods wherever the least channel might be opened! And you would not need to fear that your little needs would drain it dry! Oh, no! You would understand how there might be enough and to spare. How it might be said, "Open thy mouth wide, and I will fill it." How the promises might read, "Bring ye all the tithes into my storehouse. . .and prove me now herewith. . .if I will not open you the windows of heaven, and pour you out a blessing that there shall not be room enough to receive it." The great oceans of divine love are never drained dry. Let Christians but bring in their tithes and make ready their vessels to receive, and then, having fulfilled the conditions, they may "stand still and see the salvation of God." Oh, how those mountain floods of mercy run over and pour themselves all abroad till every capacity of the soul is filled! Oh, how your little vessels will run over as in the case of the prophet when the widow's vessels were all full and he cried out, "Oh, hasten, hasten! Is there not another vessel?" Still the oil flows on, "Is there not another vessel?" "No more," she says; "all are full." Then and only then was the flowing of the oil stayed. How often have I thought of this in seasons of great revival when Christians really get into a praying frame and God seems to give them everything they ask for. Until at length the prophet cries out, "Is there not yet another vessel? Oh, bring more vessels, more vessels yet, for still the oil is flowing and still runs over." But ah, the Church has reached the limit of her expectation. She has provided no more vessels. And the heavenly current is stayed. Infinite love can bless no more, for faith is lacking to prepare for and receive it.

REMARKS

Many people, being told that God answers prayer *for Christ's sake*, overlook the condition of obedience. They have so loose an idea of prayer, and of our relationships to God in it, and of His relationships to us and to His moral government, that they think they may be disobedient and yet prevail through Christ. How little do they understand the whole subject! Surely they must have quite neglected to study their Bible to learn the truth about prayer. They might very easily have found it there declared, "He that turneth away his ear from hearing the law, even his prayer shall be an abomination." "The sacrifice of the wicked is an abomination to the Lord." "If I regard iniquity in my heart, the Lord will not hear me." All this surely teaches us that if there be the least sin in my heart, the Lord will not hear my prayer. Nothing short of entire obedience for the time being is the condition of acceptance with God. There must be a sincere and honest heart, or else how can you look up with humble confidence and say, "My Father"? Or how else can you use the name of Jesus as your prevailing Mediator? Or how else can God smile upon you before all the eyes of angels and of pure saints above?

When people come before God with their idols set up in their hearts and the stumbling block of their iniquity before their face, the Lord says, "Should I be inquired of at all by them?" Read and see, Ezekiel 14: 3–5. The Lord commissions His prophet to declare unto all such, "I, the Lord, will answer him that cometh [thus] *according to the multitude of his idols.*" Such prayers God will answer by sending not a divine fullness, but a wasting leanness; not grace and mercy and peace, but a barrenness and cursings and death.

Do not some of you know what this is? You have found in your own experience that the more you pray, the harder your heart is. What, do you suppose, is the reason? Plainly there can be no other reason than this. You come up with the stumbling block of your iniquity before your face, and God answers you accordingly, not to His great mercies, but to the multitude of your idols.

Should you not take heed how you pray?

Because of their *past sins*, people never need to hesitate to approach God with the fullest confidence. If they now repent and are conscious of fully and honestly returning to God with all their heart, they have no reason to fear being repulsed from the footstool of mercy.

I have sometimes heard people express great astonishment when God has heard and answered their prayers after they had been very great and vile sinners. Such astonishment indicates but little knowledge of the matchless grace and lovingkindness of our God. Look at Saul of Tarsus. Once a bitter and mad persecutor, proud in his vain Pharisaism, but now repenting, returning, and forgiven. Take note! What power he has with God in prayer! In fact, after penitence, God pardons so fully that as His Word declares, He remembers their iniquities no more. Then the Lord places the pardoned soul on a footing where he can prevail with God as truly and as well as any angel in heaven can! So far as the Bible gives us light on this subject, we must conclude that all this is true. And why? Not because the pardoned Christian is more righteous than an angel, but because he is equally accepted with the purest angel, and has besides, the merits and mediation of Jesus Christ all made available to him when he uses this all-prevalent name. Oh, there is a world of meaning in this so-little-thought-of arrangement for prayer *in Jesus' name*! The value of Christ's merits are all at your disposal. If Jesus Christ could obtain any blessing at the court of heaven, you may obtain the same by asking in His name: it being supposed of course that you fulfill the conditions of acceptable prayer. If you come and pray in the Spirit of Christ, His Spirit making intercession with your spirit, and your faith taking hold of His all-meritorious name, you may have His intercession before the throne in your behalf. And whatever Christ can obtain there, He will obtain for you. Ask, therefore, now, so Christ himself invites and promises, "Ask and receive, that your joy may be full."

Oh, what a vantage ground is this upon which God has placed Christians! Oh, what a foundation on which to stand and plead with most prevailing power! How wonderful! First God bestows pardon, then takes away the sting of death, restores peace of conscience and joy in believing, gives the benefit of Christ's intercession, and then invites Christians to ask what they will! Oh, how mightily, how prevalent, might every Christian become in prayer! Doubtless we may say that a church living with God, and fully meeting the conditions of acceptable prayer, might have more power with God than so many angels. And shall we hear professing Christians talk of having no power with God! Alas! Alas! Such surely know not their blessed birthright. They have not yet begun to know the Gospel of the Son of God!

Many continue the forms of prayer when they are living in sin and do not try to reform and even have no sincere desire to reform. All such people should know that they grievously provoke the Lord to answer their prayers with fearful judgments.

It is only those who live and walk with God whose prayers are of any avail to themselves, to the Church, or to the world. Only those whose conscience does not condemn them and who live in a state of conscious acceptance with God pray. According to our text, they receive whatever they ask because they keep His commandments and do the things that are pleasing in His sight.

When those who have been the greatest sinners will turn to God, they may prevail as really as if they had never sinned at all. When God forgives through the blood of Jesus, it is real forgiveness, and the pardoned penitent is welcomed as a child to the bosom of infinite love. For Jesus' sake God receives him without the least danger of its being inferred that He does not care about sin. Oh, He told the universe once for all how utterly He hated sin. He made this point known when He caused His well-beloved Son to bear our sins in His own body on the tree, and it pleased the Father to bruise Him and hide His face even from the Son of His love. Oh, what a beautiful, glorious thing this gospel system is! In it God has made such manifestations of His regard for His law that now He has nothing to fear in showing favor to any and every sinner who believes in Christ. If this believing sinner will also put away his sin, if he will only say, "In the name of the Lord, I put all my sins away, all, now, forever," let him do this with all his heart and God will not fear to embrace him as a son. This penitent Christian need fear nothing as long as he hides himself in the open cleft of this blessed Rock of ages.

Look at the case of the prodigal son. Famished, ragged, poor, ready to perish, he remembers his father's house and the plenty that abounds there. He comes to himself and hence looks upon things once more according to their reality. Now he says, "In my father's house there is bread enough and to spare, but here I am perishing with hunger." But why is he ready to perish with hunger? Ah, he ran away from a bountiful and kind father and spent all his substance in riotous living. But he comes to himself. There, see him drawing near his father's mansion, once his own dear home. See, the father rushes to embrace him. He hastens to make this penitent son most welcome to his home and to his heart. So God makes haste to show that He is not afraid to make the vilest sinner welcome if he only comes back repentant and rests on the name of Jesus. Oh, what a welcome this is!

Follow on that beautiful illustration the Savior has given us. Bring forth the best robe. Invite together all our friends and neighbors. Prepare the music. Spread the table and kill the fatted calf. It is fit that we should make merry and be glad. Lead forward this long-lost son and put on him my best robe. Let there be joy throughout my house over my returned and penitent son.

And what does all this show? One thing, that there is joy in the presence of the angels of God, and joy in the very heart of God himself, over one sinner who repents. Oh, I wonder that sinners will not come home to their Father in heaven!

Sinner, if you will come back to the Lord, you may not only prevail for yourself, but for your associates and friends. I was once in a revival where a large company of young men banded themselves together under a mutual pledge that they would not be converted. Father Nash was with me in that revival season, and on one occasion, while the young men alluded to were all present, he made a declaration which startled me and almost shocked himself. Yet, as he said afterward, he dared not take it back, for he did not know how he came to say it and thought perhaps the hand of God might be in it. "Young men," he said, "God will break your ranks within one week, or He will send some of you to hell."

It was an awful time. We feared that possibly it might not prove to be so, and that then the result would be exceedingly bad upon the minds of that already hardened band. But it was spoken, and we could only cry unto God.

Time rolled along. About two or three days after this declaration was made, the leader of this band called to see me, all broken down and as mellow as he could be. As soon as he saw me, he cried out, "What shall I do?" I asked, "What are you thinking about"? "About my wicked companions," he answered. "All of them in the way to hell!" "Do you pray for them?" I asked. "Oh, yes," he responded, "I cannot help praying for them every moment." "Well then," I stated, "there is one thing more; go to them and entreat them in Christ's name to be reconciled to God." He darted out of the room and began this work in earnest. Suffice it to say that before the week was closed almost all of that band of young men were converted.

And now let me say to unrepentant sinners. If others do not labor to promote a revival, begin at once to do it yourself. Learn from this illustration what you can do. Don't you think you could do something of the greatest value to souls if you would seriously try? You who are unrepentant, don't you believe that if you yourself would repent, you might then go and pray and labor and secure the conversion of others, perhaps many of your companions?

Sinners are usually disposed to throw all the responsibility of this labor and prayer upon Christians. I throw it back upon you. Do right yourselves and then you can pray. Do right, and then none can labor with more effect than yourselves in this great work of bringing back wandering prodigals to their father's house.

Oh, Christian, is it not a dreadful thing for you to be in a state in which you cannot prevail with God? Let us look around. How is it with you? Can *you* prevail with God; and *you—and you?* Who are they, and how many are there, in such a state that their prayers avail nothing? And who know before they pray and while they are praying that they are in no fit state to offer prevailing prayer? One of the brethren said to me at a recent church meeting, "I have lost my power to prevail with God. I know I am not ready for this work." How many others are there still in the same awful condition?

Oh! How many are there who are the salt of the earth, whose prayers and redeeming influence save the community from becoming perfectly putrid with moral corruption? I hope they will be found alive and at work in this trying hour. Oh! we must have your prayers for the unrepentant, for the anxious, for backsliders. Or if you cannot pray, at least come together and confess your sins. Tell your brothers and sisters you cannot pray, and beg of them to pray for you that you may be brought back to the light and the peace and the repentance of real salvation.